THE POETICS OF DECLINE IN BRITISH ROMANTICISM

Anxieties about decline were a prominent feature of British public discourse in the late eighteenth and early nineteenth century. These anxieties were borne out repeatedly in books and periodicals, pamphlets and poems. Tracing the reciprocal development of Romantic-era Britain's rapidly expanding literary and market cultures through the lens of decline, Jonathan Sachs offers a fresh way of understanding British Romanticism. The book focuses on three aspects of literary experience – questions of value, the fascination with ruins, and the representation of slow time – to explore how shifting conceptions of progress and change inform a post-Enlightenment sense of cultural decline. Combining close readings of Romantic literary texts with an examination of works from political economy, historical writing, classical studies, and media history the book reveals for the first time how anxieties about decline impacted literary form and shaped Romantic debates about poetry and the meaning of literature.

Jonathan Sachs is Professor of English at Concordia University in Montreal. He is the author of *Romantic Antiquity: Rome in the British Imagination, 1789–1832* (2010) and coauthor of *Interacting with Print: Elements of Reading in the Era of Print Saturation* (2017).

T0381617

CAMBRIDGE STUDIES IN ROMANTICISM

Founding Editor
Marilyn Butler, *University of Oxford*

General Editor
James Chandler, *University of Chicago*

Editorial Board
John Barrell, *University of York*
Paul Hamilton, *University of London*
Mary Jacobus, *University of Cambridge*
Claudia Johnson, *Princeton University*
Alan Liu, *University of California, Santa Barbara*
Jerome McGann, *University of Virginia*
David Simpson, *University of California, Davis*

This series aims to foster the best new work in one of the most challenging fields within English literary studies. From the early 1780s to the early 1830s, a formidable array of talented men and women took to literary composition, not just in poetry, which some of them famously transformed, but in many modes of writing. The expansion of publishing created new opportunities for writers, and the political stakes of what they wrote were raised again by what Wordsworth called those "great national events" that were "almost daily taking place": the French Revolution, the Napoleonic and American wars, urbanization, industrialization, religious revival, an expanded empire abroad and the reform movement at home. This was an enormous ambition, even when it pretended otherwise. The relations between science, philosophy, religion, and literature were reworked in texts such as *Frankenstein* and *Biographia Literaria*; gender relations in *A Vindication of the Rights of Woman* and *Don Juan*; journalism by Cobbett and Hazlitt; poetic form, content and style by the Lake School and the Cockney School. Outside Shakespeare studies, probably no body of writing has produced such a wealth of comment or done so much to shape the responses of modern criticism. This indeed is the period that saw the emergence of those notions of "literature" and of literary history, especially national literary history, on which modern scholarship in English has been founded.

The categories produced by Romanticism have also been challenged by recent historicist arguments. The task of the series is to engage both with a challenging corpus of Romantic writings and with the changing field of criticism they have helped to shape. As with other literary series published by Cambridge University Press, this one will represent the work of both younger and more established scholars, on either side of the Atlantic and elsewhere.

See the end of the book for a complete list of published titles.

THE POETICS OF DECLINE IN BRITISH ROMANTICISM

JONATHAN SACHS

CAMBRIDGE
UNIVERSITY PRESS

CAMBRIDGE
UNIVERSITY PRESS

University Printing House, Cambridge CB2 8BS, United Kingdom

One Liberty Plaza, 20th Floor, New York, NY 10006, USA

477 Williamstown Road, Port Melbourne, VIC 3207, Australia

314-321, 3rd Floor, Plot 3, Splendor Forum, Jasola District Centre, New Delhi - 110025, India

79 Anson Road, #06-04/06, Singapore 079906

Cambridge University Press is part of the University of Cambridge.

It furthers the University's mission by disseminating knowledge in the pursuit of education, learning and research at the highest international levels of excellence.

www.cambridge.org
Information on this title: www.cambridge.org/9781108413688
DOI: 10.1017/9781108333115

First published 2018
First paperback edition 2020

A catalogue record for this publication is available from the British Library

ISBN 978-1-108-42031-0 Hardback
ISBN 978-1-108-41368-8 Paperback

Cambridge University Press has no responsibility for the persistence or accuracy of URLs for external or third-party internet websites referred to in this publication, and does not guarantee that any content on such websites is, or will remain, accurate or appropriate.

For Cecily and Sasha

Contents

Figures

Acknowledgments

This book took shape as a series of talks. I hope that its present form maintains the accessible and conversational tone of those occasions and that readers will use it as a book to "think with" and will feel welcome to take its ideas in different and unexpected directions. That I think so much about writing in relation to conversation is no doubt a reflection of the concern of so much Romantic writing with orality. But it is also a reflection of how vibrant and multivocal the field of Romantic studies remains – of how much I have learned from talking to students and colleagues and how much I want to say to them and hear from them in return. Indeed, this book would have been impossible without so many occasions for talking, from annual conferences to themed workshops, from graduate and undergraduate courses to invited lectures and seminars, not to mention the various cafes, restaurants, and bars where this book really took form.

Despite all of these opportunities for engagement, this book simply would not have been possible without considerable institutional support, from my home institution in Montreal and beyond. The book began during a visiting fellowship at Clare Hall, Cambridge and continued during a subsequent visiting fellowship at Trinity Hall, Cambridge. Thanks to the Masters and Fellows of both colleges for their support and to Martin Ruehl for initiating the Trinity Hall gig. The initial drafting of this book was completed at that paradise for scholars, the National Humanities Center in North Carolina with the support of a Benjamin N. Duke Fellowship of the Research Triangle Foundation; its final copy edits and proofs were corrected at the Institute for Advanced Study in Princeton, during the first weeks of a Membership at the School of Historical Studies. Thanks to both institutions for the kind of unparalleled working conditions that make scholarship possible and pleasurable. Throughout, this project has received generous research support from the Social Sciences and Humanities Research Council of Canada.

Further institutional support has come from many libraries and the Cambridge University Press. Thanks to Vince Graziano at the Concordia University Library. Extra special thanks to Brooke Andrade and Sarah Harris for a magical year of bibliographic ease at the National Humanities Center with its always to be missed and never to be forgotten library resources. Thanks also to the John Soane Museum, Boston Rare Maps, and the Cambridge University Library for permission to reproduce the images from their collections. A shorter version of Chapter 1 was published in *Modern Intellectual History*, while an earlier version of Chapter 3 appeared in the *European Romantic Review*. Cambridge University Press has been a welcome home for this book, from its commissioning by Linda Bree and James Chandler to its rigorous and thorough review by Ian Duncan and one further anonymous press reader.

Beyond this institutional support there are so many individuals to whom I owe such considerable debts, but it seems wrong not to begin by giving what Cordelia Flyte would call her special love to those who have commented on a number of the chapters and given my work such thoughtful attention in recent years and especially in the later stages of the project in both formal and informal contexts: Andy Franta, Paul Keen, Deidre Lynch, Jonathan Mulrooney, Anahid Nersessian, and Andy Stauffer. Each is a tremendous scholar in his or her own right and my debt to them is a pleasure to pay back in daily installments. What Jim Chandler has taught me since even before I started graduate school could fill a book of its own and will certainly be seen on every page of this one. Late in the game two further mentors came on board, and this would have been a very different book without the lessons, support, and encouragement of Jon Klancher, to whom I cannot overestimate the scale of my debt, and Jo McDonagh, whose presence out there sustains my faith in the field. My Montreal writing group of Omri Moses and Andrew Piper has possibly read every word of this book in multiple drafts. Kevis Goodman and Andrew Piper (again!) shadow every sentence of this book. Not only the model of their impeccable scholarship, ever fresh and new, but also their conversation and general support have shaped the way I think and pushed me again and again both to clarify and to complicate my ideas as they exposed me to new insights and helped me to grow my arguments in directions I otherwise might not have dared.

Four groups, "thought collectives" in the greatest sense of those words, have marked aspects of this book from memorable conversations rooted prior to its beginning to anticipated conversations that I expect will continue long after its publication: the Nineteenth-Century Writing

Group at the National Humanities Center (Noah Heringman, Jo McDonagh, and Yasmin Solomonescu); the Montreal-Ottawa Working Group on Romanticism (with particular thanks to my co-convener Ina Ferris, but extending also to those who have shared so many conversations, meals, and drinks for over ten years now: James Brooke-Smith, Frans de Bruyn, Ian Dennis, Lauren Gillingham, Paul Keen, Sara Landreth, April London, Julie Murray, Mark Salber Phillips, Andrew Piper, Fiona Ritchie, Peter Sabor, and Michael Sinatra); the Multigraph Collective (Mark Algee-Hewitt, Angela Borchert, David Brewer, Thora Brylowe, Julia Carlson, Brian Cowan Susan Dalton, Marie-Claude Felton, Michael Gamer, Paul Keen, Michelle Levy, Michael Macovski, Nick Mason, Tom Mole, Andrew Piper, Dahlia Porter, Diana Solomon, Andrew Stauffer, Richard Taws, Nikola von Merveldt, and Chad Wellmon – may our blood oath long continue); and, finally, the Interacting with Print Research Group, a subset of the above, but deserving special mention nonetheless: Susan Dalton, Peggy Davis, Tom Mole, Andrew Piper, and Nikola von Merveldt.

In addition to these groups and individuals, there have also been informal conversations with too many people to name. The list is long, long enough to make me wonder if I deserve to put my name alone on the cover of this book. With apologies to those whom I may have overlooked, I want to thank a phenomenal and supportive group of scholars, Romantic and otherwise, for their insights and conversation: Alan Bewell, Scott Black, Chris Bundock, Miranda Burgess, Tim Campbell, David Collings, Alex Dick, Angela Esterhamer, Joel Faflak, Mary Fairclough, Mary Favret, Libby Fay, Dino Felluga, Tom Ford, Sean Franzell, Tim Fulford, Billy Galperin, Marilyn Gaull, Kevin Gilmartin, Amanda-Jo Goldstein, Evan Gottlieb, Devin Griffiths, John Hall, Jill Heydt-Stevenson, Sonia Hofkosh, Noel Jackson, Colin Jones, Paul Keen, Terry Kelley, Maggie Kilgour, Greg Kucich, Celeste Langan, Nigel Leask, Tina Lupton, Mark Lussier, Charles Mahoney, Tilar Mazzeo, Brian McGrath, Maureen McLane, Rob Mitchell, Jesse Molesworth, Jeanne Moskal, Michael Nicholson, Matthew Ocheltree, Danny O'Quinn, Emma Peacocke, Adam Potkay, Padma Rangarajan, Arden Reed, Alexander Regier, Chris Rovee, Matthew Rowlinson, Chuck Rzepka, John Savarese, Stuart Sherman, Charlotte Sussman, Elisa Tamarkin, Patrick Vincent, Andrew Warren, Paul Westover, Dan White, Matthew Wickman, Laurence Williams, Karen Wiseman, and Tristram Wolff. I also want to thank all of my colleagues in the English Department at Concordia University, especially Danielle Bobker, Nathan Brown, Greg

Ellerman, Mary Esteve, Marcie Frank, Omri Moses, Sina Queras, Kate Sterns, Darren Wershler, Jason Camlot, Jill Didur, and Andre Furlani. These last three served successively as chairs through the book's composition and helped make possible the occasions for its research and writing. And last but not least at Concordia, Craig Melhoff stepped in at the last minute and heroically helped assemble the book's index.

I also want to acknowledge the many audiences who heard versions of these chapters, including groups at the University of Bristol, the University of Glasgow, McGill University, York University (UK), the California Institute of Technology, Oxford University, Cambridge University, the University of Essex, the University of Western Ontario, Harvard University, the UCLA Romantics Group, the University of Colorado at Boulder, the CUNY Graduate Center, the University of California, Berkeley, University College Cork, the University of North Carolina, the University of Victoria, the University of Toronto, the University of Indiana, and the New York Public Library. Some of this was also delivered as conference papers at several gatherings of NASSR, the MLA convention, ASECS, and BARS. Particular thanks to Liz Prettejohn and Charles Martindale for nominating me for a Benjamin Meaker Visiting Professorship at the University of Bristol in 2010, where so many of the ideas here began. In addition to those who heard and responded to these talks, thanks are due to all who generously extended invitations and organized the talks listed above, with special mention in this context for the hospitality and camaraderie of John Brewer, Jeff Cox, Claire Connelly, Kevis Goodman, Anne Mellor, Susan Oliver, Jake Risinger, Tilottama Rajan, Terry Robinson, Ian Thomas-Bignami, and Nancy Yousef.

Closest to home I want to thank friends and family in and out of the academy, especially, David Baumflek, Tamara Griggs, Tinka Piper, Ara Osterweil, Neda Ulaby, and Anya Zilberstein; Colette Camden and Will Pryce, shelter always despite my decadent eccentricities; Susan Lato and Erik Hilsdale, for the roof and so much more; and Sora and Marvin Sachs, well, for everything thus far.

Finally, Cecily Hilsdale: If I cannot imagine what this book might have been without all of those mentioned above, then I cannot imagine what my life would have been like without her. This book is dedicated to her. And to Sasha, whose arrival split the book's process of composition neatly in two and whose early morning shouts of "Daddy!" carry me instantly from text to world. These days his steady nightly request is for "something to help me go to sleep." Maybe someday he'll read this book, but for now I know just what to give him.

Abbreviations

For works frequently cited in the text, the following abbreviations are used.

CH   Reinhart Koselleck. *The Practice of Conceptual History: Timing History, Spacing Concepts*, trans. Todd Samuel Presner and others. Stanford, CA: Stanford University Press, 2002.

CPA   William Playfair. *The Commercial and Political Atlas, Representing by Means of Stained Copper-Plate Charts, the Progress of the Commerce, Revenues, Expenditure, and Debts of England, During the Whole of the Eighteenth Century.* 3rd ed. London: printed for Greenland and Norris, 1801.

CS   Adam Ferguson. *An Essay on the History of Civil Society.* Edited by Fania Oz-Salzberger. Cambridge Texts in the History of Political Thought. Cambridge: Cambridge University Press, 1995.

CW   Samuel Taylor Coleridge. *The Collected Works of Samuel Taylor Coleridge.* Vol. 3, *Essays on His Times in "The Morning Post" and "The Courier."* Edited by David V. Erdman. Princeton, NJ: Princeton University Press, 1978.

DF   Edward Gibbon. *The History of the Decline and Fall of the Roman Empire.* Edited by David Womersley. 3 vols. London: Allen Lane, Penguin Press, 1994.

EML   Vicesimus Knox. *Essays, Moral and Literary.* 2 vols. London: Edward and Charles Dilly, 1778.

EPP   T. R. Malthus. *An Essay on the Principle of Population.* Edited by Geoffrey Gilbert. World's Classics. Oxford: Oxford University Press, 1993.

EW   Charles Darwin. *Evolutionary Writings.* Edited by James A. Secord. Oxford World's Classics. Oxford: Oxford University Press, 2008.

FP   Reinhart Koselleck. *Futures Past: On the Semantics of Historical Time*. Translated by Keith Tribe. Studies in Contemporary German Social Thought. Cambridge, MA: MIT Press, 1985.

GCW   Oliver Goldsmith. *Collected Works of Oliver Goldsmith*. Edited by Arthur Friedman. 5 vols. Oxford: Oxford University Press, 1966.

IPC   William Playfair. *An Inquiry into the Permanent Causes of the Decline and Fall of Powerful and Wealthy Nations*. London: printed for Greenland and Norris, 1805.

LB   William Wordsworth. *Lyrical Ballads* (1798, 1800). In *Wordsworth and Coleridge: Lyrical Ballads*, 2nd ed., edited by R. L. Brett-Smith and A. R. Jones. London: Routledge, 1991.

LJ   Adam Smith. *Lectures on Jurisprudence*. Edited by Ronald L. Meek, David D. Raphael, and Peter G. Stein. The Glasgow edition of the works and correspondence of Adam Smith. 1978. Reprint, Indianapolis, IN: Liberty Fund, 1982.

MCW   John Stuart Mill. *Collected Works of John Stuart Mill*. 33 vols. Toronto: University of Toronto Press, 1963–91.

MS   Adam Smith. *The Theory of Moral Sentiments*. Edited by David D. Raphael and Alec L. Macfie. The Glasgow edition of the works and correspondence of Adam Smith. Indianapolis, IN: Liberty Classics, 1982.

SP   Peter Fritzsche. *Stranded in the Present: Modern Time and the Melancholy of History*. Cambridge, MA: Harvard University Press, 2004.

SPP   Percy Bysshe Shelley. *Shelley's Poetry and Prose: Authoritative Texts, Criticism*. Edited by Donald H. Reiman and Neil Fraistat. 2nd ed. A Norton critical editon. New York: Norton, 2002.

WDQ   Thomas De Quincey. *The Works of Thomas De Quincey*. Vol. 16, *Articles from Tait's Edinburgh Magazine*, etc. General Editor Grevel Lindop. London: Pickering and Chatto, 2000–2003.

WE   Vicesimus Knox. *Winter Evenings, Or, Lucubrations on Life and Letters*. 3 vols. London: Charles Dilly, 1788.

WN   Adam Smith. *An Inquiry into the Nature and Causes of the Wealth of Nations*. Edited by Edwin Cannan. 1904. Reprint, Chicago: University of Chicago Press, 1976.

Introduction

The crumbling ruin stands lit from the east. A sharp ray of light penetrates the clouds, making its way through a recess in the dome and illuminating the activities of the figures at the center of the painting. One holds a pickaxe in mid-swing while two others look on. A fourth tends to a fire over which a tripod holds an iron pot. A small pile of crumbled marble stands ready to meet the axe and in the foreground of the canvas larger piles still, having broken off in chunks from the original structure, suggest that they, too, may soon meet the same fate. To the right, beneath the clouds and bathed in an ethereal light, an elaborate series of columns and arches rise, partially crumbled, and partially intact, all in the process of being reclaimed by weeds and ivy, flowers and trees. The abundant revenge of nature's vegetation slowly creeps in to reclaim the ornate and mannered workings of culture. On the left side of the painting, the process seems complete as a thick grove of trees and overgrowth obscures the view of the building. The activities of the group at the painting's center are framed and to an extent overshadowed by the glorious, crumbling dome that sits above them open to the sky, its oculus edged by a series of statues, but it, too, is threatened by the relentless growth of vines and creepers (Figure 0.1).

With the flames of the small fire literally burning the past for the uses of the present, the painting might be read as one of a series of reminders that nothing man-made endures and that the needs of the present always trump the remnants of the past. Were we to pipe in the vespers of barefooted friars, the scene would come even more to resemble that which inspired Edward Gibbon to undertake his monumental work amid the ruins of Rome on October 15, 1764. And yet, modeled though it is on the ruins of antiquity and the aesthetic tradition of the picturesque through which they were seen by eighteenth-century Grand Tourists, this is no Roman scene. Neither does it represent any old building. Rather, the rotunda, and the larger complex of marble structures of which it stands as the monumental centerpiece, are meant to be John Soane's Bank of England, a building

Figure 0.1: Joseph Gandy, *Architectural Ruins — A Vision* (1798; 1832)

that, at the time of the painting's initial composition in 1798 by Soane's draftsman, Joseph Gandy, *had only just been built.* As Surveyor to the Bank of England, Soane had received a commission for rebuilding the bank and completed some of his designs, but construction had only begun on the rotunda in 1794, shortly before Gandy initially composed his painting.[1]

What are we to make of the fantasy of a building that has only just begun to exist projected into the future as a ruin? What, moreover, might be the significance that the ruined building is not a temple or a public forum, but a bank, *the* Bank of England, the symbol – depending on one's perspective – of the risks and dangers of speculative capital, or the stable, dependable foundation of a credit economy? If the light touch of Gandy's picturesque mode is any indication, the possibility of ruin is not one that inspires dread or fear. If anything, painting the fancied ruin would seem to be an act of confidence rather than crisis. The image of the ruined bank naturalizes credit-based forms of modern capital into a recognizably ancient and enduring form: yes, all things pass, the image suggests, but when this building passes, its ruin will not disappear or be forgotten; it will instead continue to inspire the attention of the future with precisely the hold that the ruins of Rome now have over the imagination of the late eighteenth-century European present. That present will become the antiquity of the future.

Such a prospect would seem to stand for Gandy (and by extension Soane, who commissioned the painting) as a testament to England's greatness in a context where the magnitude of that greatness can only be gleaned from comparison with the most lasting examples that the Western tradition has to offer, the enduring legacy of Rome. In such a view, greatness comes not necessarily through economic, political, or imperial achievement, though this is requisite, but rather through the cultural markers of that achievement – through the built environment that celebrates it, and that, by implication, will endure if only in ruined form after the civilization that it commemorates has long passed. Culture, in other words, venerates and rescues the achievements of the empire after it has passed, never more so than in the grandest gestures of its buildings. Soane was building not for the present, but for the ages.

The image of Soane's unbuilt building in ruins suggests one way that the prospect of decline shadows later eighteenth-century Britain. And yet in Gandy's rendering such a prospect does not terrify; instead, the implied forecast of decline allows Gandy to imagine the form in which Soane's building will endure. There are, of course, other ways to imagine decline. Some saw decline as a frightening and frighteningly close prospect, a view that could often give rise to jeremiads like that of John Brown's screed against luxury and decadence, *An Estimate of the Manners and Principles of the Times* (1757), and Oliver Goldsmith's *The Deserted Village* (1770), an elegy for a lost way of life marked by the depopulation of the author's native village. Both were alarmist works – mistrustful of the new population movements, new values, and new forms of credit associated with the contingencies of commercial society – that predicted the imminent decline of the nation. Others, however, were more optimistic about the prospects of commercial life and less sanguine about whether decline was in fact inevitable.

Gibbon, for example, despite writing a monumental work on decline, considered the technological sophistication and balance of power among European states as an assurance of stability that would prevent Europe from repeating the Roman narrative.[2] Similarly, one of the enduring features of political economy in the version consolidated by Adam Smith's *Wealth of Nations* (1776) was the insistence that arguments for or

against decline needed to be quantified or measured. Taking advantage of
Smith's insistence on measurement, William Playfair later sought to combine the lessons of Smith and Gibbon into a comparative theory of empire
designed to help Britain recognize and forestall the signs of decline.
Meanwhile, alongside these responses to national and imperial decline,
a range of newspapers, periodicals, and books in an incessantly generative
market for print media speculated about the decline of literature in
a commercial age.

These works and others discussed in the pages that follow all engage
the problem of decline. By decline, I refer to a sense of continuous and
ongoing loss or reduction that seems likely to extend into the future,
where what is thought to be in decline could range from the empire,
the economy, and the national character, to the Christian religion, or
the quality of national literature and beyond. As this book will show,
anxieties about decline – national and imperial, economic and political,
cultural and literary – are a pervasive feature of British public discourse
in the later eighteenth and early nineteenth century. To follow this
discourse is to see, time and time again, books and periodical articles,
pamphlets and poems appear that are confident in their predictions
that Britain is in a state of likely irreversible decline. Sometimes the
pronouncements were limited to the literary, as when Isaac D'Israeli
declared in 1795 that "The literary character has, in the present day,
singularly degenerated in the public mind."[3] In other instances the
concerns range more widely to population, the national wealth, and the
economy. As Adam Smith suggested in the *Wealth of Nations*, "five
years have seldom passed away in which some book or pamphlet has
not been published, written too with such abilities as to gain some
credence with the public, and pretending to demonstrate that the
wealth of the nation was fast declining, that the country was depopulated, agriculture neglected, manufactures decaying and trade
undone."[4] In response to this widespread forecasting of impending
decline, Smith argued that such alarmist works were too focused on
the local and short term and missed longer trends and wider patterns.

Smith thus underscores two prominent points about decline that this
book will develop. First, the expectation of decline is a problem of time and
time horizons, and hence an index of how those predicting decline understand and anticipate the future. Second, to foresee decline as inevitable
does not make it so. Indeed, a frequent feature of declinist arguments in the
later eighteenth century (and beyond) is that the possibility of decline can
be forestalled and averted if changes are made. Such arguments show how

predictions of decline reveal a set of values. They suggest, moreover, that decline needs to be understood differently than as oppositional to progress.

But why, the question remains, was there so much concern about decline in a period when progress became the dominant paradigm of historical time? The answer, in part, relates to the expansion of commercial society and a market economy, which, while it was eventually understood to facilitate sociability and networks of interdependence, was also consistently seen, especially in the case of print culture, as pushing towards too much expansion and as producing too much stuff. This abundance of print media – the relentless proliferation of books and periodicals and newspapers and magazines and broadsides and playbills – also generated attendant temporal anxieties. Hazlitt, for example, worried that what was in print was ephemeral and could not stand the test of time as when he characterized modern literature as "a gay Coquette" that "glitters, flutters, buzzes, spawns, dies, – and is forgotten."[5] Related to Hazlitt's concerns about literature in "the bustle of the world"[6] were arguments that with so much in print there was simply no time to read it. As Vicesimus Knox noted in 1778, "in a commercial country like our own. . . only the short interval which the pursuit of gain, and the practice of mechanic arts affords, will be devoted to letters by the more numerous classes of the community" (*EML*, 2:4–5). Such concerns placed an attendant anxiety on how one used the little leisure time one had, and a sense of time pressure led to a correspondent sense of acceleration that left many feeling as if the speed of commerce would lead to social instability and inevitable decline.

But in addition to this historical explanation, the question requires a conceptual clarification. When we understand decline differently than as oppositional to progress, then the apparent discrepancy between the two blurs. Decline too can be productive of new future possibilities; moreover, because anticipations of decline see the future negatively – not as open-ended and unpredictable in the manner often associated with progress, but as closed and graspable – to expect decline, in contrast to expectations of progress, is to force a clarification of value by offering the possibility that decline can be avoided or at least forestalled. This can be seen in the range of possible remedies that commonly accompany anxieties about decline, including the renewal of national manners, the implementation of new policies, the recognition of previously hidden patterns, or in the case of the literary field, the development of new forms of literary experience.

Thinking about decline, then, enables new possibilities and new sources of value. From those who feared decline and announced its likelihood, to those who thought it was a problem that could be measured, managed, and forestalled, through the combination of these extremes and the various positions in between, engagement with arguments about decline suggests that the anticipation of decline might be understood as generative and not disabling, as we see, for example, in Gandy's painting of Soane's bank in ruins. This book is not concerned, in other words, with whether those anticipating decline were correct in their predictions. Rather, its interest lies in how decline becomes a shorthand for discussing a generalized outlook on the future and, more specifically, a reaction to the new contingencies, confusions, and contradictions of an expanding commercial economy.

Decline spanned a variety of discourses and concerns around the turn to the nineteenth century. This book will focus, however, on the literary and cultural significance of decline. There is good reason for doing so. Not only is the later eighteenth-century press full of dire prognostications about the decline of literature, but such anxieties shape debates about the very meaning and efficacy of literature itself. They also impact literary form and literary experience. For a start, there is the issue of canon. Anxieties about the decline of literature commonly relate to the omnipresence of print, its seeming saturation of public and private life. This proliferation of print culture and the expansion of the reading public generated concerns about literary decline that highlight new problems: quality and quantity come to seem opposites, and questions arise about how, with so much material in print, a standard of quality can be maintained, and further, how one could find the time to read even a small portion of what was available. And, with so many readers, not all who read could be said to read literature properly. This is what Wordsworth suggests when he condemns the preference of the reading public in 1800 for "frantic novels, sickly and stupid German Tragedies, and deluges of idle and extravagant stories in verse."[7] We should note here how the "deluges" of stories recall this commonplace sense of a flood of print, and the attendant threat implied by natural disaster. Such problems required a solution, a set of values that could narrow the mass of print media into a readily graspable selection of works: a canon of British literature. Here, quantitative overabundance translates into qualitative assessment. This book's focus on arguments about literary decline thus suggests that canon is not just a reaction to new market conditions created by changes in copyright law as William St. Clair argues, or a new economy of prestige that, in John Guillory's account, reflects the asymmetric distribution of cultural capital, but also a response to new temporal pressures and constraints that accompany commercial society, the same pressures and constraints that contributed to the forecast of literary decline.[8]

Thinking about decline also allows us to reconceptualize the significance of what is often called the Romantic cult of ruins and the aesthetic fascination such material decay held for so many Romantic writers. As numerous scholars have pointed out, ruins were everywhere in the Romantic imagination, where they were an example of decline made visible. In a society moving with apparent speed into an unknown commercial future, ruins join time past and time present and thus serve both as a discursive counterweight to and a sentimental icon of decline. Ruins have consistently been recognized as memento mori, and analyzed by recent critics for revealing a range of specific relationships to time, from the time of empire to the constructed nature of historical experience itself or the new attitudes towards futurity produced by the forward looking instabilities of a credit economy.[9] My suggestion, however, is that thinking about the temporal problems raised by ruins as the inflection of a broader range of concerns about decline reveals not particular issues with empire or history or credit, but a more generalized set of temporal instabilities generated by the rush of commercial society and by the compensatory strategies that develop in relationship to that sense of hurry and accelerated time. The Romantic ruin in this reading is about experiencing the incommensurability of multiple temporalities; it serves as an index for a series of new relationships to the future that emerge in the later eighteenth century in connection with decline.

A related but distinct counterpoint to the sense of decline associated with the rush of market society and the seemingly overwhelming expansion of print, commerce, and population is what I call "slow time," a way of experiencing time that while not necessarily stable at least offers a more secure basis of thought and new possibilities for how to live within accelerated time. The development of slow time reflects the new time pressures of a commercial economy and a society saturated with print. Slow time, however, is not simply a reaction to acceleration, but rather reveals the development of new kinds of literary experience. If, for example, the rush and press of commercial life and the seemingly endless proliferation of things to read helped to generate the sense of literary decline that we so often see articulated in the periodical press, then this might help to explain why action and event are downplayed in so much of Wordsworth's poetry and why verse like "The Old Cumberland Beggar," "Old Man Travelling," and "The Ruined Cottage" turn around the slow movement of marginal figures. In this reading, the lack of eventfulness in Wordsworth's poetry requires – and helps to generate – a particular mode of attentiveness. The experience of reading poetry that represents slow time, and that offers a close and deliberate focus on experiences that transpire beneath the threshold of ready observation, models for its dedicated readers a resistance to the newsworthy eventfulness and rapid change on which the world of commerce appears to thrive. Representations of slow time in poetry, in other words, create new forms of literary experience by deploying a particular temporal framework to generate modes of attentiveness and habits of reading that counter the market's relentless generativity, the nonstop production of more and more print, and the anxieties about decline that are so commonly attached to such proliferation.

All three of these points, which will be developed in what follows, suggest that to trace the reciprocal shaping of eighteenth-century Britain's market culture and its literary culture through the lens of decline – to observe how the literary field seeks to manage and forestall anticipations of decline – offers a fresh way of thinking about how the kinds of emergent literary experience that we associate with British Romanticism handle the problem of time. If the abundance of print and the sense that later eighteenth-century Britain was awash and drowning in what *The Connoisseur* called an "ocean of ink,"[10] contributed to acute concerns about the decline of literature at this time, then we need to recognize that whether explicitly or not, much writing that appears circa 1800 can be understood as part of an intraliterary debate about how to manage and forestall this perceived decline of literature through new forms of literary experience. Hence the persistent posing from the later eighteenth century onwards of such fundamental questions as: What is poetry and who is a poet? What should poetry do in a developed commercial economy? From the framing of these questions in Wordsworth's "Preface" to Thomas Love Peacock's dismissal of "the degraded state of every species of poetry" in the present age of advanced knowledge, to Shelley's rousing "Defence of Poetry," these responses to the perceived decline of literature shape the literary field at the turn of the nineteenth century. A focus on decline thus frames the significance of these questions in new ways and encourages us to recognize that Romanticism itself, with its valorization of poetry and the observing consciousness, constitutes new forms of literary experience as a response to the temporal pressures of commercial society and the perceived decline of literature. Maureen McLane has used these same arguments about poetry by Wordsworth, Peacock, and Shelley to show how they distinguished poetry from literature and how this very distinction helped to produce lyric poetry as the dominant form of what Jean-Luc Nancy and Philippe Lacoue-Labarthe call "the literary absolute." For McLane, this is part of a story about the origin of language and how poetry came to be linked with the origins of Man and hence with a timelessness distinct from the ephemerality associated with the contemporary sea of print and "literature" more broadly considered. Like McLane, I am interested in how poetry and imagination are consistently linked to futurity and immortality, and thus how they come to be defended from historicism, but as I develop the argument in this book, my suggestion is that lyric poetry comes to be the privileged mode of the literary as such not only because its timelessness is grounded in a form of elemental life that preceded the letter, but also due to its technical capacity to model habits of attentiveness that induce slow time.[11]

In my account, then, decline is a problem related to the new pressures on time imposed by commercial society, especially the widespread sense of urgency and rush that Adam Smith called "the hurry of life" in a commercial world, and that Hazlitt later termed "the bustle of the world."[12] My emphasis on commerce helps to explain what distinguishes my account of decline circa 1800 from accounts of "decadence" a century or so later. Stephen Arata has suggested that in decadence, the "perception of loss" outweighed its historical and material validity and he has shown how that perception was cast in narrative.[13] For Arata, the perception of internal decline produces opportunities for cultural regeneration through empire, an empire whose very strength is then understood to produce a propensity for cultural decay. Decadence, then, is an imperial problem, a symptom of Britain's perceived loss of control over its colonies and its citizens. In contrast, decline in my account is rooted in the perceived loss of control over cycles of commercial prosperity and over commercial production, especially of books whose overproduction in the literary realm produces anxieties about the decline of literature. More recently, Vincent Sherry has used the fin-de-siècle decadence movement to reveal an adverse, past-directed orientation in modernism, a movement more commonly understood as pointed firmly towards the future. Decadence, in other words, persists as a trace of "backward time" in a poetics of novelty.[14] I share with Sherry an interest in how a cultural obsession with decay exposes basic structures of time and temporality and an insistence that the "macro-narrative of cultural time may be told most closely and meaningfully... in the micronarratives of imaginative time itself."[15] Sherry locates the origins of this temporality in "the failure of the renewal of historical time in revolutionary romanticism," a lost political ideal that extended into "the feeling of declining times and exhausted time in the historical imaginary of decadence."[16] My account – which might be understood as stretching Sherry's story of conflicted temporality even further backwards by rooting it in temporal complexities associated with the continued spread of commercial society through the eighteenth century – also sees politics here but one more closely grounded in the temporal effects of eighteenth-century cycles of commerce rather than revolutionary failure.

Such distinctions aside, my account of decline shares with arguments about later decadence like those of Arata and Sherry an understanding of decline as a way of anticipating the future negatively, not as a locus of improvement and progress but as a falling away or a withering of strength and value. Accordingly, at the dawn of the nineteenth century as at the dawn of the twentieth, decline and the structure of arguments about decline shift across discursive boundaries. While one of the goals of this book is to show what is distinctive about decline in the literary field, I also want to emphasize a common set of concerns that characterize anticipations of decline circa 1800 across a range of discourses. Decline understood as a general outlook toward the future is not readily constrained to economic, imperial, cultural, or literary terms and apprehensions of decline typically move across these categories of analysis. That is why this book, which has a particular investment in the analysis of literary and cultural decline, also engages attempts to analyze, predict, and prevent decline in a broad range of other discourses. Whether one frets about the decline of national wealth or the loss of territory within the empire or the lapse in the quality of the national literature, anxieties about decline can be understood broadly as worries that arise from a sense of rapid change and an awareness of the increasing uncertainty of the future. Thus, one salient feature of all concerns about decline is that, like the present-day discussion of climate change, such concerns raise questions not only about why decline happens, but <u>when</u>.

Decline, in other words, is a temporal problem keyed to new ways of perceiving time and the future in the later eighteenth century. What distinguishes decline from progress is the anticipation of the future as closing down and narrowing rather than opening up into uncertain realms of improvement. Nonetheless, decline is not necessarily oppositional to progress and might be understood as complementary to it in a number of ways. In all of my examples, new cultural practices, from political economy to statistical graphics to new forms of literary experience, emerge from the encounter with decline, and such practices collectively enable new ways to imagine the future. This creation of new future possibilities, then, is one shared feature of both progress and decline.

In addition, both progress and decline produce new modes through which to imagine the future, but the possibilities for that imagined future, the ways that people living in the eighteenth century understood futurity as such, were changing in significant ways in the later eighteenth century. In part, this can be understood as a feature of acceleration. It was not only that people felt things changing around them, but also that they increasingly sensed a change in the rates of change themselves. As Jürgen Habermas suggests, "the *Zeitgeist*, or spirit of the age, one of the new words that inspired Hegel, characterizes the present as a transition that is consumed in the consciousness of a speeding up and in the expectation of the differentness of the future."[17] As a sense of acceleration developed, the future came to seem fundamentally different from the past and, as a consequence, past experience was less of a guide for future possibilities. Such concerns are more commonly associated with progress than with decline,[18] but my suggestion is that decline too can serve as an index for new attitudes toward the future in the later eighteenth century. Before clarifying the distinctions between progress and decline, however, I want first to elaborate my understanding of social acceleration and how it relates to the emergent temporal concerns and new ways of imagining the future that characterize the eighteenth century.

Reinhart Koselleck associates acceleration especially with the forms of progress that were becoming increasingly widespread in the eighteenth century. Acceleration, for Koselleck, takes two related forms, one structural and tied to periodization and the other phenomenological and linked to how historical change feels to those living through it from the eighteenth century onwards. As a structural issue, Koselleck suggests that what distinguishes modernity from earlier epochs is the ready use and acceptance of markers of period like Antiquity, the Middle Ages, the Renaissance, and the Reformation to distinguish one epoch from another. Only by looking backwards at certain earlier experiences deemed to have lapsed can one make periodizing distinctions that identify the deep structural determinants that say "beforehand not yet" and "afterwards no longer." Further, looking at these concepts in sequence suggests the continued shortening of temporal stages in which the duration of each epoch decreases and the identifying term that characterizes the epoch is more readily accepted as a period concept. "This shortening of temporal stages may be interpreted as a perspectival illusion," Koselleck concedes, "However, there is every reason to believe that more and more new experiences had actually accumulated in shorter and shorter amounts of time, so that with such shortened as well as more quickly established determinations of periods, a new experience of time seems also to have announced itself."[19]

The structural sense of acceleration as a more rapid movement through historical epochs also changes how those living through the later eighteenth century experience time as they come to recognize "the feeling of acceleration by which processes of economic or political change appear to be taking place" (*CH*, 168). This produces an increasing gap between what Koselleck describes as the "space of experience" and the "horizon of expectation." By "space of experience," Koselleck means the ways that people understand their relationship to a collective past, especially how they remember the events of that past and incorporate them into their present experience. By "horizon of expectation," he refers to how people imagine a range of future possibilities and bring those potential futures into their present. The two categories are of different temporal orders since experience is condensed into a focus, while expectation is spread over time, from minutes to centuries. Moreover, Koselleck argues that the relation between these two concepts is itself historical and that "historical time is not simply an empty definition, but rather an entity which alters along with history and from whose changing structure it is possible to deduce the shifting classification of experience and expectation."[20]

In this context, Koselleck characterizes a modernity that he sees emerging in the eighteenth century through the separation of experience and expectation. The anticipation of change and improvement associated with progress makes actual experience less relevant for future expectations. The significant developments to which he attributes this separation and its sense of accelerated time include increasing secularization, the discovery of the globe and the uneven conditions of its peoples, and the advances of science and technology. With these developments, change accelerates at such a rate that the past, the space of experience, becomes less and less of a guide for the future, the horizon of expectation. What we call progress, in other words, makes the future less and less knowable, more open, and more unpredictable. As Koselleck explains, "*Neuzeit* [modernity] is first understood as a *neue Zeit* [new time] from the time that expectations have distanced themselves evermore from all previous experience" (*FP*, 276). This creates what Koselleck describes as a rupture in the continuity between past and present such that "the experience of the past and the expectation of the future were no longer in correspondence, but were progressively divided up" (*FP*, 280). Koselleck sees this process as developing through the eighteenth century and leading to the French Revolution, with which "the previous world of social and political experience, still bound up in the sequence of generations, was blown apart"

(*FP*, 282). The result is that "one process of time became a dynamic of a coexisting plurality of times" (*FP*, 282).

A sense of progress, then, produces temporal plurality and breaks apart the space of experience and the horizon of expectation. The ensuing sense of transition is marked by two specific temporal determinants, "the expected otherness of the future and, associated with it, the alteration in the rhythm of temporal experience: acceleration, by means of which one's own time is distinguished from what went before" (*FP*, 252). Acceleration, then, comes to stand as a new experience of time and the rapid and widespread acceptance of modernity as a concept becomes "an indicator of an acceleration in the rate of change of historical experience and the enhancement of a conscious working-over of the nature of time" (*FP*, 245). History can consequently be understood not as the neutral background of events, but becomes itself temporalized: "Time is no longer simply the medium in which all histories take place; it gains a historical quality. Consequently, history no longer occurs in, but through, time. Time becomes a dynamic and historical force in its own right" (*FP*, 246).

With progress producing a sense of time that itself is a dynamic force of history, a series of related shifts in historical experience that recur repeatedly throughout Koselleck's writing fall into place. Central here is the suggestion that the present is always recognized as a period of transition into an open future, which carries the expectation of new and previously unknown experiences commonly articulated as progress and development. This sense of transition consolidates a series of related processes characterized by Koselleck as:

> the dynamization and temporalization of the experiential world; the task of trying to plan for the open future without being able to foresee the paths of history; the simultaneity of the nonsimultaneous, which pluralistically differentiates events in our world; arising out of it, the perspectival diversity within which historical knowledge must be gained and evaluated; furthermore, the knowledge that one is living in a period of transition in which it becomes harder and harder to reconcile established traditions with necessary innovations; and finally, the feeling of acceleration by which processes of economic or political change appear to be taking place. (*CH*, 168)

The point here is not that these experiences are unheard of prior to the eighteenth century, but that it is at this historical moment that these processes Koselleck identifies as central to the experience of modern time are coordinated with themselves for the first time.

But if progress drives the changes in temporal experience so central to Koselleck's account of modernity, what do we make of decline? Unlike progress, which develops towards an open future in which seeming advance makes that which lies ahead new in ways that cannot be antici-pated or predicted, decline indicates a potential terminus, an endpoint. Decline implies a different sense of time, but one nonetheless related to the concepts of progress that increasingly shape the sense of time in the eight-eenth century. The centrality of progress to the temporalization of history in the eighteenth century, in other words, changes the meaning and implications of decline, and it does so in at least two ways. First, with the dominant expectation of progress and the differentness of the future, decline itself can be integrated into a larger pattern of progress, much as Gandy represents ruin through the picturesque. Decline, Koselleck notes, "surfaces again and again as the aporia of progress or as the reproduction of decline through progress itself."[21] Second, and related, because the idea of progress assumes that the future will be unknown and open in ways that cannot be anticipated, decline becomes a way to close an open future by projecting into the future patterns of decline modeled on the experiences of societies and civilizations that have withered. To see the future as a repetition of past decline can paradoxically even be a comfort because it makes an otherwise unknown future known. This is perhaps why ruins, which function as a spatial symbol of temporal decay, are not only an object of fascination circa 1800 but are also commonly represented through the tropes of the picturesque and even the beautiful rather than through the sublime and the terrible keyed to catastrophe and wreck.

Koselleck offers a compelling account of the new senses of time that characterize the eighteenth century, especially as they relate to a feeling of acceleration and a fracturing of experience where a singular sense of time breaks into a coexisting plurality of times. This is why Koselleck's analysis of temporal experience and processes of acceleration is so central to the interpretation of decline that will be the core focus of this book, which treats decline as a temporal problem. One complaint about Koselleck's argument, however, might be that, as an historian focused predominantly on concepts, he works at such a broad level of abstraction that he loses the empirical details and more particular implications of the concepts in which he traffics. His narrative, after all, frequently depends on grand gestures toward complex processes like the Copernican revolution in science, the development of technology, the discovery of the globe, and the dissolution of established orders of European society.

Working off of the claims about modernity made by Koselleck, Peter Fritzsche is much more particular about what Koselleck's argument might mean for changes in the sense of time circa 1800 and the new practices and possibilities opened up by a fractured sense of time. Fritzsche argues for a new and modern conception of history that, in his view, develops around the time of the French Revolution, what he describes as "the restless iteration of the new so that the past no longer served as a faithful guide to the future, as it had in the exemplary rendering of events and characters since the Renaissance."[22] For Fritzsche, then, as for Koselleck, the European sense of history after the French Revolution is marked by a rupture with the past and a sense of the temporal acceleration of the present, one characterized by a new sense of eventfulness and a disconnection between past, present, and future. As Dorothea Schlegel remarked, "Time has now become so fully rapid. It is not possible to keep up; between one mail day and the other lies an entire historical epoch" (qtd., *SP*, 93). As Fritzsche explains, this sense of rupture might be understood as enabling, since rupture and contingency reveal new possibilities. He is eager to show how ruins, for example, expose what he calls the "half-life" of the past, the way that new structures of temporality reveal the past as a source of latent and buried possibilities, a potential for the past to pose alternatives that, for Fritzsche, "is at least as important as its ability to provide the illusion of durability and naturalness" (*SP*, 108).

Although she maintains a certain skepticism about modernity as a concept, Lynn Hunt also associates the modern understanding of time with a new relationship to the future, one that depends upon the secularization and naturalization of time in a way that makes possible concepts like progress through which historical agents appear to "gain some kind of control over the passing of time."[23] For Hunt, this sense of control arises most firmly from the French Revolution, which "opened the prospect of a new kind of voluntarism, that is, the notion that human will could consciously shape the future and thereby accelerate the effects of time."[24] Like Fritzsche, Hunt understands the French Revolution as marking a rupture with the past, out of which a "new relationship to time was the most significant change, and perhaps the defining development, of the French Revolution."[25]

Collectively, Koselleck, Fritzsche, and Hunt underscore that time itself is historical; more, their work suggests why the sense of time changes in the later eighteenth century and what these changes might mean for the felt sense of history at that time, for how historical agents perceive their relationship to time and to possibilities for the future. They offer, in other words, a historically grounded sense of how time comes to be experienced and understood differently at the turn of the nineteenth

century and a new sense of the possibility and agency generated by a sense
of temporal confusion and disconnection from the past.

Ultimately, however, this book departs from the emphasis these thinkers
place on historical rupture and the consequent centrality of the French
Revolution. Instead, this book suggests that the acceleration and abundance of commercial life, especially as manifested in the proliferation and
eventual saturation of print media, offers new ways of thinking about both
the future and the past prior to the French Revolution, in a manner that
does not necessarily depend on a sense of political rupture and discontinuity with the past. One manifestation of this that I address in later
chapters of this book is the renewed emphasis on slowness that we find
in Coleridge's analysis of the French Revolution and in the poetry of
Wordsworth. Experiences of this type – which are anticipated by the
emphasis on unseen change articulated in Adam Smith's account of
economic activity and enhanced by later eighteenth-century developments
in geology that extend estimates of the age of the earth and underscore the
importance of slow, gradual, imperceptible change – complicate both the
centrality of acceleration and the insistence on rupture in the accounts of
modernity presented by Koselleck and echoed by Fritzsche and Hunt.
In the British context, at least, new senses of time and futurity keyed both
to acceleration and slowness continue to insist on the close connection
between past precedent and future possibilities.

To clarify what I mean by changes in the understanding of time that link
past and present, we can return to Gandy's painting of Soane's bank in
ruins. The temporality implied by Gandy's painting is curious, and can
best be understood through the future perfect tense (the tense sometimes
also called the future anterior), which is used to articulate an action that
will have been completed at some future moment. Similar to the implied
temporality of Gandy's painting, the future perfect projects forward to
a future that then looks retrospectively backward at its present. It anticipates the future, but it also remains gripped by its present moment as it
imagines what that present will look like from the vantage of the future.
The future perfect is thus a fundamentally imaginative mode because it
requires both the forecast of events that have yet to occur and asks that its
present time be reconceived from the perspective of those events. It is also
the tense that best responds to anxieties about futurity as such because it
can imagine the completion of a narrative whose ending is not yet known
in order to speculate on how the present will look from the perspective of
that known future. If, as historians often suggest, truth is the daughter of
time, then historical distance is what makes knowledge of the past possible;

the future perfect seeks to accelerate that distanced perspective and to ask what the significance of the present will be as understood from some future moment when the implications of that present will become clearer. As a mode of projected retrospection that implies continuity between past, present, and future, the future perfect mode forms a central and recurring motif of this book.

Because predictions of decline, like contemporary anxieties about climate change, inevitably raise the question of when the anticipated outcome will occur, this book is ultimately about changes in how those living through the later eighteenth and early nineteenth century perceived their relationship to time and especially to the future. The understanding of decline, I argue, changes in the second half of the eighteenth century because it frequently results from the temporal confusion produced by two fundamentally different orders of time that are experienced in felt conflict during the later eighteenth century and more intensely into the nineteenth. On the one hand, there is acceleration and the sense of speeding up in the rhythm and pace of daily life. This is figured in terms that reflected what Adam Smith called "the hurry of life" in a commercial world and that the *Edinburgh Review* later described as the "universal hurry" of modern life.[26] We might call this the time of commerce since it is a response, as Smith and the *Edinburgh Review* would suggest, to the development of commercial society in eighteenth-century Britain. I would add that, as Chapter 2 suggests, the time of commerce is also related to the saturation of print media exemplified, among other features, by the development of periodicals like the *Edinburgh Review* that addressed the need for the reading public to sort through an ever-expanding array of printed material. Here, the issue is both the increased speed of communication made possible by new distribution networks like sophisticated postal systems, canals, and improved roads, and the sheer proliferation of print in what was increasingly recognized by contemporaries as a print-saturated media environment circa 1800 in which publications of all sorts – from newspapers to books to periodicals to prints and so on – were multiplying. D'Israeli offers a dizzying lament of what the apparently endless increase in the production of literature must have felt like for those experiencing it firsthand when he attempts to calculate the number of volumes that the nineteenth century must infallibly produce, only to lose himself "among billions, trillions, and quartillions," and laying down his pen at infinity.[27] It is the related development of commerce and print media that distinguish the "hurry" identified by both Smith and the *Edinburgh Review* as characteristic of a commercial society.

On the other hand, new developments in what we now call geology began in the later eighteenth century to extend estimates of the age of the earth, emphasizing just how long it took for the earth to assume its present form and extrapolating from present conditions to geoformation before human history. New attention to such processes index not a speeding up, but a slowing down; they stand as a mark of the proliferation of time that we now call "deep time," or the fact that the earth was several million years old, which underscored not how quickly things were moving, but how slowly. The early paleontological and geological research of scientists such as Georges Cuvier and James Hutton, and the emergence of a theory of evolution in the work of Erasmus Darwin, unsettled inherited assumptions about the origins and progress of human life.[28]

Neither the sense of acceleration that I understand to be a function of commercial society and of the commercial context in which print media circulate nor the opposite sense of longer time that itself intensifies with the ever-expanding estimates for the age of the earth from Buffon forward is enough to characterize the sense of time circa 1800. Together, however, these competing and complementary temporalities offer a distinct sense of how temporal experience comes to be framed at the start of the nineteenth century. The book focuses on Britain because it was, by most accounts, the most advanced commercial society in the later eighteenth century, and hence the geographical context for some of the most sophisticated and self-conscious thinking – from Bernard Mandeville and David Hume to Adam Smith and Adam Ferguson, and beyond – about the meaning of commerce for social and moral life.

In addition to its emphasis on a temporal perception that accommodates competing senses of acceleration and slowness, my account of decline departs in other ways from the understanding of time in the work of historians like Koselleck, Fritzsche, and Hunt, whose work still remains essential for any thinking about time and the eighteenth century. If decline can be understood otherwise than as opposition to progress, that does not mean that it signifies simply as progress by other means in the eighteenth century. There is a temporal complexity built into the notion of decline itself that merits closer scrutiny. Unlike progress, which develops towards an open future in which seeming advance makes that which lies ahead new in ways that cannot be anticipated or predicted, decline implies a potential terminus, an endpoint. Decline, then, suggests a different sense of time, but one nonetheless related to the concepts of progress that were becoming increasingly widespread in the eighteenth century. That is why I attend specifically to how concerns about decline produce new experiences of time and new cultural practices. The figures discussed in the pages that follow, from Adam Smith and William Playfair to William Wordsworth, Samuel Taylor Coleridge, and Anna Barbauld, use the problem of decline in a manner resonant with new ways of thinking about time as a multilayered series of processes that unfold in complementary, competing, and sometimes contradictory senses. The time of decline is heterochronic – but not always in the same way.

When thinking about the heterochronic sense of time that I associate with decline and about the plural and dynamic senses of time more generally that become increasingly common in the eighteenth century, an additional factor to consider is the relationship between new experiences of time and new visual modes for representing them. The now omnipresent timeline, for example, first appears in the work of Joseph Priestley in the later 1760s, and its development and acceptance coincides with the period of my study. The metaphor of the line has become such a common means to think about the movement of time and the timeline is now such a recognized norm for visualizing temporal change that it seems impossible to disentangle thinking about time from its linear representation. But why, if lines are such an obvious means to grasp historical time – such an ideal standard of what history looks like, and so ubiquitous to our understanding of the past – why did the timeline not appear until the middle of the eighteenth century? In response to this question, Daniel Rosenberg and Anthony Grafton suggest that the seemingly late appearance and rapid acceptance of new linear formats for visualizing time indicates that the key problem was "not how to design more complex visual schemes . . . but, rather, how to simplify, how to create a visual scheme to clearly communicate the uniformity, directionality, and irreversibility of historical time" (*CT*, 19). The watershed moment was Joseph Priestley's *Chart of Biography* (1765), which "was the first chart to present a complete and fully theorized visual vocabulary for a time map" (*CT*, 19). More, Priestley's elegant solution to the linear visualization of time "also provided an intuitive visual analogue for concepts of historical progress" (*CT*, 19). Priestley's work, in other words, sits at the convergence of new forms of graphic expression and new ways of understanding time connected to the idea of progress.

But decline also plays an important role in the development of new techniques to visualize time in the later eighteenth century, especially in William Playfair's invention of the time-series line graph (and also the bar chart and the pie chart). While Playfair developed his new visual techniques in the 1780s – and was clearly indebted to Priestley, with whom he became acquainted during his apprenticeship in Birmingham from

1777–1781 with Matthew Boulton and James Watt – he subsequently put these graphic technologies to the service of a comparative theory of empire designed to help the expanding British empire recognize and forestall the signs of decline. The focus of my discussion of later eighteenth-century innovations in the visualization of time, then, is not on the timeline, but rather on Playfair's new visual strategies for conveying quickly and at a glance large quantities of data to facilitate the recognition of gradual change over time. As we will see, Playfair's attempt to forestall decline through new ways of visualizing time and temporal process complicate and accentuate the very processes of acceleration that they allow users to track because they make it possible to see time at a glance, to see, that is, more time in less time. Or, as Playfair put it, his graphs meant that "as much information may be *obtained in five minutes as would require whole days to imprint on the memory, in a lasting manner, by a table of figures*" (*CPA*, 1801, xii, emphasis original). This is why I devote sustained attention to Playfair's work in Chapter 1 where my argument seeks to clarify both the relationship between concepts and modes of representation and a grammar for the graphical representation of time.

My analysis of Playfair's new techniques for visualizing time thus borrows from Rosenberg and Grafton the insight that the visual compo-nents of historical understanding are commonly overlooked. More, for Rosenberg and Grafton, their treatment of cartographies of time is to be understood as "a reflection on lines—straight and curved, branching and crossing, simple and embellished, technical and artistic—the basic com-ponents of historical diagrams" (*CT*, 10). The pair continue to note that "Addressing the problem of chronology . . . means going back to the line, to understand its ubiquity, flexibility, and force" (*CT*, 13). While my discussion of Playfair shares this interest in the line, I also want to extend Rosenberg and Grafton's insights away from the visual and towards a different kind of line: the straight even lines that characterize most printed texts in the eighteenth century, and ultimately, the lines that make up a poem. Priestley's representation of temporal change in linear form brought new problems, most notably that historical narrative is not solely linear and thus the timeline flattens the many intersecting trajec-tories of time that characterize temporal experience and historical narra-tive. Accordingly, much of the later part of Rosenberg and Grafton's history concerns alternative visual and verbal metaphors for time and other less linear modes of representing its passing.

This is what I uncover not in visual modes, but in the *versus* of poetry, in my reading of lines that have their own complex logic, one that has much to teach us about the temporal experiences of decline and progress at the turn of the nineteenth century and also about the capacity of poetry to integrate linear time with other nonlinear, irregular, and contradictory temporal experiences. In my account, poetry that takes as its occasion various possibilities of decline struggles with futurity and gives shape and form to the heterochrony so central to the experience of modernity. This shaping quality of poetry, its capacity to sustain multiple possibilities and contradictions without resolution, both in its content, but also in its formal qualities, make it a fruitful site for uncovering temporal complexity and for further developing the intricate sense of time emphasized by Rosenberg and Grafton and also by Koselleck, Fritzsche, and Hunt.

This, then, is my primary point of departure from the historical work that has influenced how I address time in this study: in addition to using decline to complicate what is often perceived as a one-sided process of acceleration and to move away from an emphasis on rupture, I focus on poetry because it is a way of writing framed by meter and rhythm, with temporal functions built into its very basis. Even more importantly, the explicit handling of temporal problems in later eighteenth- and early nineteenth-century poetry documents, as I will show, a temporal sense and a capacity for articulating new kinds of temporal experience that are even more richly layered than the already complicated sense of time offered by those discussed above. This is why I refer to a "poetics" of decline, an imaginative working out of the possibilities of decline that I analyze in relation to the complex forms of temporality that such a working out continuously invokes.

This is not to say that poetry is the only locus for working through temporal complexity. I take it as my focus, however, because in addition to the reasons outlined above, poetry has received less critical attention than the novel in this context. Scholars like James Chandler, Katie Trumpener, and Ian Duncan, for example, have shown how the novel serves as a major site for developments and refinements in the representation of nonsynchronous time. Such work has tended to focus on the problem of uneven development and to derive its force from an analysis of the fiction of Walter Scott and those who influenced him or who worked in what Duncan calls "Scott's shadow." For these critics, the novel circa 1800 offers the most sophisticated and consequential reflection on the layering of different historical scales, from the personal to the national – a series of scalar incommensurables that Adelene Buckland has now extended also to the longer times of natural history.[29]

Prose journalism could also be a useful place to articulate the perception of heterochrony, perhaps never more so than Samuel Taylor Coleridge's 1802 essays that address the establishment of the French Empire under Napoleon. There, Coleridge insists that the rise of Napoleon and the transition from republic to empire in France is not just parallel to the establishment of the Roman Empire by Augustus, but that the more recent event is a precise repetition of the past, with the only difference being "the degrees of rapidity with which the same processes have been accomplished." As Coleridge insists, "The reigns of the first three Caesars have been crowded into the three first years of the reign of Bonaparte."[30] For Coleridge, this speed of accomplishment also augers a similarly rapid decline. The temporality of Coleridge's understanding of the relation between Rome and France, as I discuss in Chapter 5, is distinctive. Even as Coleridge acknowledges the increased speed at which modern events unfold, he also insists on continuity between antiquity and the present because "As human nature is the same in all ages, similar events will of course take place under similar circumstances."[31] This is precisely the sort of exemplary thinking that, in Koselleck's argument, falls away with the French Revolution,[32] but for Coleridge, the slow timescale of antiquity as seen in Roman history and the fast timescale of the present as seen through events in France do not preclude comparison. Indeed, it is through such a comparison that one can be confident that Britain will triumph over France. For Coleridge, in other words, the speed of the present and the seemingly accelerated rate of change in his contemporary moment does not invalidate a comparison with earlier and slower historical eras, and one can use the slower pace of past events to anticipate the future on the fly.

For others, however, a sense of different timescales experienced simultaneously produced not a cohesion, but a barely articulated sense of conflict or irresolution. What I described above as an abrupt juxtaposition of fast and slow timescales produced a temporal dissonance that made it increasingly difficult to imagine what Koselleck describes as an "open future," and the traces of this dissonance can be found in particular literary forms. This is why poetry plays such an important role in my understanding of decline generally and in my analysis of how anxieties about decline relate to new experiences of time developing in the later eighteenth century. In Charlotte Smith's poem *Beachy Head*, for example, the immediacy of the speaker's lyric voice reveals an awareness of temporal richness and a deep past as it alludes to the discovery on "hills so early loved" of "fossil forms" and "enormous bones" "with the pale calcareous soil mingled."[33] Smith's poem uses a lyric present, an enduring sense of now, to unfold the rich layers of time accruing beneath that present. In this way a complex spatial stratigraphy, and Smith's particular connection to the landscape of the South Downs, comes to stand also for the layers of temporal complexity so richly mined by Smith out of the various historical times layered into Beachy Head on the chalky southeastern coast.

A similar sense of temporal multiplicity, of different timescales unfolding with a tangled simultaneity, can also be found in Anna Barbauld's *Eighteen Hundred and Eleven* – the subject of Chapter 3 – which shows well the felt tension between accelerated time and slow time. Barbauld's poem describes women left behind by war poring over newspapers: "Oft o'er the daily page some soft-one bends / To learn the fate of husband, brothers, friends."[34] The repetitive and daily quality of this newspaper reading recalls, of course, the dated specificity produced by the poem's title, but the affect produced by the reading – the "anxious eye" (35) that fears "wrecked... bliss" (37) – threatens to encompass such predictability with the more mute and shapeless feelings of anticipated loss and dread. But time in the poem is marked not only by these daily activities whose aggregation produces the year eighteen hundred and eleven, but also by a less specific, less linear manner of marking time through stone and rock as the poem uses the mode of the future perfect to imagine how future visitors to a ruined London will commemorate Britain's past. Barbauld's reference to stone "mined by time" (171) might also be understood in connection with a different kind of mining than that of the poem's later reference to "the ponderous ore" (227), which when drawn from its bed serves to initiate the motor force of commerce. It might be linked – especially given the way that Barbauld's plow recalls the uncovering of weapons and bones in Virgil's *Georgics* – to the digging up of bones and fossils and to the extended timescales that these objects come to represent in the later eighteenth century and into the nineteenth.

While the poem does not explicitly refer to new developments and disputes in natural history, the time of ruin in the poem is itself a kind of slow, or perhaps even deep time, a time that in its intentional incomprehensibility and confusion – can London really fall into ruin in the manner of Rome? – stands for the closest regular human time can come to the vast and incomprehensible timescales of earthly change, to a timescale where the earth itself might be understood as "mined by time." Barbauld, then, shows us simultaneously a sense of compression (the "universal hurry" of modern life) and expansion (prolonged, slower time) that disrupted progressivist historical assumptions, as the theological future of the past became the secular, market-driven future of the present.

Wordsworth's poetry, as I explain in Chapters 4 and 6, also articulates a related sense of temporal contrast that he too associates with decline – though Wordsworth sees decline marked not on the grand scale of national monuments as we see in Barbauld's poem and Gandy's painting but rather through the marginal figures and common structures whose slow decline forms the basis of much of his poetry. Here, I have in mind his analysis of the increased speed of contemporary life characterized by "great national events" – by which he presumably means the British response to the French Revolution and the subsequent Revolutionary and Napoleonic wars – that have caused a "craving for extraordinary incident" in new, crowded urban populations.[35] Further, this craving is fulfilled "hourly" by "the rapid communication of intelligence," by which he refers not only to the increasing capacity of print to fulfill a desire for news, but to do so "rapidly" (*LB*, 249). This lexicon of speed matches that of Coleridge in his analysis of France and suggests how both understand what we might call "informational time" as contributing to the felt acceleration of social life. But instead of using an awareness of this time to anticipate future events, Wordsworth moves in a direction different than Coleridge. He introduces his poetry as an explicit response to this craving for news and event, as an attempt to enhance the capability of his readers for "being excited without the application of gross and violent stimulants" (*LB*, 248) and he adds that the "endeavour to produce or enlarge this capability is one of the best services in which, at any period, a Writer can be engaged" (*LB*, 249).

This, I argue, is why so much of Wordsworth's poetry – especially his early poetry from the *Lyrical Ballads* through to *The Excursion*, whose initial portions were also composed at this time as "The Ruined Cottage" – focuses on the slow, uneventful movement, commonly of old men, through the landscape. Given its link to the rapidity of accelerated time, I argue, such slowness needs to be understood as a hortatory slowness, as a valuation of the slow generally that works in conjunction with the steadying rhythms of poetic meter as a means to heighten perception and repair the wound to attention inflicted by the increasingly common craving for eventfulness that Wordsworth so resents in the "Preface." Such slow time is not deep time per se, but it is a pushback against speed that aims to sensitize its readers to slow, often invisible processes of change, processes that are necessary for an imaginative purchase on deep time, as Chapter 6 suggests in speculating about what Darwin might have learned from Wordsworth.

Read this way, for Barbauld, Wordsworth, and others poetry expresses a particular kind of temporal feeling in its use of rhythm and meter to regulate pace and the movement of language, but also in its capacity to represent a sense of time that often operates below the level of explicit articulation, the presence of which can be extrapolated from the traces left behind. Inchoate temporal experience, in other words, registers in poetry as a sense of disturbance or incoherence that, in turn, preserves and makes available for later critical uncovering a sense of time that would otherwise be unknowable. The simultaneous representation and thematization of slowness suggest temporal structures of reception built into poetry itself. This is not to say that poetry is the only place that such embryonic and often amorphous experiences register, but I am particularly interested in how, in the case of Wordsworth, the lyric as a mode of mediated imme-diacy seeks to commemorate particular present moments while also remaining shot through with the traces of other times and temporalities. Similarly, while Barbauld's satire *Eighteen Hundred and Eleven* is not a lyric per se, in taking its title from a date meant to represent the present it too works to mark a present moment while also complicating the temporalities that surround that moment through its future perfect structure.

In formulating my understanding of poetry thus, it might be compared to recent foundational work in Romantic studies by Kevis Goodman and Mary Favret, work to which this book owes a considerable debt. Goodman follows Raymond Williams in demonstrating how literary works can be understood as privileged sites for preserving the flux of historical process, what Williams calls history "in solution." Literary works can thus help us to grapple with what Goodman describes as "the difficulty of recording and recognizing history-on-the-move," which registers affectively "as *unplea-surable* feeling: as sensory discomfort, as disturbance in affect." Such an amorphous and difficult to articulate "noise of living" contrasts to "sha-pely, staged, or well-defined emotions."[36] Literary writing is then under-stood as registering the affective and cognitive dissonances that lie beneath formed ideas, and such writing preserves an affective residue that records an otherwise unknowable history. In the context of media saturation and the ensuing sense of accelerated eventfulness that this book calls informa-tional time, Goodman explains how a literary mode, georgic in her case, can act not only "as a shield against the possibility of sensory over-extension" but also as "an *aperture*, disclosing the pressures it might seek to cover."[37]

But such an aperture, of course, is not exclusive to the georgic mode. Mary Favret extends the sense of affective disturbance that so interests

Goodman as the more general mark of wartime. Romanticism, in this account, "gives its distinctive voice to the dislocated experience that is modern wartime: the experience of war mediated, of time and times unmoored, of feeling intensified but also adrift."[38] Reading the uneasy feelings produced by this dislocation offers a new way to tell the time of war, a time that eludes models associated with historical linearity and periodicity. For Favret, affect of this sort can be understood as a productive response that she contrasts explicitly with the cognitive work done by the date in Barbauld's poem as described above, since affect, in Favret's interpretation, resists the linearity preserved by markers of calendar time. As Favret suggests, "If we take wartime less as an object of cognition bounded by dates – a period – and more as an affecting experience which resonates beyond the here and now, then wartime literature becomes an attempt to trace and give shape to such affect, to register its wayward power."[39] There is thus a particular tension between the date – in its largest sense as a marker of a temporal moment but also as a periodizing impulse – and the feelings understood to be produced by the date, a tension between counted, dated experience, and what Anne-Lise François calls "uncounted experience," the unconsidered or commonplace anxieties about time and the present that are close to cognition but never fully articulated.[40]

Poetry, then, might help us to recognize history-on-the-move and "in solution," while revealing traces of temporal process that allow insight into how present (now historical) events feel to those experiencing them through various levels of mediation. In drawing upon Goodman and Favret for this account of poetry, temporal experience, and affect, I am interested less in the kind of troubled affect so central to both of their accounts, and more in the particularities of temporal affect, or a feeling for disturbances in time. This is a disturbance that this book, following Goodman, locates in an emphasis on how eighteenth-century media produce a sense of acceleration and overextension that marks literary form, and also, like Favret, in a sense of wartime. Ultimately, however, my account does not locate the source of temporal disturbance solely in the accelerated time of media or war; instead, I aim to show how both senses of time are complemented and complicated by competing processes of slow, or deep time, time whose manifestations and movements work on a level that often escapes perception. This is not to suggest that time is simply nonlinear. Rather, time is linear, and the poems I treat in this book follow a narrative thread that we might understand as akin to a gridded historical timeline; but they also point to other times in a manner that cannot be readily placed within a historical grid, and they thus reveal how what we consider the past was experienced as the present for those living through it. The past never exists except as a realm outside of a continuum of particular presents, moments that are in turn dissolved into the past with each passing moment.

Decline is a relative concept. As such, one quality that inevitably links arguments about decline across different discourses is their comparative quality, whether implicit or explicit. Sometimes, in debates about national decline or the decline of national literature, this comparison is between two extant nations, often where one is understood as rising and the other as declining; at other times, the comparison can be between a contemporary power and a past example of decline.[41] Such comparisons can also be internal, as when aspects of a nation's present are judged negatively against its past.[42] Decline is also a notoriously slippery category. One of the most important developments associated with political economy generally is the shift away from understanding decline as a moral problem (as we see in John Brown and Oliver Goldsmith) and toward an insistence that decline must be measured and quantified. To speculate about decline, in other words, requires that one identify what is in decline as a quality to be measured and then track the changes in that quantity over a significant period of time. Accordingly, this book argues that important standards for the measurement and understanding of decline emerge in the later eighteenth century in the work of Adam Smith, Edward Gibbon, and Smith's self-proclaimed acolyte, William Playfair.

Chapter 1, on decline and political economy, opens in 1776 when colonial revolt gave those worried about decline a concrete set of events on which to pin their fears. They also had, with the publication of the first volume of Edward Gibbon's *Decline and Fall of the Roman Empire* (also in 1776), a powerful new model to explain decline through its prior occurrence in antiquity. The convergence of these events tapped into a deep strain of concerns about the social and political implications of what we would now call commercial modernity. The chapter shows how Adam Smith sought to address these concerns by proposing quantifiable categories through which relative decline could be measured and by insisting on the century as the proper timescale in which such quantities could be observed. What might appear to be a process of decline and fall, Smith suggested, could, with a shift to the long view, be explained instead as part of a normal business cycle. Smith, then, encourages us to think about decline through the abstract comparison of particular qualities measured over a century, while Gibbon, who is less invested in the measurement of particulars and more in the course of time during which they need to be observed, shifts the scale of evaluation to the millennium. William Playfair, in turn, draws both on Smith's quantification measured over a century and Gibbon's broader millennial scale to visualize more easily the patterns Smith sought to identify and to produce a comparative account of imperial decline structured around novel graphic images that can be readily understood at a glance.

The quantitative analysis of decline – associated here with Adam Smith and William Playfair – and political economic thinking about decline scaled to the time span of a century might be understood as imaginative insofar as its rendering of decline allows for the perception of long term trends that can be revealed not just in the past but also projected forwards into the future. This is what the speculative continuity of trends and linear patterns to the right of known quantities in the typical time-series line graph invites us to do. If, then, there is an imaginative aspect to the treatment of decline in more quantitatively based political economy, there is also a quantitative element to thinking about decline in association with imaginative writing and the perceived decline of literature. In the case of culture broadly and literature in particular, measuring the relative decline associated with political economy is simply not possible, and judgments of decline tend to be more evaluative and grounded in perceived lapses of taste. Nonetheless, as Chapter 2 explains, perceptions of the decline of literature circa 1800 might be thought of as a quantitative problem insofar as the rapid proliferation of print media, what we might think of as the saturation of print, is a quantitative issue.

By the decline of literature, I refer to three related contemporary perceptions: decline in the quality of literature itself, decline of the importance of "literature" in British culture, and decline in the intellect of readers, what Wordsworth called the "savage torpor" of the audience for poetry circa 1800. All three were a product of the increasing commercialization of cheap print media, which also enabled more people to engage literature than ever before. This chapter observes the tendency to discuss the decline of literature as an outgrowth of a quantitative problem – the vastly increasing number of works in print – in which concerns about the quantity of literature stand also for concerns about similar increases in the number of authors and, especially, of readers. When, for example, D'Israeli suggested that the literary character had degenerated in the example above, his claim was followed by a projection of the future output of the press stretching from billions of volumes ultimately to infinity. D'Israeli's speculation about the continued growth of print is borne out by the bookseller

James Lackington's estimate in his 1791 *Memoirs*, that "more than four times the number of books are sold now than were sold twenty years since."[43] More recently, William St. Clair, in his comprehensive study of the Romantic reading nation, has affirmed that "Despite virtually continuous wars from 1793 until 1815 and high taxes on paper and advertising for long afterwards, the British book industry boomed as never before. In the year 1822 Longman was reported to have sold five million volumes, employed sixty clerks, and given employment to two hundred and fifty printers and bookbinders."[44]

When commentators acknowledge this rapid expansion of print media negatively, we see one of the ways that discourses of decline in political economy and literature resemble each other. The implicit, and frequently explicit, suggestion of arguments for decline based on quantity follows the political economic logic whereby a greater supply of a good results in a lower price. Translated into the qualitative evaluation of the literary marketplace, the argument is one whereby a greater quantity of literature must inevitably be of a lower quality and must also therefore reflect a falling off from the standards of past literary production. By the later part of the eighteenth century such moves are further distinguished by the increasingly common contiguity of anxieties about the expanding quantity of print and the decreasing quantity of time in which to read. Proliferation, in other words, becomes a temporal problem and the chapter ultimately suggests that the sense of hurry and rush both described and exacerbated by print contributes to the emphasis on duration and timelessness in arguments for the value of literature by Wordsworth, Shelley, and De Quincey.

Questions about the relationship between decline and quantification frame the first two chapters of the book. Ultimately, I argue that on the subject of literary decline, quantitative overproduction produces qualitative judgment. But cultural discourses like literature and painting that escape (at least during the period of my study) most forms of quantitative analysis nonetheless contain an imaginative quality that enables them to flesh out and develop future possibilities that may happen but have yet to occur. They invite us to consider the horizon to the right of Playfair's time-series line graph, that uncharted and uncharitable region of time that we call the future, where the only guide is the perceived extension of a trend-line continuing beyond the most recent known measurement. Gandy's image of Soane's bank is one such example. We can also think in this context of Anna Barbauld's *Eighteen Hundred and Eleven*, the subject of Chapter 3 and a work that, like Playfair's graphics, asks us to visualize decline but this time through the careful description of England's ruined empire projected into the future.[45] Barbauld, neé Aikin, was a classically educated member of a prominent dissenting family whose father, John, taught at the Warrington Academy. Barbauld was exceptionally well versed in the intellectual discourse of her day and, in a claim derived from political economy, her poem suggests that global warfare would wreck economic prosperity and produce national decline.

The poem describes England's projected ruins in careful detail, but when Barbauld imagines a ruined England as the antiquity of the future, her poem helps to figure not the decline of England but the enduring value of English literature, which will become the "classics" of an empire whose center has shifted to North America. The work closely resembles Gandy's fantasy of Soane's bank because in each case, decline is not measured but assumed, and both Barbauld and Gandy provide an example of how cultural achievement compensates for the inevitable loss of power and territory. In the year prior to the date of *Eighteen Hundred and Eleven*, the last poem that Barbauld wrote, she published a fifty-volume series of *The British Novelists*. The close links between the canon of national culture established in *Eighteen Hundred and Eleven* and the canon of novelists that appeared just before it support my insistence that while canon can and should be understood in connection with the asymmetrical distribution of cultural capital, it also must be considered as a response to anxieties about the decline of literature and the new temporal pressures intensified by print proliferation circa 1800.

From projected future ruin and its inevitable questions about the set of values that would remain after the decline of Britain that I characterize as an often-overlooked feature of canon formation, the book turns to a series of chapters that explain how the fear of decline frames new contingencies in Romanic understandings of time. Chapter 4 offers a close reading of Wordsworth's "The Ruined Cottage" to show that the Romantic fascination with ruins can productively be understood as a representation in space of the confusion produced by discord between a sense of accelerated time and experiences of slowness and gradual change. This chapter introduces what I call "temporal parallax" as a way of referring to these competing senses of time and their felt incommensurability signified by the experience of ruin.

The book's final two chapters then develop an account of what I call "slow time," as a counterpoint to the overwhelming propagation of media, people, and commerce that so frequently generated anxieties about decline. As developed in the poetry of Wordsworth and the prose of Samuel Taylor

Coleridge, slow time offers a way of experiencing time that was, if not stable, at least secure as a basis for thought and meditation about how to live within time. Chapter 5 considers Coleridge's use of the ancient Roman example in developing his ideas about the aftermath of the French Revolution. Coleridge's reflections on the links between Napoleonic France and imperial Rome are part of his effort to understand the initiation of "revolutionary time," that ostensibly new sense of time thought by many circa 1800 to be a product of the French Revolution that sees the future as cut free from the constraint of past precedent. In the context of this seeming rupture between past and present, Coleridge comes to associate Roman antiquity – and the transition from republic to empire most pointedly – with a particular pace and rate of change, and with slowness generally, a slowness that serves as a marked contrast to the apparent speed of his present moment. What can be gained by comparison between two such temporally uneven durations of time? Is it even possible to link two series of events that are understood to unfold at different speeds? In response to these questions, this chapter shows how Coleridge's slow time is inextricable from the seeming speed and acceleration with which events were understood to develop in the aftermath of the French Revolution. Coleridge returns processes of slow and gradual change into the French Revolution's seeming rupture with the past. Following Coleridge, the overall argument of this book reconstitutes at the level of its thesis a stress on gradual models of structural change over and against the seeming rupture with the past preferred by more catastrophic models.

In keeping with this argument, Chapter 6 develops what I describe as a poetics of slowness that characterizes Wordsworth's poetry. For Coleridge, slow time is an explicit mode in the analysis of historical decline and a means to help forecast the outcome of events in France; for Wordsworth, in contrast, slow time is not a historical mode and his work is less about the contingencies and particularities of decline on a national scale. Rather, Wordsworth is concerned with the impact of national issues like war, poverty, and economic crisis on particular individual lives. Decline is crucial to this poetics, not only because Wordsworth's "Preface" fits easily into the type of "decline of literature" jeremiad written against contemporary taste and the habits of the later eighteenth-century reading public (as discussed in Chapter 2), but also because the poetry itself represents explicit processes of decline, as in the case of "The Ruined Cottage"; and also because in other instances the figures depicted in Wordsworth's poetry themselves might be understood as being in decline or, as Wordsworth says of the old Cumberland beggar, as representative of a way of life facing what he calls "extinction." Reading works by Barbauld, Coleridge, and Wordsworth through the lens of decline reveals the perceived acceleration of modernity not as a rupture with the past, but as closely related to new kinds of slowness and a new appreciation for the infinitesimal rates of change that would later become central to Darwinian evolution.

With its speculative attention to how time might feel to those experiencing it not as past but as present, *The Poetics of Decline in British Romanticism* seeks to understand the layered, uneven, heterochronic temporality that complicates and complements the progressive, even time of historicism. It thus focuses not on a precise range of dates in which time is understood to change definitively, but rather on an approximate time span, circa 1800. This is not to suggest that time and temporal experience are somehow simple and clear prior to this historical moment; rather, the sense of time that this book tracks requires the presence of two contradictory senses of time that emerge fully only in the eighteenth century and it understands these time senses as complementary and integral to temporal experience circa 1800: the informational, media time of commercial society and the slow, deep time commonly associated with geology and developed in my examples by Coleridge and Wordsworth.

My particular focus on decline derives from both senses of time. With the development of the idea of progress through the eighteenth century, the meaning of decline also began to change. Decline, the book suggests, comes to be understood not as terminal and definitive, as the precedent to an inevitable fall, but often as a temporary setback within a larger pattern of progress and advance. But with progress also comes an increasing sense of the contingency, or openness, of the future and apprehensions of decline can also be understood as a reaction to this new sense of uncertainty associated with the progress of a commercial society. Indeed predictions of decline, I suggest, often seek to close an open future by projecting patterns of the past, especially the model of decline and fall in the model of Rome, forward into the future. And so, this Introduction also closes where it opened, with the lingering image of Gandy's crumbled dome, a structure that was indeed destroyed in the 1920s but of which no traces now remain: its afterlife was not as Gandy imagined it would be. Past is prologue, but not always in the ways that we anticipate.

From Morals to Measurement: Scaling Time, Anticipating the Future, and Quantifying Decline in Gibbon, Smith, and Playfair

> Be assured, my young friend, there is a great deal of ruin in a nation.
> – Adam Smith, letter of 1777

Introduction

After the British surrender at Saratoga in October of 1777, a young correspondent wrote to Adam Smith of his fear that the British loss was a sign of national ruin. Many must have shared his distress. It would have been hard not to read the potential loss of a large and productive colony as anything other than a sign of decline, especially for those invested in mercantilist understandings of empire as the source of national wealth and prestige. Though certainly related to colonial events, such anxieties might also be understood as indicative of more widespread changes in the way those living in the later eighteenth century understood their relationship to the past and, as a result, their expectations for the future. Reinhart Koselleck, as we saw in my Introduction, argues that a widespread sense of time speeding up makes it more difficult for those living in the eighteenth century to imagine the future. This is because what he calls the "space of experience" (the past that people use to relate to their present) no longer matches the "horizon of expectation" (their imagination of a potential future).[1] For Koselleck, in other words, with the Enlightenment understanding of progress comes the possibility that the future will be fundamentally different from the past because new ways of understanding the world create future possibilities that are conceived as new in a way that cannot be entirely derived from previous experience.

Koselleck is not the only one to make this claim, and it correlates with, for example, J. G. A. Pocock's argument about the implications of public credit for the sense of the future in the British context. Pocock proposes that "the growth of public credit obliged capitalist society to develop as an ideology something society had never possessed before, the image of a secular and historical future," which he further characterizes as "the spectacle of a society advancing at high speed into a world it can only imagine as existing in the forms which it may desire."[2] Pocock describes a shift from a theological future to a market future in which markets and credit structures are contending with a religious notion of futurity as they seek to replace a religious teleology with a market teleology.[3] Here, it is not just that public credit produces the "image of a secular and historical future" but also that in a credit-based economy, such a future seems to be arriving "at high speed." It is thus not just daily life in commercial society that can be understood as fast and accelerating, but also the more general and widespread sense that such a society imagines itself moving through time.

As this book's Introduction clarified and as Koselleck and Pocock confirm, this is a period of increasing self-consciousness about the uncertainty of the future and a period of increasing awareness of the speed at which the future seems to be arriving. My point is that while late eighteenth-century anxieties about decline might be linked with particular events like the loss of colonies, as they clearly are for Smith's correspondent, such anxieties might also reflect broader changes in time-sense that make it more difficult to imagine the future at all. Fear of decline can be understood as a response to this problem, whereby imagining imminent decline helps to contain an open future by making it knowable. The future will be a repetition of past decline. Saratoga initiates national ruin.

But decline is not the only way to imagine the future and Smith's (perhaps phlegmatic) composure in answering his correspondent is telling in this regard. "Be assured, my young friend," he replied, "there is a great deal of ruin in a nation."[4] Smith's response forms the basis of the present chapter, which will consider how discourses of decline can help to index changes in the scale on which time is imagined and experienced in the later eighteenth century. In its focus on Smith's "great deal of ruin in a nation," my argument's debt to Donald Winch, who uses this reply as the title of an essay on Smith and the problem of decline, will be obvious. Winch claims that, for Smith, "centuries were the relevant timescale for some of his observations."[5] Similarly, in another work more obviously focused on decline, Gibbon rejects his contemporaries' fears of Roman-style decline and produces an argument for European security in part through an expansion of the timescale through which decline can be recognized. The fall of Rome may have been a setback for European manners, but a shift in perspective to the many millennia that surround Rome's rise and fall reveal, according to Gibbon, a broader pattern of progress.

My argument, then, is that in the later eighteenth century, decline becomes a problem not of morals, but of measurement. It is, moreover, a temporal problem insofar as recognizing decline requires, according to Smith and Gibbon, a properly distanced perspective. One of my fundamental claims will be the obvious one that 1776 marks a key moment in the political and intellectual understanding of decline in the conjunction between Smith, Gibbon, and the American Revolution.[6] This is why I choose to read Smith alongside Gibbon: both works offer a response to widespread perceptions of national and cultural decline, and in each case, the repudiation depends on a rejection of the moralizing that characterizes much of the literature of decline in favor of a focus on the effects of temporal rescaling and resizing. In addition to this connection, I want to suggest further that the 1770s generally, and the work of Smith and Gibbon in particular, mark a moment in which understandings of temporal scale are reordered in a variety of discourses, including historiography, political economy, and natural history. While consistent with Michel Foucault's much-repeated point about the temporalization of knowledge in the later eighteenth century,[7] I will suggest that we can understand the implications of this reordering of temporal scale as a problem of distance that needs to be considered along broader representational axes, both verbal and visual.[8] My close reading of patterns of progress and decline in Gibbon and Smith will therefore suggest how various kinds of distancing and measurement force a reconsideration of arguments about decline and convert apparent decline into a larger pattern of progress. Such patterns then form the basis of the novel graphic techniques of William Playfair, the focus of the second half of the chapter whose charts of time give visual form to the temporal scales used by Gibbon and Smith to evaluate decline.

Gibbon

Greece and Rome were particularly important in connection with eighteenth-century anxieties about decline because they presented a surviving record of societies that had gone through the cycle of rise, growth, decline, and fall. For those who believed in a cyclical model of history or in the relevance of historical parallels between temporally and geographically distinct events the example of antiquity offered the challenge of finding a way to prevent the repetition of a cycle that brought the ancient world to an end. As Michael Sonenscher suggests, "Chronologically the modern world was [the ancient world's] heir. What came to matter in the eighteenth century was whether it might also have its fate... [whether]

eighteenth-century Europe might have to face the prospect of a replay of
the ancient cycle of decline and fall under modern conditions of war and
debt." As Sonenscher continues to explain, the threat to European prosperity and power "was not so much the inequality and luxury that, according
to a long-standing tradition of political and historical analysis, had been
responsible for earlier cycles of decline and fall, but the new financial
instruments and fiscal resources that had accompanied the transformation
of warfare during the seventeenth and eighteenth centuries."[9] For
Sonenscher, the problem of decline and fall becomes a problem of debt
and credit. His comments suggest that Gibbon's monumental history
should be understood as part of a protracted concern that eighteenth-
century Europe would share the fate of late imperial Rome.

One curiosity of Gibbon's work, however, is that it begins neither with
decline nor fall. Instead, we are offered an extended picture of Roman
prosperity under the Antonines, which leads up to Gibbon's encomium
(adapted from Robertson): "If a man were called to fix the period in the
history of the world, during which the condition of the human race was
most happy and prosperous, he would, without hesitation, name that
which elapsed from the death of Domitian to the accession of
Commodus."[10] Such prosperity does not last, but Gibbon never offers
a detailed parceling out of cause; he never provides an account that would
explain the relative importance of internal and external factors in the
eventual triumph of barbarism and religion.

Indeed, such a precise account of causality is not Gibbon's point, as
Arnoldo Momigliano long ago pointed out.[11] Instead, Gibbon is more
concerned to draw distinctions between ancient Rome and modern Europe
in consistent but brief insights that have bearing on his contemporary
moment.[12] These insights culminate in volume 3 of the *Decline and Fall*
with the "General Observations on the Fall of the Roman Empire in the
West" (1781). As its omission from the chapter's title would suggest, cause is
not central here. Gibbon indicates that "the decline of Rome was the
natural and inevitable effect of immoderate greatness," and adds,
"The story of its ruin is simple and obvious; and instead of inquiring
why the Roman empire was destroyed, we should rather be surprised that it
had subsisted so long" (*DF*, 2:509). His explanation of this "awful revolution" is then distinguished by a willingness to venture into sustained
historical parallelism "for the instruction of the present age" (*DF*, 2:511).
For Gibbon, Rome's fall does not contain a moral lesson for Europe;
instead, he suggests that the lack of an external threat, a system of balanced
powers, and the development of arts and technologies like gunpowder

distinguish Europe from Rome. Collectively, this adds up to an optimistic claim for the durability and permanence of civilization on a grand scale of millennia: "the experience of four thousand years should enlarge our hopes, and diminish our apprehensions: we cannot determine to what height the human species may aspire in their advances towards perfection; but it may safely be presumed, that no people, unless the face of nature is changed, will relapse into their original barbarism" (*DF*, 2:515). Ultimately, then, Gibbon's optimism about European security depends upon substituting a broad temporal scale of millennia for the narrower historical parallel between Rome and Europe.

Such optimism is what J. G. A. Pocock calls "the enlightened narrative." It suggests that the decline and fall of Rome can be seen at "a remove by an age which had solved their problems, yet found their values an effective criticism of the world which had replaced them."[13] Manners and the balance of powers define the difference between European modernity and ancient virtue, while a belief in commerce and plurality serves as a critique of antiquity and its problem of imperium. The Romans sought to conquer others when they should have traded with them. In the face of anxieties about European decline, standing armies, and the loss of ancient virtue, Rome provides not a warning lesson for Europe, but rather a counterexample to Europe's more developed state of manners and commerce, even while the "analogy to Roman history could be effective in historical conditions recognized as different."[14] In connection with Sonenscher's point that eighteenth-century Europe was concerned that it "might have to face the prospect of a replay of the ancient cycle of decline and fall under modern conditions of war and debt," Gibbon suggests that these very conditions create stability – debt can be associated with the manners developed by commercial society, while the expensive technologies of warfare that debt supports protect Europe from barbarians (or civilize the very barbarians who learn to produce them).

In calling attention to this narrative, I want to underscore how it turns apparent decline into progress by recalibrating to a particularly grand temporal scale. Gibbon looks back nearly two millennia to Rome and then, in eliciting a rationale for European security, he expands his scale another two millennia to what he terms "the experience of four thousand years" (*DF*, 2:515). His "Observations" make clear Gibbon's willingness to think through historical parallels, but by adjusting his temporal scale away from a pointillistic comparison between imperial Rome and eighteenth-century Europe – between, in other words, two distinct temporal points in the typical manner of exemplary history or what Koselleck calls *historia magistra vitae*[15] – and toward the scale of four thousand years of recorded history, Gibbon expands his temporal scope. He explains Rome's decline and fall not as a moral problem and not as part of a cycle that all advanced civilizations are doomed to repeat, but rather as part of a longer narrative of the advance of civilization. This is a story that at moments down the scale, like the first half of the first millennium BCE, may appear to be a narrative of decline and fall, but that in its broader scale is ultimately one in which civilization makes a series of advances that prove more lasting and more permanent than momentary collapse. The key is an adjustment of perspective that moves from smaller (but still comparatively large) scales of time like centuries upward to even larger units like millennia.

Smith, the Scaling of Time, and the Quantification of Decline

Where Gibbon ends his historical account of Western Rome's decline, Smith begins his narrative of the progress of European society. *Wealth of Nations*, book 3, the short, historical book on landownership and land tenancy in Europe after the fall of Rome's Western empire, begins with Smith's theory that the progress of civilization should develop by directing capital first at agriculture, then at manufacture, and finally at foreign commerce. The irony, of course, is that in Europe this supposedly "natural" order has been inverted. In an effort to explain the discrepancy, Smith offers an extremely compressed history of Europe in which the thriftiness of the urban bourgeoisie, its persistent reinvestment of capital in manufacturing and eventually land, produces European agricultural development. This is a narrative of progress and advance. As such, it is not at all anomalous in a work whose first sentence has as its grammatical subject "improvement."[16] But it is also a story of decline, and specifically of the decline of the great proprietors who sell their birthright, "for trinkets and baubles, fitter to be the playthings of children than the serious pursuits of men" (*WN*, 439).

What from Smith's long timescale is a process of aristocratic decline may, from the narrower perspective of the wealthy, luxury-obsessed landowner, be a kind of progress: where he once had an army of retainers and wore rough clothes, now he has fine diamond buckles. Indeed, the great proprietors may never become aware of the magnitude of this exchange because they lack the distant, cultivated perspective of one observing the process from a later point in time. In this sense, Smith's compressed history illustrates the conventional assumption of historical distance: that increasing clarity comes with the passage of time; or, perhaps more accurately, with the detached observation made possible by the passage of time.

The distance required here, however, is not solely an issue of temporality, and we might productively think about it along the axes of representation, affect, ideology (implications for action), and cognition (fundamental assumptions about explanation and understanding) – the four distinguishable but overlapping distances that Mark Phillips locates as central to his recent rethinking of historical distance and that he calls form, affect, summoning, and understanding.[17] Broadening the category of historical distance along the lines suggested by Phillips can help us better to understand the implications of Smith's history of European civilization. As he moves from the theoretical chapter on the natural progress of opulence (book 3, chapter 1) to the historical narrative of European development (book 3, chapters 2–4), Smith uses the advantage of distance to cultivate detached observation that can offer greater clarity, but he also must bridge this temporal gap to make the events seem closer and more immediate to his reader. The technique that Smith adapts for this is one of compression. His account of thirteen centuries unfolds in a scant forty pages and contains relatively few references to particular dates and a similarly limited number of references to specific places. Particularities of time and space blur into a generalized story of European development as Smith performs a variant of conjectural history on European society itself. What Smith is doing here, in other words, is re-distancing and rescaling social processes. He is making the long history of Europe after Rome short and compressed so that it can be appreciated as a kind of montage. Smith bridges temporal distance by choosing a mode of explanation that trades detail, nuance, and temporal precision for the enhanced understanding and cognition enabled by compression.

Once he has explained the means by which luxury produces the security of Europe, Smith then concludes:

> A revolution of the greatest importance to the public happiness, was in this manner brought about by two different orders of people, who had not the least intention to serve the public. To gratify the most childish vanity was the sole motive of the great proprietors. The merchants and artificers, much less ridiculous, acted merely from **a view** to their own interest, and in pursuit of their own pedlar principle of turning a penny wherever a penny was to be got. Neither of them had either knowledge or foresight of that great revolution which the folly of the one, and the industry of the other, was gradually bringing about. (*WN*, 440, emphasis mine)

In this passage, the focus on cognition and understanding mediates other aspects of distance and scale. Further, as the emphasis on perspective and point of view indicates, the formal and the affective aspects of distance are particularly close here. Both the merchants and the proprietors have a distinct point of view, "a view to their own interest." Neither, however, can see or understand the other's point of view. We are reminded here of the impartial spectator not only because Smith's account faults both merchants and proprietors for their interestedness and lack of impartiality, but also because the passage turns on viewing and spectatorship.[18]

The meaning of the events described here might be understood as a conflict over focalization in which the privileged perspective is reserved for the narrator of the passage, whose greater temporal distance from events affords an opportunity to see what the participants cannot. It is the narrator of the passage who emerges by virtue of his distance from the events at hand as an impartial spectator, and this is why we experience Smith's history as a narrative of progress and not decline. Furthermore, although Smith presents himself as a distanced, objective observer of events, the affective dimensions of his account remind us of the moral qualities of distancing and make clear that he is not neutral. The great proprietors, who are characterized by "childish vanity" and "folly," come off the worst here. The merchants are "much less ridiculous" but they operate in pursuit of what Smith rather dismissively calls a "pedlar principle." Neither acts with any view to public service but "merely from a view to their own interests." This might seem, then, like history without heroes, and Smith's depriviledging of agency makes the work's ideological dimension, its implications for action, difficult to read. The focus on techniques of distancing in the passage and the broader narrative, however, allows us to recognize that the hero of the story is the narrator himself, what Smith called in his earlier work the "impartial spectator." We might even describe the philosophical historian as an impartial spectator, one capable of recalibrating distance and scale to perceive significant patterns and to understand the outcome of unintended actions (what Smith here calls a "revolution") and the lessons that this history carries for those seeking to measure and grow the wealth of nations.

Recognizing Smith's suggestive use of temporal rescaling, his play with the plastic and multivalent effects of historical distancing in book 3 of *The Wealth of Nations*, returns us to Smith's claim about there being a "great deal of ruin in a nation" and to the larger problem of decline as characterized in *The Wealth of Nations*. Just what does Smith mean when he makes this claim? In part, it links to Smith's antimercantilist argument in *The Wealth of Nations* in which he questions whether there would be adverse effects from the loss of the colonies because, as currently administered, the colonies bring in less in tax revenue than they cost for war and protection. More abstractly, Smith is clearly suggesting that not every local setback can be played into a grand narrative like that of decline and fall. A single undesired outcome, or even a long series of them, does not necessarily indicate irreversible decline. It is again a question of distance and perspective, and one that relates to both time and space: space because Smith's point is that local moments like Saratoga need to be understood as part of events happening elsewhere in the nation and the empire; and time because whether or not Saratoga marks a turning toward descent can only be known to one privy to a longer narrative and a distanced perspective.[19]

Smith had taken up this very issue the year prior to Saratoga in the first edition of *The Wealth of Nations*, most notably on those occasions when he acknowledges fears of decline and ruin in order to reject them for their failures of measurement and perspective.[20] In a chapter on the accumulation of capital and productive and unproductive labor, for example, Smith observes the regular appearance of jeremiads predicting Britain's imminent decline, jeremiads whose failed predictions do not prevent audiences from taking them seriously each time they appear. In rejecting these arguments, Smith shifts from a microeconomic and often local focus to macroeconomic indicators, and in so doing he also eliminates the moralizing tone of a jeremiad. His response aims to identify quantifiable economic criteria through which decline might be measured, but it also emphasizes the need to calibrate one's temporal perspective for the longer term. In addition to the emphasis on quantification, Smith's attempt to bring change into time, to encourage comparisons not only between the country and the city but of the "state of the nation" as a whole "at two different periods" (*WN*, 365) is crucial here.

Smith acknowledges the popularity of decline jeremiads – and his comments indicate just how preoccupied those living in later eighteenth-century Britain were with the problem of decline. Smith notes that every five years, some book or pamphlet demonstrating "that the wealth of the nation was fast declining, that the country was depopulated, agriculture neglected, manufactures decaying, and trade undone" (365) gains credence with the public. Although Smith does not identify his sources here, similar comments in the *Lectures on Jurisprudence* suggest that he may have been thinking of Joshua Gee's *The Trade and Navigation of Great-Britain Considered* (1729) or Swift's *A Short View of the State of Ireland* (1727–28).[21] He may also have had in mind John Brown's more recent moralistic attack on luxury and the feminization of English manners in *An Estimate of the Manners and Principles of the Times* (1757), while another likely target would have been Oliver Goldsmith's 1770 poem, *The Deserted Village.*[22]

In response, Smith explains the need both to identify quantifiable economic criteria through which decline might be measured and to calibrate one's temporal perspective for the longer term through the particular example of post-Restoration Britain, in what he calls the "happiest and most fortunate period of all," which has nonetheless included "the fire and plague of London, the two Dutch wars, the disorders of the revolution, the war in Ireland, the four expansive French wars of 1688, 1702, 1742, and 1756, together with the two rebellions of 1715 and 1745" (*WN*, 366). Taken singly or collectively, these events could be read as indicators of decline, but a wider perspective reveals that despite government profligacy, private frugality and prudence have slowly counteracted these circumstances.[23]

Smith describes a slow, almost invisible process that is contingent on calibrating one's perspective for a broader distance and scale. "To form a right judgment of it," Smith notes,

> we must compare the state of the country at periods somewhat distant from one another. The progress is frequently so gradual, that, at near periods, the improvement is not only not sensible, but from the declension either of certain branches of industry, or of certain districts of the country, things which sometimes happen though the country in general be in great prosperity, there frequently arises a suspicion, that the riches and industry of the whole are decaying. (*WN*, 365)

Smith emphasizes gradual change, frequently imperceptible to human observation, which suggests that the analysis of apparent decline and its inversion produces an awareness of the slow time that will become so important in literary responses to decline. Smith's insistence on "periods somewhat distant from one another" reveals also how problems of scale and the confusion of the short term for the long term can productively be understood as an issue of closeness and distance. Smith's insistence on the need for distance gives him a powerful argument against what he perceives as the regular appearance of and credence given to jeremiads predicting national decline.

These predictions, Smith argues, result from a confusion of scale. They read the small scale as the large scale, the local ("certain districts") as the national ("the country in general"), and the short term as the long term:

> The annual produce of the land and labour of England, for example, is certainly much greater than it was, a little more than a century ago, at the

restoration of Charles II. Though, at present, few people, I believe, doubt of this, yet during this period, five years have seldom passed away in which some book or pamphlet has not been published, written too with such abilities as to gain some authority with the public, and pretending to demonstrate that the wealth of the nation was fast declining, that the country was depopulated, agriculture neglected, manufactures decaying, and trade undone. (*WN*, 365)

What might appear to be a process of decline and fall, Smith suggests, could with the shift in perspective to a longer timescale of "a little more than a century" be explained instead as the vicissitudes of a normal business cycle.

Smith's response to jeremiads of decline, then, pushes away from the imprecise moralism implicit in a perceived loss of virtue in favor of measuring concrete and quantifiable factors like the produce of land and labor and the accumulation of capital. It further emphasizes that such factors should be measured annually and compiled across the larger unit of the century. This can be seen most clearly in the defense of free trade from book 4 of the *Wealth of Nations* in which Smith reflects on widespread predictions of decline not just in England, but throughout all commercial economies. As he asserts:

There is no commercial country in Europe of which the approaching ruin has not frequently been foretold by the pretended doctors of this system, from an unfavorable balance of trade. After all the anxiety, however, which they have excited about this, after all the vain attempts of almost all trading nations to turn that balance in their own favour and against their neighbours, it does not appear that any one nation in Europe has been in any respect impoverished by this cause. Every town and country, on the contrary, in proportion as they have opened their ports to all nations, instead of being ruined by this free trade, as the principles of the commercial system would lead us to expect, have been enriched by it. (*WN*, 522–23)

Once again, we see Smith confronting pervasive anxieties about decline – anxieties about supposedly "certain ruin" articulated "with all the passionate confidence of interested falsehood" (*WN*, 522) – only to suggest that they are focused on the wrong metric.

He proposes instead that the annual balance of production and consumption "necessarily occasions the prosperity or decay of every nation" (*WN*, 523):

If the exchangeable value of the *annual* produce, it has already been observed, exceeds that of the *annual* consumption, the capital of the society must *annually* increase in proportion to this excess. The society in this case lives within its revenue, and what is *annually* saved out of its revenue is naturally added to its capital, and employed so as to increase still further the *annual* produce. If the exchangeable value of the *annual* produce, on the contrary, fall short of the *annual* consumption, the capital of the society must *annually* decay in proportion to this deficiency. The expence of the society in this case exceeds its revenue, and necessarily encroaches upon its capital. Its capital, therefore, must necessarily decay, and together with it, the exchangeable value of the *annual* produce of its industry. (*WN*, 523, emphasis mine)

For my purposes here, Smith's relentless focus on the annual suggests how he naturalizes the year as a temporal category and encourages his readers to think about the future as a neatly progressive unfolding of commensurate units of time, units which can then be scaled and gridded in relation to each other to allow ready and easy comparison.

Decline, in this reading, can be recognized as part of a quantified pattern, a pattern that repeatedly measures the same quantity annually in order to observe changes over longer and more significant spans of time.

Smith, Malthus, Goldsmith, and the Time of Decline

Smith's emphasis on annual measurement and his insistence that the annual accrues significance slowly and gradually in relation to the larger accumulation of time marked by the century emerges clearly as a response to the moralization and misperception of decline. Smith's emphasis on the chronological gridding of the year and the century and the distinct temporal modes related to decline become clearer when we compare Smith's handling of time with two other works that focus on decline: Oliver Goldsmith's *Deserted Village* (1770) and Thomas Robert Malthus's *Essay on the Principle of Population* (1798). Goldsmith's poem – one of Smith's targets for his shift from moral to measure in the assessment of decline – reads the movement of time as a shift away from stability and value, but Goldsmith does not account for the temporal process of that shift. Malthus, in contrast, shares Smith's emphasis on measure and is similarly focused on the relationship between the year and the century, but he puts the relation between the two temporal units towards a distinct vision of the future: where Smith's future is open-ended and expanding,[24] the future for Malthus is constrained and cyclical. It is, as he repeatedly describes it, a future of "oscillation."

In *An Essay on the Principle of Population*, Malthus targets the fantasy of future perfectibility put forward by William Godwin and the Marquis de

Condorcet, both of whom look to the future and see what Koselleck would characterize as an "open future," one in which potential problems, including the problem of population, can be solved.[25] For Malthus, in contrast, the future is always similar to the past because the principle of population guarantees the persistence of vice and misery, while "gigantic inevitable famine stalks in the rear."[26] For Malthus, decline is both inevitable and perpetual.

Decline is, furthermore, a temporal problem. As Charlotte Sussman observes, for much of the eighteenth century, population was a problem of space, something to be solved through geography, through emigration. For Malthus, however, population is not a local problem to be solved by geography because the world does not have infinite space.[27] When Malthus considers "the whole earth" instead of locally and nationally delimited spaces, he recasts population as a temporal problem, and this is one of the major points of Malthus's argument – a point, in turn, that has significant implications for how Malthus understands time and temporal progression. On the one hand, Malthus, like Smith, understands time as measured, regular, and repetitive and he, too, is concerned with calibrating the changes in relevant metrics over what he considers to be the proper duration. Again, we see the interplay between the year and the century as Malthus looks at the growing separation between increases in food supply and increases in population over the course of a century in chapter 2 and when he later insists in chapter 7 that the happiness of a nation hinges solely "upon the degree which the *yearly* increase of food approaches to the *yearly* increase of an unrestricted population" (*EPP*, 60, emphasis mine). In order to get the proper picture of a nation's health, such annual data, in turn, must be understood over "a period of a hundred years" (*EPP*, 55). Here and elsewhere, Malthus – like Smith before him – assumes that time is regular and uniform, that it can be measured in discrete units, which can then be compared to each other.

On the other hand, for Malthus, the timescale of such patterns and the way that they develop matters less because, insofar as the problem of population persists – and Malthus insists it always will – one millennium will be the same as the next. As Malthus says, "It is probable that the food of Great Britain is divided in as great plenty to the inhabitants, at the present period, as it was two thousand, three thousand, or four thousand years ago" (*EPP*, 60). Given the problem of population, the future starts to look less like something difficult to imagine, with unbounded possibilities for progress, and more like a repetition of the past. In this way, Malthus might be understood to represent the bounded time of decline; in contrast to the open-ended, unpredictable time of progress with its sense of futurity, decline is always enclosed. Decline binds time and narrows the aperture of an open future.

Reading Smith alongside Malthus reveals how political economy comes to regularize time and to naturalize its division into years that must be understood from the perspective of centuries or millennia. Crucial here is the insistence on grounding arguments for temporal processes into long-term units, most commonly the century, and the emphasis on national patterns rather than local ones. The project of classical political economy as consolidated by Smith and taken up by Malthus thus promises to make questions of decline more objective – economic rather than moral – by offering the possibility of measurable categories through which anxieties about decline can be confirmed or refuted.

This insistence by Malthus and Smith on the measurement of decline calibrated between annual changes and their accrual over a century differs markedly from the time of decline depicted in Goldsmith's *Deserted Village*. Goldsmith's lament over rural depopulation and the lost joys of a simple country community is a poem about decline: the decline of a mode of agricultural production but even more so the decline of a corresponding rural way of life. One of the distinctive features of Goldsmith's interpretation of rural decline is that he does not see it as in any way inevitable. It is neither a natural result of senescence nor part of a cyclical pattern. Instead, Goldsmith blames decline specifically on the loss of common land that results from the desire for picturesque landscapes and the tendency of the newly rich or the conspicuously consumptive to turn agricultural land into pleasure parks.[28] As a result, the rural poor were driven off of their land into cities or to the far-flung regions of a growing colonial and commercial empire. Such changes are understood as related to the desire for wealth and luxury generated by commerce, which assumes full responsibility for the decay of rural life in Goldsmith's account.

For Goldsmith, in other words, decline is a moral problem related to luxury. In identifying Goldsmith's poem as one of Smith's targets, Donald Winch situates *The Deserted Village* in relation to eighteenth-century debates about luxury and uses the poem to clarify the differences between Goldsmith and Smith regarding the degree to which the consumption of the rich produced a diffusion of benefits to others of lesser fortune. Winch emphasizes that, from the perspective adapted by Smith in *The Wealth of Nations*, "Goldsmith's mistake was exactly that noted when dealing with other popular writings on luxury and decline: a failure to take a sufficiently long or broad view of the real sources of a nation's wealth, of its accumulating stock of capital and rising labour productivity."[29] In my reading, which extends Winch's point about temporal horizons, the juxta-position between Goldsmith's poem and Smith's rejection of its claims clarifies Smith's efforts to grid the transition between past and present in the accumulation of a set of measurable quantities mapped over a series of recurring annual units.

Goldsmith's poem works by type. He is specific about the lost joys of rural life, but there is nothing particular about Auburn that distinguishes its scenes and populace from the scenes and populace that mark rural life elsewhere. The opening scene, for example, is marked by cottage, farm, brook, and mill; it is peopled by the swain, the virgin, and the matron, by young and old. The village preacher and the village schoolmaster are given more detailed descriptions and were likely based on actual figures from Goldsmith's youth, but, even so, each functions within the poem as a carefully described type of rural person. Such typologies extend to a series of further distinctions around which the poem turns as the contrast between young and old in the opening scene expands into a series of oppositions between country and city, rich and poor, trade and agriculture, and – most importantly for our purposes here – now and then.[30] Written largely in the past tense, *The Deserted Village* develops a sharp contrast between an idealized rural past and a depopulated rural present. There once was a time when villages like Auburn were the nation but now "times are altered" (63). Between the now and the then we know only that "many a year elapsed" (79). Though the poem calls our attention to ways of marking time, with the "varnished clock" (228) clicking behind the door of the village pub or the village schoolmaster who could "terms and tides presage" (209), we are offered only a minimal sense of time's *motion*, of its passing. In a rare exception to the poem's resistance to marking the passing of time as process, and one of the few indicators of speed in the poem, we are told that "Trade's proud empire hastes to swift decay" (427). In contrast to this haste and swiftness, "self-dependent power can time defy" (429). In a poem whose nostalgic rural typologies represent the apex of virtue, such defiance of time becomes the ultimate value, and this may help to explain why the poem elides temporal process in favor of the stark contrasts it creates between past and present. Further, although it is not character-ized as such, one senses as well that the decline of Auburn itself has been "swift" in that it was unexpected and has transpired within the speaker's own lifetime.

The speed characteristic of a commercial society – and, the poem suggests, of its decay – has come to mark village life. As an alternative to

such speed and to temporal process more generally, the *Deserted Village*
brings rural life out of time, which is why its reliance on typology is
significant: because types, like the idealization of rural life the poem
presents, are meant to be unchanging, timeless. As characterized here,
they do not respond to time and are immune to the perceived speed of
commercial society. Distinctive here is that for Goldsmith, the contrast to
the rapid changes provoked by commercial society is not the reduction of
pace, a slowing down commonly associated with rural life, but rather
a move out of time. Speed and slowness are not mutually entwined in
Goldsmith's poem, and this separation is what distinguishes Goldsmith's
response to perceived acceleration from later responses like Wordsworth's
"Preface" or even, as we will see in Chapter 5, Keats's "Grecian Urn," that
"foster-child of silence and slow time." For both Wordsworth and Keats,
slowness mediates between a perceived speed and a projected timelessness
and consequently becomes entangled with speed such that neither pole can
signify independent of reference to its opposite. For Goldsmith, in contrast, slowness does not yet stand in opposition to speed and haste and
hurry are instead contained by a fantasy of timeless permanence.

Despite Goldsmith's identification of himself in the poem's dedication
as a "professed ancient" on the subject of luxury,[31] his poem of rural
decline became an occasion to celebrate perceived progress. Reviewers for
both the *Monthly Review* and the *Critical Review* acknowledged the
pleasure given by Goldsmith's poem but then continued, as Smith
would later, to insist that luxury is not a problem, but rather the source
of cultivation and prosperity. Reviewing Goldsmith's poem thus offers an
opportunity to celebrate perceived progress and the superiority of the
moderns over the ancients.[32] This is a frequent feature of arguments for
decline, one that we will see more clearly in Chapter 2: in provoking
a response, pronouncements of decline help to consolidate value by
identifying qualities that they perceive as lost to the present and future
while also forcing those who oppose their assessment to counter with the
identification of different qualities and values that are understood to
persist.

The contrast between Goldsmith and Smith is significant for a further
reason: it reveals the impact of commercial development on eighteenth-
century understandings of time. It does so by exposing the tensions
between a moralized understanding of time keyed to distinctions between
a corrupt now and an idealized past and a more regularized, less sharply
divided time grounded in the regularized annual movement of time whose
significance can be understood across the temporal unit of a century. This

latter progressive time sense represents time as moving consistently and irreversibly in regular units toward that fundamental conceit of modernity that Peter Fritzsche calls "the restless iteration of the new."[33] But Goldsmith's temporal understanding, which seeks to preserve the past for its accumulation of foreclosed possibilities, does not just disappear. It leaves behind traces and residues that can be recovered to clarify snaps, discontinuities, and tensions in the progressive, even time of years and centuries. It is thus episodes like the contrast between Smith and Goldsmith that establish the conditions of possibility for what Fritzsche describes as the "paradox" that "the synchronization of historical time rested on... the acknowledgement of diachronic difference" (*SP*, 53), a recognition that in his account initiates a particular kind of historical thinking and creates "a specific temporal identity not unlike the feeling of generation" (*SP*, 53).

For Fritzsche this is part of an argument that the French Revolution represents a rupture in the understanding of the past – "the perception of the restless iteration of the new so that the past no longer served as a faithful guide to the future" (*SP*, 5). In the English context, Fritzsche links this sense of rupture to Cobbett's *Rural Rides* (1830), which, he insists, "developed an emphatically national optics by which the fresh ruins and displaced people came prominently into view, and it was Cobbett who signposted a totally mobilized landscape that had to be understood historically. By systematizing the debris of the countryside within a comprehensive national and historical context, he created an image of the nation as broken" (*SP*, 137). What I am suggesting, however, is that the understanding of time that Fritzsche and others want to read as following from the French Revolution actually begins to emerge before it, and that this temporal sense assumes a degree of shape in arguments centered around the problem of decline in modern, commercial society. In this reading, Goldsmith may not systematically place the ruins of the countryside in a national context (this is Smith's rebuttal), but he does want Auburn to stand for the nation (his mistake, in Smith's view). Goldsmith's emphasis on rural depopulation also works – like Fritzsche's account of Cobbett, but well before the French Revolution – to sunder the past from the present and future, a tearing that it laments and regrets while also seeking, like the supposedly post-revolutionary historical consciousness that so interests Fritzsche, to re-enliven the past "with the identification of foreclosed possibilities" (*SP*, 7).

Decline, the Expansion of Timescale, and the Visualization of Time

The emphasis on longer timescales and slow, gradual processes of change that I have identified in Gibbon and Smith correlates also with developments in natural history. Buffon, for example, argued in *Les époques de la nature* (1778) that the earth could be 75,000 years old, and not the more biblically acceptable 5,000, while speculating privately that the figure might well be more like 3 million.[34] From Buffon forward, debate over the age of the earth and the efforts to reconstruct the process of geological development that produced present conditions intensified.[35]

Martin Rudwick is particularly clear about how this debate develops a new conceptual space: "In contrast *both* to the short and finite timescale of traditional chronology *and* to the infinitely long perspective of traditional eternalism," those disputing the earth's age begin "to open up the conceptual space for a third (and modern) option: that timescale might be unimaginably lengthy, *yet not infinite.*"[36] In linking the human time of Smith and Gibbon to the rescaling of time on an even longer natural and geological basis, I am not insisting on a model of direct influence, though Rudwick is keen to show how those working on Earth's history borrowed metaphors and evidential techniques from biblical historians and antiquarians. Rather, I am suggesting a correlation of new possibilities from 1770 onward for thinking about time and scales of time across a range of emergent disciplines and modes of inquiry.[37] This rescaling of time was not limited to movements up the scale across larger swaths of time but also extends downward into smaller units. The last decades of the eighteenth century, after all, are where E. P. Thompson locates the increasing prominence and precision of timepieces as minutes and seconds begin to matter due to the increased synchronization of labor.[38]

As thinkers in a variety of disciplines continued to recalibrate the relevant timescales to measure change and coordinate events, one prominent challenge was how best to represent such recalibrations. If change happened gradually and slowly, too slowly to register at the level of perception, if it was frequently "not sensible" (*WN*, 365) in Smith's phrase, how could it be grasped? One novel solution was to transpose abstract time into visual space on a printed page. This, too, must be understood as a problem of distance in that such graphic representations sought to make a diverse array of events that spread across a broad swath of time close and comparable by joining them in a single visual field. In 1769, for example, Joseph Priestley produced his *New Chart of History* (1769, 2nd ed. 1770; Figure 1.1). In his companion

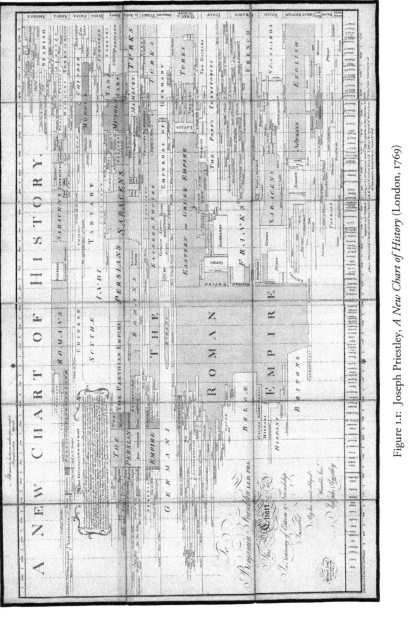

Figure 1.1: Joseph Priestley, *A New Chart of History* (London, 1769)

description of this chart, Priestley argued that all time could be represented as a line. "Time here," Priestley insists, "flows uniformly, from the beginning to the end of the tablet. It is also represented as flowing *laterally*, like a river."[39] With a horizontal axis of years and a vertical axis of territories, Priestley hoped to show both the temporal duration and the spatial expanse of empires at a glance, and hence to impress the imagination "indelibly" and efficiently with "a just image of the rise, progress, extent, duration and contemporary state of all the considerable empires that have ever existed in the world."[40] Spatially and temporally distant events could be brought close through techniques of linear representation. Looking horizontally would show all changes in the government of a particular territory, while a vertical glance would allow for the comparison of various territories.[41]

Priestley's graphics would subsequently be taken up by William Playfair, who enhanced Priestley's historical chart and extended its linear and geometric principles to the financial measurement of relative prosperity and decline. Like Priestley's *New Chart*, Playfair's graphs and charts turn abstract time into something that can be imagined and visualized concretely as a continuous linear progression. They attempt to bridge the distance between territories and events by uniting them in a single visual plane. We have seen how Smith's rebuttal to decline jeremiads in *The Wealth of Nations* downplayed the significance of seemingly profound setbacks like wars, bad harvests, and uprisings in favor of gradual processes that cannot be seen. Playfair's response to the problem of decline similarly de-emphasizes traditional events in order to make visible the very processes that Smith characterized as "not sensible."

The abstract rescaling of Smith and Gibbon receives form and shape in Playfair's "linear arithmetic." As Playfair describes his charts, they "bring into one view the result of details that are dispersed over a very wide and intricate field of universal history."[42] The key here is uniformity of scale, a development located in the mid-eighteenth century by Rosenberg and Grafton in their history of the timeline. "Once that uniformity had been achieved," they note, "projecting other kinds of quantitative data into the chronographic space was not difficult."[43] It may not have been difficult, but it certainly was not common. Collectively, Playfair's graphs and charts help to underscore his argument that decline is a relative category, that it can be quantified and measured, and, more, that it can be easily visualized through lines, shapes, and colors plotted to show comparative national prosperity and productivity, most commonly over an interval of a century, but also by examining the movement of empires over a nearly four-thousand-year period.

Mapping Decline after Smith: The Statistical Graphics of William Playfair

William Playfair plays a central role in my argument about later eighteenth-century efforts to identify, predict, and forestall decline. The younger brother of John Playfair – the champion of James Hutton's *Theory of the Earth* who became professor of mathematics and natural philosophy at the University of Edinburgh – Playfair is perhaps best known for his contributions to statistical graphics: he was the inventor of the time-series line graph, the bar chart, and the pie chart.[44] He was also the editor of the first critical edition of Smith's *Wealth of Nations* in 1805.[45] In the same year that his edition of Smith appeared (a year during which he was incidentally convicted at the King's Bench for fraud), Playfair also published a lengthy and substantial book on decline, *An Inquiry into the Permanent Causes of the Decline and Fall of Powerful and Wealthy Nations*. This universal history of wealth and power, whose title combines Smith's *Wealth of Nations* with Gibbon's *Decline and Fall*, sought to demonstrate the value of commercial wealth, which in Playfair's argument was unlike wealth gained through conquest because it could be preserved perpetually.

Decline, in Playfair's hands, was therefore not something inevitable that would be the fate of all great nations and empires, but rather something that new commercial regimes might be able to forestall and manage if one knew what signs to look for and how best to respond to those signals. If the signs of decline could be more easily recognized, Playfair suggested, decline might be avoided perpetually. The best way to recognize the signs of decline, he insisted, was through the use of time-saving visual graphics. Though largely textual, Playfair's argument in his *Inquiry* was organized around four such graphic images: a geographical timeline of "universal commercial history" that spans three millennia and shows the comparative progress and decline of all known empires, from ancient Egypt through modern Europe to the Americas (Figure 1.2); a circle chart showing the extent of population and revenues in Europe's principal nations; and two time-series line graphs, one showing British exports and imports across the whole of the eighteenth century updated to 1805 (Figure 1.3) and the other showing increases in the exports and imports between England and France from the start of the seventeenth century to the declaration of war between the two countries in 1793 (Figure 1.4).

All of these graphic forms had been previously introduced by Playfair beginning with his *Commercial and Political Atlas* in 1786

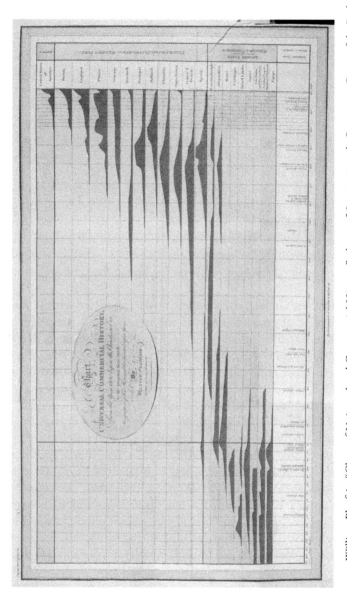

Figure 1.2: William Playfair, "Chart of Universal and Commercial History," plate 1 of *Inquiry into the Permanent Causes of the Decline and Fall of Powerful and Wealthy Nations*. London: printed for Greenland and Norris, 1805

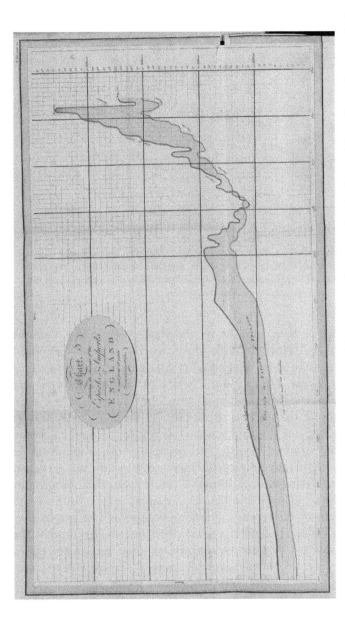

Figure 1.3: William Playfair, "Chart Showing the Amount of the Exports and Imports of England, to and from all parts from 1800 [sic] to 1805," plate 1 of *The Commercial and Political Atlas, Representing by Means of Stained Copper-Plate Charts, the Progress of the Commerce, Revenues, Expenditure, and Debts of England, During the Whole of the Eighteenth Century*. 3rd ed. (London: printed for Greenland and Norris, 1801)

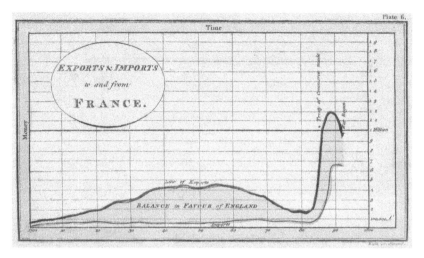

Figure 1.4: William Playfair, "Exports and Imports to and from France," plate 6 of
*The Commercial and Political Atlas, Representing by Means of Stained Copper-Plate
Charts, the Progress of the Commerce, Revenues, Expenditure, and Debts of England,
During the Whole of the Eighteenth Century.* 3rd ed. (London: printed for Greenland
and Norris, 1801)

and continuing in new editions of the *Atlas* (1787, 1801) and the
Statistical Breviary (1801).[46] With these works, Playfair developed
a succession of time-series line graphs that showed the balance of
trade between Great Britain and a series of trading partners and
imperial colonies over the course of what the full title of the *Atlas*
calls "the whole of the eighteenth century."[47] Playfair's work was so
definitive that, as one leading scholar of statistical graphics notes,
"time-series line graphs are seen in essentially the same form as
today."[48] Such charts not only enable their users to link the particular
data of a year to a pattern spread across a century, but they also assume
in their very form and scale that all annual data must be subsumed into
the larger pattern of the century. Playfair's time-series line graphs thus
develop Smith's insistence on the move from the smaller scale to the
larger scale, from the year to the century. In their use of aggregated
annual data to reveal patterns across a century, Playfair's charts raise
a series of questions about scale – questions about the relationship
between the year and the century, the annual and the centurial, about
the way that the relationship between them is imagined to produce
knowledge, and about the scale on which knowledge is produced.

Visually arresting, clearly engraved, and colored to make their presentation of information even more clear, Playfair's charts are striking documents. Their assumption that every numerical quality (the years of a life or the duration of a historical event) could be readily translated into a line clearly draws on Priestley's *Chart of Biography* (1765) and his more ambitious (and more visually arresting) *New Chart of History* (first ed. 1769, second in 1770, [Figure 1.1]). Charts by both Playfair and Priestley require the assumption of temporal uniformity and naturalize the regular, measured time of calendar and clock. While they enable the perception of simultaneity, they work against a sense of unevenness, of temporal layering and multiplicity – against the competing temporal senses that might help to explain this period's fascination with ruins and anxieties about decline more generally.

Playfair's charts differ from Priestley's however in their visual clarity, as a comparison of Priestley's *New Chart* (Figure 1.1) with Playfair's universal commercial history (Figure 1.2) will show. Priestley's chart is crowded. It aims for comprehensiveness and seeks to show a plethora of transitions in political rule across a broad swath of territories and a broad swath of time. Playfair's chart also aims for universality, but by limiting its focus to significant empires, it achieves greater economy than Priestley. Its color-coding, furthermore, allows for temporal distinctions between the empires of antiquity and those of the common era, while also allowing a sharp distinction between European empires and those emergent in the Americas. Consequently, Playfair's image allows its viewers to track the movement of empire and the oscillations of ascent and decline inherent in those movements. Playfair's chart, in other words, makes a more ready and lasting visual impression on its viewers, and this was precisely Playfair's intent. As he explains, "The advantages proposed by this mode of representing matters are the same that maps and plans have over descriptions, and dimensions written in figures; and the same accuracy is in one case as the other; for, whatever quantities can be expressed in numbers may be represented by lines; and, where proportional progression is the business, what the eye does in an instant, would otherwise require much time" (*IPC*, 214).

How, then, do Playfair's graphs allow us to think about decline in a different way? For a start, the charts reveal a particular understanding of the timescale that frames decline, both in the manner that they organize time through the relation between the year and the century and in the way that Playfair conceives of the chart as a time-saving device that can maximize an economy of time for busy men. Repeatedly, Playfair insists on the psychological efficacy of the graphic representation of quantitative information. To see numerical data as geometric shapes, he asserts, reveals its significance more quickly, makes it easier to remember, and saves time for those "of high rank, or active business" (*CPA*, 1801, xiv). To aid this endeavor and to initiate the unfamiliar, he offers a brief explanation of how to use the charts so that "those who do not, at first sight, understand the manner of inspecting the charts" can read "the few lines of directions facing the first Chart, after which they will find all the difficulty entirely vanish, and as much information may be *obtained in five minutes as would require whole days to imprint on the memory, in a lasting manner, by a table of figures*" (*CPA*, 1801, xii, italics in the original).[49]

Playfair promises that he can reduce days of work into the space of "*five minutes*," and his emphasis is thus on the time-saving qualities of visualization. Playfair's charts can therefore be understood as a direct response to the profusion of knowledge and information that we associate with the Enlightenment specifically and with the eighteenth century more generally. This seeming explosion of information – the sheer proliferation of raw data – is of course what enables Playfair's time-series graphs.[50] But for Playfair, the proliferation of information does more than provide raw data for visualization, it practically mandates such techniques and is necessary for those busy men with increasing demands on their time: "As knowledge increases amongst mankind, and transactions multiply, it becomes more and more desirable to *abbreviate* and *facilitate* the modes of conveying information from one person to another, and from one individual to the many" (*CPA*, 1801, vii). As this point suggests, in the later eighteenth century, the proliferation of data and the information overload to which Playfair explicitly responds helped to drive a sense of the distinct form of acceleration that Hartmut Rosa suggests defines modernity, a function whereby more data seemed to indicate more things happening and happening faster, a sense that, as I have been suggesting, enhanced anxieties about decline.[51]

In this context, one of the benefits of Playfair's graphs is their ability to stop time. They show "in an instant" through a single image an abstract process as it is perceived to develop over a century, one that they then fix and make concrete. But in the way that such charts are scaled, they also participate in and advance this sense of acceleration because they enable viewers to see large swaths of time at a glance. Those men of high rank and active business whom Playfair imagines as his audience are suddenly enabled to take in as much information in "*five minutes*" as would require "*whole days*" if seen as a table. Time itself takes less time to see.

Further, Playfair's charts emerge at a particular historical moment – the later eighteenth century – that, with the increasing proliferation of print media generally and periodical writing in particular, was becoming an age of serialized, often annualized regularity. This was a century when new, more accurate timekeeping technologies converged with new ways of representing this regular, even, and calibrated time in diaries, newspapers, and travel narratives in what Stuart Sherman characterizes as "diurnal form."[52] More, by the later eighteenth century, as E. P. Thompson has shown, this measured time came also to serve the routine, commodified time of industrial production.[53] The periodical press, with its production of evenly spaced issues that could be gathered into yearly volumes with predictable, structured regularity, was a central part of this culture of temporal precision and rigorously scheduled time. But if this made the later eighteenth century the "age of the annual," it was also the age of the centurial, and the historical moment when the interplay between the annual and the centurial assumed an enhanced importance. "The use of centuries as time designations," as Lynn Hunt notes, "only became common in the seventeenth century, at least in English and French" (119), and this manner of comprehending time assumed increased explanatory power in the eighteenth century.[54]

With their interplay between the year and the century, Playfair's charts present time as fundamentally "homogeneous," as a series of even, numbered, and continuous years that can be arranged in a grid to compose decades and, ultimately, a century. They thus resemble the regular continuous time that Mark Turner calls "periodical time," but despite their regularity, as Turner is careful to point out, periodicals also produce what he calls "temporal asymmetry" because "while there *is* a repetition of cycles, a regularity to the press in one sense that could lead to a synchronic social experience, there is no single cycle, no single motion which somehow contains it all."[55] Playfair's charts, however, seek to consolidate this time into an uninterrupted, continuous time and they fill the supposed emptiness of such homogeneous time in rich and intricate ways.

For Walter Benjamin, the emptiness of homogeneous time is filled by progress, while in his account of the origins of nationalism Benedict Anderson suggests that such time is filled by the nation.[56] Playfair fills homogeneous time with data proportioned to the equally divided and accumulative units of his analysis, years grouped into centuries, one of the newly emergent structures for organizing time in the eighteenth century. The uniform, annual units of Playfair's analysis facilitate filling and completion through the addition of quantitative data, but they also demand such filling since a time-series graph with broad temporal discontinuities would prevent the apprehension of significant patterns. The manner in which Playfair's charts fill homogeneous time works similarly to the measured and continuous time of Samuel Pepys's diary, where the uniform durations (the day for Pepys and the year for Playfair) "function as isochronic containers that in the uniformity, specificity, and seriality of their temporal dimensions make it possible to reckon fullness and hence to 'realize' it: to embody it palpably on the page."[57]

Like Pepys's diary, then, but in an even more graphic manner, Playfair's charts show time and its passage on the page as a visual image. They figure homogeneous time as full rather than empty by what Stuart Sherman describes as "a strategy of double containment": there is a plenum of data within each year, and a plenum of years within each chart. As in Pepys's diary, the measure of time defines the contour to be filled (the annual in Playfair's case and not the day as in Pepys) and the fulfillment of the data (after the one hundred years of the horizontal axis) produce the temporal fullness of each chart. Each year accounted for in the chart occupies a place in the fullness of time so constructed and contained.[58] Charts like this thus help to naturalize the annual as a way of perceiving time and measuring data.

Playfair's charts allow their users to connect the particular data of a year to a pattern spread across a century, but, more importantly, they assume in their very form and scale that the significance of annual data can only be grasped as part of the larger pattern of the century. Time, which seemed to be accelerating, could be made to yield to measured regularity. In these ways, then, Playfair's graphic charts and his method of what he calls "lineal arithmetic" would seem to crystallize his moment. Nonetheless, despite Playfair's repeated publication of his charts and graphs in edition after edition of the *Commercial and Political Atlas* and other publications like the *Statistical Breviary* and his reuse of certain graphics in the *Inquiry*, one remarkable feature of Playfair's charts was that despite their apparent prescience they failed to catch on and had virtually no impact or imitators in England until William Stanley Jevons began to engage Playfair's work in the later nineteenth century.[59]

Still, Playfair's graphic statistics develop new ways of seeing time that respond to a sense of the time pressures of life in commercial society. Their techniques of visualization ideally shorten the time required to understand complex economic data and make it possible to see time more quickly. The charts thus work both as a response to and an intensification of the kind of social acceleration associated with the development of commercial society, what Adam Smith called "the hurry of life" in a commercial world.[60] The graphics are intended to save time for busy men of commerce and politics, to enable them to process and analyze information more quickly. Insofar as commercial life contributes to that press on time, Playfair's charts respond to it through his characterization of them as time-saving; but they also intensify that sense of acceleration because they allow their users to "see" larger swaths of time quickly and thus their very efficiency allows users to pack the reception of more information into smaller intervals of time.

The time represented by these charts might therefore be understood as "informational time." Such time is closely related to commercial society in two senses: first, the charts represent commercial activity over time, most commonly the unit of the century; and second, the charts both respond to and intensify the perceived acceleration of social life in commercial society. Informational time suggests a combination of the steady accumulation of information and data that arises from the particular combination of the growth of commercial society and the corresponding abundance of media that accompanies it. Though built out of the seemingly regular and steady accumulation of data over days, months, and years such time is anything but regular. Its gradual accumulation is a sign of the slow processes that Smith calls "not sensible," but the sheer proliferation of data and information also gives rise to a sense of acceleration, a sense that more things are happening and that they are happening faster than before.

Playfair's charts, however, figure not just as time-saving devices consistent with the new accelerated rhythms of commercial life, but also as a means to see and analyze the hidden causes of commercial events in a way that allows those busy with matters of policy to anticipate problems. This is my second point about how Playfair's charts allow us to see and understand decline differently: they highlight repeatable events whose significance must be understood in the aggregate and thus make visible and comprehensible complex and often concealed processes that develop slowly over relatively long periods of time. Because Playfair's charts rely on aggregate data and the repetition of a particular kind of measurable commercial event (exports and imports) over a series of annual dates (years), they raise questions about whether decline is caused by unique events – like the loss at Saratoga in 1777 – or by a series of repeatable episodes whose cumulative effects make themselves known over an expanded timespan. In this sense, I want to associate Playfair with a model of historical interpretation that relies not on a narrative of seemingly unique events, but rather on the standardization and repetition of events and episodes that, while seemingly insignificant in themselves, could be perceived as significant in their aggregate. This is a model related to the growth of statistics and what we now call the social sciences, a model that relies on data and one that might be described as fundamentally informational.

This point becomes most clear in connection with Playfair's *Inquiry into the Permanent Causes of the Decline and Fall of Powerful and Wealthy Nations* (1805), which is both a universal history of comparative empire that tracks the movement of empire and prosperity from Egypt through Europe to North America and an attempt to imagine the future possibilities for Britain's commercial empire and commercial society more broadly. Both issues hinge on the problem of decline. In the *Inquiry*, Playfair argues for a distinction between wealth acquired by conquest, which in his account is impossible to sustain and therefore will lead to an inevitable decline, and wealth acquired by commerce, which can be maintained indefinitely. Although Playfair's broad survey of past empires suggests that decline is unavoidable, the relative novelty of a nation whose power is based in commercial wealth creates new possibilities.

This is an issue with which Playfair had been concerned since the publication of his first major work, the *Commercial and Political Atlas* (1786). There, Playfair noted that the rapid increase in England's trade during the eighteenth century "must come in time to a point which it cannot pass, as nothing is infinite; it is therefore of great importance to trace and find out to what causes we owe our commercial superiority, that we may endeavour to prolong it as much as possible" (*CPA*, 1801, 2). This is precisely the challenge that Playfair takes up in the *Inquiry*.

The problem is heighted by the fact that the causes of "commercial superiority" accrue slowly and are often imperceptible or "not sensible." The recognition of such slow, gradual change was not new, and here Playfair likely benefitted from his awareness of Scottish Enlightenment thought, which consistently emphasized gradual change, change that although significant cannot be readily perceived or recognized. Of particular interest for thinkers like Adam Smith, William Robertson, David Hume, John Millar, and Lord Kames were the slow and gradual changes in manners that formed the backbone of the increasingly self-conscious program of historical studies that we associate with the Scottish Enlightenment.[61] Kames, for example, in his *Historical Law Tracts*, says of the transition from private revenge to penal codes that, "A Revolution so contradictory to the strongest propensity of human nature, could not by any power, or by any artifice, be instantaneous. It behooved to be gradual, and in fact, the progressive Steps tending to its completion, were slow, and, taken singly, almost imperceptible."[62] Given the invariably slow nature of progress and progressive change, how could it be noticed or demonstrated? How can you know what you cannot see?

If, for the Scottish Enlightenment, slow, gradual, imperceptible change was a problem associated with progress, for Playfair such change is crucial for understanding decline. Because Playfair sees decline as a structural problem, one that cannot be prevented by individual morals or agency, it must be the subject of concerted government policy before its signs appear. The challenge, according to Playfair, is to recognize the problems before they are acute and to prevent them from worsening, but the problem is one of rate or pace: because decline happens slowly, it is easy to miss the signs and decline often appears to be a direct result of a particular event. In this sense, Playfair's understanding of decline is like Smith's account of progress in that both are understood as developing from gradual changes that, in Smith's phrase, are "not sensible." Playfair, then, resists the notion of historical rupture built around the singular event, preferring instead a model of aggregated data whose significance (and eventfulness) is constituted only by examining change over a relatively long, centurial timescale. As he further elaborates in the *Inquiry*, "The single and unforeseen cause that overwhelms a man in the midst of prosperity, never ruins a nation: unless it be ripe for ruin, a nation never falls; and when it does fall, accident has only the appearance of doing what, in reality, was already nearly accomplished" (*IPC*, xii). Decline is structural, and if its onset is difficult to discern among martial kingdoms, it has become even more so in commercial nations.

In his insistence on the institutional causes of decline and the differences between martial and commercial nations, Playfair's *Inquiry* can be compared to Adam Ferguson's argument about the decline and corruption of nations in the final two books of his *Essay on the History of Civil Society* (1767). For both Ferguson and Playfair, decline is largely a problem of internal decay. In Ferguson's account, it occurs because the "national spirit" cannot create the conditions that secure its preservation. Unlike Playfair, Ferguson is a moralist. He is deeply skeptical about the supposed progress of commercial society because it creates specialization and a division of labor that improves material well-being but separates a people's private and commercial life from their public allegiances, leaving the individual divided and the nation weak. The cost of refinement, in other words, is the loss of virtue. But decline is not inevitable and occurs due to a failure of will. Ferguson explains that when matters of public concern "cease to animate, nations may be said to languish; when they are during any considerable time neglected, states must decline, and their people degenerate."[63] Decline can be prevented by proper institutions and is therefore more a problem of virtue than of time.[64]

Perhaps because he is most concerned with the moral qualities of decline, Ferguson (like Goldsmith) is not concerned with dates, nor is decline for him something that can be measured. It is not numerate, either in relation to quantities like annual production or through dates that would allow comparison of those quantities over fixed periods of time. This is the key distinction that separates accounts of decline like those of Playfair and Smith from those of Ferguson and Goldsmith. To put it briefly: Smith and Playfair do not see decline as a moral problem, but rather as a problem of numbers. Decline can be measured and quantified and possibly prevented. Moreover, for Playfair, far from weakening the national spirit, commercial society offers the possibility of overcoming decline and folding it into a larger pattern of progress. Playfair agrees with Ferguson that luxury and military success were incompatible since the development of refined tastes weakened virtue and prevented military discipline. For Playfair, however, this changes with the development of commerce. In commercial society money can buy the engines of war and "by this means, the decline of nations is, at least, now become a less natural and slower process than formerly" (*IPC*, 18). Playfair, then, believes that decline is a slow and gradual process, one that has become even slower and more gradual in commercial societies and one that can therefore be forestalled by preventative measures if its early signs can be recognized.

An understanding of decline that is based on the tracking of aggregated data and not particular events requires new epistemological techniques to make it recognizable. Playfair's charts might be understood in relation to the rise of statistical thinking described by Theodore M. Porter, and to the increasing importance of numbers in state policy and public life more generally, as characterized by Mary Poovey.[65] Neither Porter nor Poovey make any mention of Playfair since his work does not contribute in a significant way to statistical methodology. What Playfair's work does, however, is insert the diagram front and center as a representation of quantitative data. Unlike the Scottish Enlightenment thinkers who sought to characterize the less visible, sluggish processes of gradual change through a philosophical method designed to reveal them, Playfair offers his statistical charts and graphs as a different methodological response to track slow and gradual developments. In the third edition of the *Commercial and Political Atlas* (1801), Playfair claimed that he was "the first who applied the principles of geometry to matters of Finance" (*CPA*, 1801, viii). This may be true, but Playfair's use of lines and circles does not rely on advanced geometric principles, nor was he the first to plot figures on a Cartesian coordinate system.[66] What is important about Playfair, however, is that unlike his predecessors, who used the abscissa (x-axis) and ordinate (y-axis) coordinates to plot abstract mathematical functions, Playfair was a pioneer in his use of graphs to represent a concrete set of unique historical data.

Playfair's charts suggest that the recognition of patterns of decline from the aggregation of large quantities of data into readily graspable charts could perhaps postpone decline indefinitely. They can thus help to turn what might initially appear to be a pattern of decline into an occasion for renewed progress, and this transposition of decline into progress is the third salient feature of Playfair's charts. Central to Playfair's argument throughout the *Inquiry* are the new possibilities for perpetual progress enabled by commercial wealth.[67] In conquering empires the reward of conquest is often luxury, which corrupts the populace and thus makes further conquests, and eventually even defense, impossible. By contrast, "Wealth procured by commerce, far from degrading a nation more than wealth procured by conquest, does not degrade it near so much; and the reason is easily understood. Whenever a commercial nation becomes too corrupted and luxurious, its wealth vanishes, and the evil corrects itself" (*IPC*, 33). Playfair suggests, in other words, that the apparent decline of a commercial nation can be better understood cyclically, and that decline might actually be precedent to further progress. It is a pattern that lends itself more to the population cycles of Malthus than Gibbon's grand narrative of decline and fall, except that it more closely resembles the inverse stamp of the principle of population. If for Malthus, any apparent progress and perfectibility is precedent for an eventual catastrophe that will decrease population, for Playfair, any apparent decline in a commercial nation simply paves the way for retrenchment and eventual recovery. And if this is the case, then the decline of commercial empire is not inevitable and relative permanence is possible.

Though he takes decline as his subject, Playfair does not think that England is in decline. Rather, he raises the specter of decline to encourage attention to preservation. As Playfair explains in the preface to his *Inquiry*:

> Though the career of prosperity must necessarily have a termination amongst every people, yet there is some reason to think that the degrada-
> tion, which naturally follows, and which has always followed hitherto, may
> be averted; whether it may be, or may not be so, is the subject of the
> following Inquiry; which, if it is of importance to any nation on earth,

must be peculiarly so to England; a nation that has risen, both in commerce
and in power, so high above the natural level assigned to it by its population
and extent. A nation that rises still, but whose most earnest wish ought to be
rather directed to preservation than extension; to defending itself against
adversity rather than seeking still farther to augment its power.

Playfair's comments here indicate that even in states that we would consider to be rising, like Great Britain in the early nineteenth century,
anxieties about decline are never far off. Strategies of retrenchment, then,
though we may associate them with falling empires and states in decline,
may also be just as essential for navigating a graceful rise and for perpetuating empire into the future.

   This issue of futurity, in turn, is a final significant issue related to decline
that Playfair's graphs allow us to rethink. Here, we should note that the
only new chart to appear in Playfair's *Inquiry* is his universal commercial
history (Figure 1.2), which is meant to show the life cycle of all commercial
empires from antiquity to the present. This is also the only chart that
contains no concrete and verifiable data.[68] Of the remaining three charts,
two are time-series line graphs: one showing British exports and imports
from 1700 to 1805 (Figure 1.3) and another showing the increase of annual
revenues of England and France from the start of the seventeenth century
to the French Revolution (Figure 1.4). As noted, both of these had already
appeared in all three editions of Playfair's *Commercial and Political Atlas*.
There the imports and exports chart showed a history of increasing
commercial prosperity and provoked a reflection on inevitable decline,
while a consideration of the comparative revenues of England and France
produced Playfair's disclaimer that "This work is intended to represent the
past, and by no means to lead to observations on its future increase" (*CPA*,
3rd ed., 1801, 83). But in their new context – amid a protracted argument
about the causes of decline and the preventative measures that can be taken
in response to these causes – these charts turn conjecture into projection.
The backward-looking techniques of the Scottish Enlightenment, the
conjectural method for reconstructing the development of human society
from its origins to its apex in commercial society, is redirected into a future
projection by a visual turn. The charts project an implicit assumption of
large-scale regularity and they further imply that such regularities continue
into the future because they arise from the structural stability of society.
Put differently, the charts, in their new context, continue to show aggregate data and evident trend lines, but read as part of an argument about
how to postpone and avoid decline in commercial society, they now invite
their reader to imagine the continuity of the trend lines to the right of the

graph and off the page – into the future. Worrisome trends can thus be anticipated and corrected before their impact is felt, while trends that suggest continuity and strength can be maintained.

What this means, then, is that a detailed representation of past data becomes the implicit basis for forecasting, for thinking about how past patterns of economic data shape future possibilities, including the possibility that properly managed commerce can form the basis for a potentially perpetual prosperity, one that keeps decline at bay by using economic indicators to delay and subvert the symptoms of its onset. One crucial factor here is the avoidance of conquest in favor of trade: it is only commercial empire that Playfair sees as at all sustainable. When Playfair deploys his graphic techniques to create visual patterns from large sets of assembled data, in other words, the result is a thoroughgoing attempt to affect a different understanding of the past and the relationship between economic indicators and more traditionally understood historical events. But it also represents the deployment of a method whose techniques might be understood as inviting a shift from conjecture about the past to projection of the future (as would certainly be the case when the formal discipline of economics turned its statistical methodology more explicitly to models designed for forecasting).[69]

To get a clearer sense of how projection works in Playfair's argument, we can return to the point with which this chapter began: Adam Smith's rejection of jeremiads predicting imminent national decline. Like Smith, Playfair was also attuned to jeremiads of this sort, especially those that took the rising national debt as the root cause for projecting imminent disaster. Playfair notes that the debt "has been a continual object of terror since its first creation; not a public terror merely amongst the ignorant, but the most profound and enlightened statesmen. Calculators, and writers on political economy, have served to augment the uneasiness by their predictions of a fatal termination" (*IPC*, 234). While Playfair admits that extensive borrowing cannot go on indefinitely, the question becomes at what point the crisis will begin, and this is a problem of projection, one susceptible to uncertain events. Nonetheless, Playfair insists that those who foretell approaching decline overlook two important factors: first, that necessity breeds industry and an increased output will counteract the tendency to decline; and, second, that the value of money decreases with time, thus inevitably lessening the debt burden. In expanding upon his understanding of necessity, Playfair notes that the high taxes paid to service the national debt are also often held up as an indicator of decline. Yet, far from lowering national wealth, Playfair suggests that taxes increase wealth "so that the flourishing state of England is a very natural effect of heavy taxation" (*IPC*, 237).

To support this point, Playfair introduces a curious example. He notes how many poor people from the country choose to emigrate to London despite its having the highest taxes in the kingdom, and then asks his reader to imagine that "if the nature of things could have admitted of people *changing centuries* as they *change countries*, the people of the seventeenth century, with light taxes, would have emigrated to the nineteenth century, with all its heavy taxes, just as those Irish and Scotch come to London" (*IPC*, 238). This, Playfair declares, proves his point. Those versed in more contemporary debates about the temporal-spatial assumptions in the concept of uneven development will not be at all surprised that "The common expression. . . that one part of the country is a century behind another, or twenty years, or fifty years, is exactly the same idea, expressed in other words, for it is a comparison between the changes which a lapse of time makes in one case, and a removal of place in the other" (*IPC*, 238).[70] In the context of Playfair's graphics the episode underscores the limitations of charted, visualized time, which understands temporal processes as operating only in a continuum of even, mappable time. In such a continuum, those "out of time" or "out of place" are interchangeable because they can simply shift positions on the grid. This transcription of time into space, considered alongside the visualization of time in Playfair's charts, suggests that, for Playfair, space itself can be made to encode temporal difference. After Foucault, it has become difficult to understand space as a marker of temporal change, but this is exactly what Playfair's charts do: When Playfair turns the flat table – "the non-temporal rectangle" described by Foucault – into a visual chart, he shifts from tabulation to series and converts time into space, thus showing one way that space itself can offer a visual record of time even within the Classical episteme.[71]

Collectively, Playfair's charts imply that decline is a relative category, one that can be quantified and measured. More, to this emphasis on quantification, Playfair insists that decline can be seen visually, that it can be represented through lines, shapes, and colors plotted to show comparative national prosperity and productivity, most commonly over an interval of a century, but also by examining the movement of empires over nearly four thousand years. In other words, it is not only in his title that Playfair combines Gibbon and Smith; the visualizations of change over time that he offers utilize a combination of the millennia that in Gibbon's argument showed the development of prosperity if one adapted a perspective of four thousand years (chart 1 Figure 1.2,) and the unit of the century that Smith insisted was the appropriate timescale for observing significant patterns of increase or decrease (chart 3, Figure 1.3, and chart 4, Figure 1.4).

My analysis of decline as understood by Smith and Playfair, then, reveals an attempt to use decline as an occasion to reflect on how it might be measured and avoided and on the appropriate timescale for considering such measurement. Smith and Playfair disagree about exactly what should be measured, but they both agree on the need for measurement and they further concur that whatever measure one chooses, the timescale of a century is necessary to reveal a significant trend. Further, in each instance, the perceived threat of decline is something that can be managed, and through its management, diffused. Considered thus, we might understand decline as distinct from fall, as a threat that is potentially disabling but not necessarily so and therefore as a cultural problem that motivates a range of culturally productive responses. And sometimes, as Chapter 2 will suggest, culture itself can serve as both compensation for and solution to perceived decline.

The Decline of Literature: Acceleration, Print Saturation, and Media Time

> When I reflect that every literary journal consists of 50 or 60 publications, and that of these, 5 or 6 at least are capital performances, and the greater part not contemptible, when I take the pen and attempt to calculate, by these given sums, the number of volumes which the next century must infallibly produce, my feeble faculties wander in a perplexed series, and as I lose myself among billions, trillions, and quartillions, I am obliged to lay down my pen, and stop at infinity.
> – Isaac D'Israeli, *Essay on the Manners and Genius of the Literary Character*
> (1795)

Chapter 1 of this book considered arguments about decline in political economy. Adam Smith emphasized the need for a standard – annual production – by which to measure decline and then insisted that this standard had to be tracked over a significant period of time, notably the century. William Playfair, instead, emphasized the balance of trade between nations, but as his attempts to picture and chart this standard indicate, he, too, measured the significance of trade balances wherever possible across one hundred year periods. For both Smith and Playfair, their data only made sense when considered in the context of a particular and particularly long timescale. Further, both addressed the effects of temporal acceleration; for Smith, such acceleration was part of the "hurry of life" in a commercial world, while Playfair imagined his charts as being of immense use for men of rank and active business because they represented time in a manner that took less time to see. The kinds of commercial charts devised by Playfair, then, at once respond to the acceleration of commercial life and intensify it by allowing for the processing of information in ever-faster ways. This is why I call this accelerated time "informational time" and associate it further with the time of commerce and commercial society.

In this chapter I want to speculate about the connection between commerce and print media in informational time. In this context, the regular appearance of an ever-proliferating quantity of printed materials – from books to broadsides, pamphlets to periodicals, annuals to almanacs, prints to playbills, newspapers to magazines – exacerbated the sense of hurry in commercial life because the accumulation of print often made it seem as if more things were happening and as if what was happening were happening more quickly. More print, in other words, meant more to read and pressured the amount of time in which to read it, thus creating an effect of intensification as a people already busy with the rush of commercial life experienced even greater demands on their time. Since all these forms of print were also part of a commercial society, we might ask about the relationship between commerce and print media as related qualities within informational time and a more general sense of temporal acceleration. This chapter takes up this question by looking at accounts of the decline of literature from the 1750s forward, notably those of Oliver Goldsmith, Vicesimus Knox, and John Stuart Mill. Not only do these accounts show how anticipations of decline cut across what we now understand to be separate categories like political economy and literature, but they also show how literary production contributed to the sense of temporal acceleration and a fractured, heterochronic sense of time – a key feature of the understanding of decline circa 1800 – and how print saturation produced correspondent concerns about the decline of literature in particular.

In thinking about accounts of literary decline, my argument draws upon my previous explanation of how Smith and Playfair handle arguments about decline to make two main points. First, I want to suggest that accounts of literary decline share with related accounts of national, imperial, and economic decline a sense of the increasing complexity of the modern world, a complexity that often results in the signs of decline remaining hidden from view. But while political economy seeks to sustain this complexity and to manage it through quantification, accounts of literary decline more commonly acknowledge the decline of literature as a quantitative problem but then try to manage this complexity by winnowing it, by selecting certain works or certain kinds of works from the abundance of material in print. This represents, in other words, a strategy for managing complexity by shifting from the quantitative to the qualitative, one that we commonly associate with the problem of taste. Next, however, I will argue that we need to read complaints about the decline of literature as more than simple laments over abandoned standards of taste. This point also relates to perceptions of the greater complexity and contingency of contemporary life, and my suggestion is that the increasingly common tendency to decry the state of

contemporary literature, often in apocalyptic terms, can be better understood as an objection not to the decline of taste but to this new sense of
contingency and complexity produced by the saturation of books. Concerns
about decline, then, mask concerns about the difficulty of understanding or
mapping an increasingly complex literary field.

If this is the case, there are two further implications for my claims. For
a start, my suggestion here is that print media both represent anxieties
about the increasing hurry of life in commercial society and participate in
the creation of these kinds of anxieties. "The Press," in this sense can be
understood to allude both to the media of print culture, but also to what
I am here characterizing as the sense of hurry and hustle that such media
produce in those who engage them. It is no accident, then, that the first line
of George Crabbe's poem *The Newspaper* (1785) begins with "A time like
this, a busy, bustling time" or that Hazlitt's essay on "The Periodical Press"
(1823) similarly declares that "we exist in the bustle of the world."[1]
Repeatedly, awareness of the increasing output of the press, the proliferation and eventual saturation of print, in later eighteenth- and early
nineteenth-century culture links up to anxieties about time, to new senses
of temporality, and in particular to an awareness of pressure associated with
time. Such pressure maps onto worries that there is not enough time to
read or even to keep track of the seemingly endless flow of print and to
related concerns about the temporal duration of different kinds of writing.
Further, this sense of haste, of rush, and of the perception of increasing
pressure on time as distinguishing characteristics of the present from the
later eighteenth century onward, I want to suggest, paves the way for
a correspondent sense of despair and, ultimately, decline.

The confusion, bafflement, and bewilderment readers experienced when
faced with the ever-expanding world of print media, in other words,
established a sense not only of complexity but also of precariousness, one
that underscores the fragility of the system and suggests, for some, its
unsustainability and inevitable decline. My concerns here might be understood to correlate with the shift from print proliferation to print saturation
described by Clifford Siskin and William Warner when they distinguish
between print proliferation as productive of shared, confident enterprises
to organize or mediate a comprehensive range of knowledge and print
saturation as the condition in which such reconciliation became less and
less likely.[2] My emphasis, however, is not on how this turn might be
understood as part of the history of mediation, but rather on the effect of
this shift on the felt pressure of time, especially as a sense of the future turns
from what Siskin and Warner call "something that could be accomplished:

a better and more perfect whole made collectively out of more and more parts"[3] into a future understood as fragmenting and multiplying, as incapable of organization and, hence, in decline.

Finally – and this is the second further implication – by reading accounts of the decline of literature against the grain, we can better see how they might be understood, like the accounts of decline discussed in Chapter 1 of this book, as generative and not disabling. In this reading, to lament the decline of literature is not necessarily to concede that it is a problem without remedy, and such arguments frequently counter their negative assessment of the state of contemporary literary production by emphasizing works that stand out from the fray as valuable, whether this value is a quality of length, of genre, of style, or of moral worth. Concerns about the decline of literature, in other words, might help to consolidate both the need for a vernacular canon of works whose value seems beyond doubt and set the kind of standards understood to guide the selection of these works, especially as they relate to timelessness, permanence, and durability. In the case of political economy and literature, then, an awareness of the threat of decline becomes a means for identifying value and for proposing how to forestall decline such that decline becomes not an end point, but rather part of a larger pattern of potential progress and improvement.

Decline as a Quantitative Problem: Political Economy and the State of Literature

With these issues in mind, I want to review the relationship in Adam Smith's political economy between the function of quantity and the problem of complexity. This will enable a comparison between Smith's account of economic and national decline and Oliver Goldsmith's account of literary decline in his *The Present State of Polite Learning* (1759). Both Smith and Goldsmith respond to the frequency with which decline is invoked in their respective subjects, but the juxtaposition of their responses suggests how accounts of decline in political economy and assessments of the state of literature handle the problem of quantity differently in the later eighteenth century.

Smith's response to the decline jeremiad, as we saw in Chapter 1, was to insist on the need to measure and quantify a standard of decline and to consider changes to that standard in the context of a prolonged timescale. One effect of this reassessment was a shift in emphasis from particular and seemingly significant events, like the loss at Saratoga in 1777, to the proliferation of repeatable and seemingly insignificant events, like the repeated measurement of annual production and capital reinvestment across the century. A shift of this sort depends on the collection and comparison of large amounts of data and serves as an indication of the increasing complexity of national life. Wealth and related concerns about national welfare, Smith insists, are much more complicated than a simple tally of precious metals kept in the national storehouse nor should we necessarily consider as powerful a country with more exports than imports. It is not just any number or set of numbers that can represent the relative welfare of the nation. Some numbers have more significance than others: For Smith, annual production is a more valid measure than the quantity of precious metals. In offering his assessment, Smith implies a complex and contingent world in which change is frequently "not sensible." This is a world governed by the mechanisms of an invisible hand, sure, but in this case the emphasis is more on an invisible world of private frugality – a nation of savers in which the private habits and motivations of hundreds of thousands, even millions, of anonymous individuals create a system of capital reinvestment that is powerful enough to advance the annual production of land and labor despite government profligacy and the waste of maintaining costly foreign wars and colonies that, Smith elsewhere makes clear, do not pull their weight. The issue is that this intricate system of private savings cannot be seen, while other aspects of national life, like wars and demographic movement from the country to the city, are much more visible.

When Goldsmith, for example, complains in 1770 about the depopulation of Auburn and the decline of agriculture and village life, he is not mistaken, but the particular fate of Auburn is but one element in the increasingly complex and invisible system that might elsewhere be thriving as Auburn suffers. The same goes for John Brown's earlier *Estimate* from 1757 in which Brown insists that "We are rolling to the brink of a precipice that must destroy us."[4] As Smith makes clear regarding the decline jeremiad, "Many of them have been written by very candid and intelligent people; who wrote nothing but what they believed, and for no other reason but because they believed it."[5] What such estimates miss, however, is the increasing complexity of the commercial system. As Paul Keen notes, condemnations of the present state of things reflect "fundamental questions about the deeper structural implications of Britain's evolving commercial order" and, consequently, the "problem that critics often identified as a consumer-driven decline into personal and social *corruption* was, at a certain level, actually one of *complexity*."[6] It is the complex and hidden nature of this system that Smith's work is so astute at manifesting.

One of the key features of the debate over national decline as clarified by Smith was the attempt to quantify the problem. Indeed, we might understand this to be one of the major contributions of an emergent political economy: It turned anxieties about the national future and qualitative judgments of national health, manners, and morals into problems that could be assessed numerically by looking at measurable quantities like annual productivity. As the work of William Playfair showed us, such numbers, in turn, could be characterized through lines and readily mapped onto a visual field, eventually making it even easier and faster to assess the significance of quantity. Playfair's visual representations remind us that numbers here function on two levels: they work concretely as a form of measurement, but they also work symbolically, in this case as an indication of the relative welfare of the nation. The system itself cannot be seen, but the numbers that measure its relative status can be. Faced with the problem of complexity, political economy attempts to maintain complexity through quantification. Numbers represent a complex economy that has too many moving parts – all those private individuals saving and striving who for Smith help to maintain national prosperity even in times of government profligacy and corruption – that cannot be seen or grasped except through numerical representation.

Smith's comments from 1776 about the prevalence of jeremiads predicting national decline recall Goldsmith's earlier claims in *The Present State of Polite Learning* (1759). There, Goldsmith opened his account with the observation that "It has been so long the practice to represent literature as declining, that every renewal of this complaint now comes with diminished influence. The publick has been often excited by a false alarm, so that at present the nearer we approach the threatened period of decay, the more our fatal security increases."[7] Both Goldsmith and Smith note how frequently pronouncements of decline are issued in their respective fields. Smith emphasizes the consistent success of such accounts at gaining "some authority with the public" (*WN*, 365), while Goldsmith, by contrast, suggests that the more common such pronouncements become, the more likely the reading public is to tune them out and hence produce a false sense of security. As he continues Goldsmith proceeds to defend contemporary letters. He suggests, as Smith will later in a different context, that claims for decline are inaccurate, that they favor "declamation" over the "calmness of deliberate inquiry."

In his attempt to correct such declamations and to clarify and improve polite learning, Goldsmith not only quantifies the problem, but he understands it as a relation between quantities. He is acutely aware of numbers, particularly the increasing number of critics. He suggests that "the genius of every country" diminishes in proportion to the increase in critics, but as learning spreads and matures, "critics must be proportionately more numerous" (*GCW*, 1:287) and this "always portended a decay" (*GCW*, 1:288). With his emphasis on proportion Goldsmith here sounds like a political economist discussing the relation between two dependent variables, like price and supply, while the specific relationship Goldsmith describes appears – to our modern eyes that have become accustomed to charts, graphs, and the visualization of quantitative data – like a function that could be easily graphed. According to Goldsmith, the problem with critics is that they judge from rule and not from feeling.

But while he discusses the problem in proportional terms that resonate with the kind of analysis prominent in Smith, Goldsmith offers a different solution. He shifts from a quantitative problem, a problem of proliferation, to a qualitative response by introducing the standard of taste: "The man, the nation, must therefore be good, whose chiefest luxuries consist in the refinement of reason; and reason can never be universally cultivated unless guided by Taste, which may be considered as the link between science and common sense, the medium through which learning should ever been seen by society" (*GCW*, 1:337). Goldsmith's discussion of taste here falls in between two of the eighteenth-century's most important statements on that subject: Burke's *A Philosophical Enquiry into the Origin of Our Ideas of the Sublime and the Beautiful* (1757) and Adam Smith's *Theory of Moral Sentiments*, published just after Goldsmith's work in April 1759. Linked as it is to morals and manners, taste in Goldsmith's account becomes the "standing evidence" through which "we can, with precision, compare the literary performances of our fathers with our own, and from their excellence, or defects, determine the moral, as well as the literary merits of either" (*GCW*, 1:337). Both Goldsmith's rejection of decline and his argument in defense of modern learning thus rely on numbers and ratios – more learning means more critics; the rise of critics is in proportion to the decrease in genius – but his argument ultimately retreats from quantitative proportions and instincts in favor of a qualitative standard of comparison, taste. Goldsmith does not need numbers; he contends that taste allows for a comparison "with precision" between past and present.

In this regard, Goldsmith might be understood as typical of responses to the perceived decline of literature. The pattern of such responses, as this chapter will explore in detail, often parallels responses to perceived decline in other contexts, notably national, imperial, and economic decline, whereby some deny the basis of decline, some insist that decline is terminal and beyond repair, some understand decline as part of a necessary cycle of birth, growth, and decay, while still others recognize the signs of decline, but hope to transform them into repair and ultimately progress. But the logic of responses to the perceived decline of literature differs sharply from that of political economy. Political economy as a mode of analysis is premised on quantification and measurement. Faced with the increasing complexity discussed above, political economy maintains complexity, which it seeks to comprehend through measurement. In contrast, when confronting similar problems of complexity and contingency, the tendency of those seeking to provide an account of the literary field is to quantify its increasing complexity by consistent reference to a seemingly ever-expanding universe of print (in Goldsmith's case, all those critics and all those representations of literature's decline), but then to narrow and refine this perceived complexity by assigning value to a reduced segment (in Goldsmith's case, via the standard of taste). The premise, roughly, is akin to the explanation political economy offers for the relationship between price and supply: A greater supply of something lowers its price. In the case of literature, the suggestion is that because so much is being published, the value of literature must be declining, and the response is to restore perceived value by, in a sense, reducing supply, by selecting a small category of merit from the larger field of print.

The Hurry of Modern Life: Print Proliferation and the Problem of Time

Goldsmith's rejection of arguments for the decline of literature, and his insistence that taste can serve as "standing evidence" with which to compare past and present literary works alludes to a common feature of the eighteenth-century literary landscape: an awareness of the ever-increasing output of paper, what Johnson called the "superfoetation" of the press and what present-day scholars have described variously as the explosion, proliferation, or saturation of print. To be sure, such worries are not new in the later eighteenth century, and for earlier examples, we need think no further than Dryden's reference in *Mac Flecknoe* (1678; published 1682) to discarded print as "the scattered limbs of mangled poets" destined to become "martyrs of pies, and relics of the bum," or Pope's vicious satire on the early eighteenth-century print explosion, *The Dunciad* (1728–1743). This is why some attribute the massive expansion of print production to the early eighteenth century and the abuses of the press mocked in the satiric

writings of Pope and Swift.[8] Others, however, suggest that there was an
even greater magnitude of writing in the later eighteenth century, which
has been called the age of print saturation.[9] Still others claim that complaints about overproduction were coeval with the advent of printing.[10]
My point here is not to settle the dispute but to observe that what is
significant about later eighteenth-century complaints about the proliferation of print is the way that these claims increasingly come to bear on the
problem of time. More print is a problem because there is less time to read
the output of the press. Johnson here might serve as an appropriate
example. According to Boswell, in a 1778 conversation with Allan
Ramsay, Johnson reported: "It has been maintained that this superfoetation, this teeming of the press in modern times, is prejudicial to good
literature, because it obliges us to read so much of what is of inferior value,
in order to be in the fashion; so that better works are neglected for want of
time."[11] Johnson ultimately rejects the position on the grounds that more
print means more general diffusion of knowledge such that it can reach
those, including women, who were not previously counted among the
reading public. Still, Johnson succinctly calls attention to the proximity
between the proliferation of print and anxieties about time.

Worries that better works would be neglected for want of time suggest
that time was increasingly an issue in relation to print in the later eighteenth century, and raise questions about how we might think about
changes in time in relation to the history of print. The issue here turns
on two related developments: first, the impact of advances in chronometry
that allowed more accurate timekeeping and the increasing sophistication
of clocks and watches with ever more dependable minute hands from the
seventeenth century forward; and, second, the register of these timekeeping technologies in new prose forms like the diary, the daily and weekly
newspapers, and the travel journal. This is what Stuart Sherman calls
"diurnal form," the writing of a new kind of time that is regular, steady,
and continuous and that competes with religion in organizing narratives of
everyday life.[12] Central here, of course, is the growth of the periodical press,
whose repetitive rhythm John Sommerville describes as fundamentally
forward looking, hinged on concepts of change and movement and
hence, for Sommerville, productive of instability – not of steadiness and
predictability.[13] We might even say, following Deidre Lynch, that time
itself changes from roughly 1750 forward in response to the growth of
periodical culture and the emergence of a domestic culture that turns
around the emergence of daily, weekly, and monthly rituals pitched to
the time of the clock. Time becomes more regular, more routine, and more

measured as diaries, daily papers, and more precise clocks produce a heightened consciousness of time. For Lynch, this more regular sense of time values literature for its steadiness and constancy to such a degree that long forms, like the novel, come to have increased value for their commitment to "the longueurs and recursive rhythms of common life"[14] – as a response to the overexcitement generated by the hurry and bustle of modern life.

Thinking about these accounts in relation to accounts of the decline of literature helps us to see that what distinguishes later eighteenth-century complaints about the expansion of print from those earlier in the century is the convergence of these complaints with the heightened awareness of time. Even if one remains skeptical of the claim that time itself changes in the later eighteenth century, it seems undeniable that the kind of changes sketched above were felt as new. As Ann Blair notes in her account of information overload, "the feeling of overload is often lived by those who experience it as if it were an utterly new phenomenon, as is perhaps characteristic of feelings more generally or of self-perceptions in the modern or postmodern periods especially."[15]

To see the point more clearly, we can compare Goldsmith's argument above with Vicesimus Knox's survey of the literary field nearly twenty years later. An Oxford-educated clergyman and headmaster of Tonbridge School, Knox was a prolific writer on contemporary literature, a moralist whose essays underscore the need to address a broad general audience, who is also skeptical both of pedantry and of the fashionable excess of the literary scene. He is perhaps best known for his *Elegant Extracts* in both prose and verse (1784, 1789) – one of the works that Mr. Martin reads in Jane Austen's *Emma* – collections whose very form caters to the increasing pressure on time characteristic of the later eighteenth century by offering gobbets of works deemed elevating and morally valuable. My discussion of later eighteenth-century anxieties about the decline of literature focuses on Knox because he shows how accounts of literary decline respond to quantitative problems with shifts to qualitative solutions, but the qualitative standards for which he advocates reveal his acute awareness of the time pressures of commercial life. Moreover, when he uses the proliferation of print as an opportunity to define new standards of taste and composition, Knox shows the generative potential of concerns about decline. As such, Knox can be understood not as unique, but as representative of the later eighteenth century. The kinds of issues raised by Knox, as we will see, help to frame later arguments for the value of literature, the place of poetry in a crowded literary field, the relationship between literature and political economy, and the ways that all these issues are shadowed in the Romantic period by new perceptions of time and new anxieties about the future.

Knox opens his 1778 essay "On Modern Literature" with a comment that echoes closely Goldsmith's complaint about the profusion of commentators remarking on the decline of literature in the opening of *The Present State of Polite Learning*. "To complain of the present, and to praise the past," Knox observes, "has so long been the favourite topic of disappointment, or of ignorance, that every stricture on the degeneracy of the times is looked upon as the effusion of ill-nature, or the result of superficial observations: but the absurdity of declamatory invective, ought not to preclude the cool remarks of truth, reason and experience."[16] The frequency with which critics observe decline, Knox insists, might lead us to dismiss this as a kind of crankiness, an "effusion of ill-nature" that has now become an empty, "superficial" trope but, when examined closely, such claims might prove to have merit. They might justify an examination of "the justice of the charge of literary degeneracy in the present age, and, if it be well founded, to discover the causes of it" (*EML*, 1:36). In response, Knox also produces an argument about quantity, in his case one that sets its terms opposite to those of Adam Smith. For Smith, greater productivity was a sign of greater wealth, of more value, value that it turned out was being managed productively by a whole series of private (and invisible) hands. For Knox, however, more writing can only be a mark of its lesser quality: "It has however been observed, that the learning of the present age is not deep though diffusive, and that its productions are not excellent though numerous" (*EML*, 1:37).

Quantity, then, is one of the defining features of the literary field, but for Knox, quantity is not a sign of the greater wealth of literature; rather, it raises a series of problems related to time, from haste of production to decreasing time for consumption. Books, Knox implies, represent a different kind of good, one whose value is diminished by increases in production. Furthermore, not all products of the press are alike. In his *Winter Evenings* (1788), Knox suggests that,

> The dignity of the republic of letters is much lowered by the publication of many novels, pamphlets, and newspapers. . . . Illiterate readers are easily misled by [newspapers]. No books can counteract their effects; for where one book is introduced and read, a thousand newspapers have had the advantage of a previous perusal. I do not intend to insinuate, that the papers are always culpable and delusive; but, from the frequency of their appearance, and the quantity which they are obliged to furnish, it will happen that trash and falsehood will often occupy an ample space in the best among them."[17]

Here, we see how speed, or frequency of appearance, drives quantity. Numeracy for Knox becomes a mark of haste, and a sign of "mercenary motives" (*EML*, 1:38), for "The multiplicity of compositions is an argument of their hasty production; and hastiness is, at least, a presumptive proof of their want of merit" (*EML*, 1:37). Speed of composition is here equated with a lack of quality, with the implication that its opposite, slowness, is a sign of durability and quality, and within this sensibility, newspapers are fast and books are slow. Not all products of the press, then, keep the same time, and while "informational time" might be linked to the haste and hurry of "commercial time," we can see here how the situation is inherently more complicated, encompassing temporalities that at once keep the time of commerce in the daily, weekly, monthly, quarterly, and annual turnout of a certain kind of newspaper and periodical production, but also those that resist commercial time, that are slow, and that function as a path to the timelessness and endurance, which later Romantic critics like Wordsworth, Shelley, and De Quincey come to see as the defining feature of their preferred modes of literary value.

The contrast between hasty and deliberate methods of production leads Knox to assimilate natural and literary production:

> In this point, the literary and natural world resemble each other. The productions of nature, whether vegetable or animal, as they are either of a slow or speedy growth, are known to be durable or transitory, solid or unsubstantial. The oak and the elephant are long before they attain to perfection, but are still longer before they decay; while the butterfly and the tulip perish as they arose, almost within a diurnal revolution of the sun. The works of Virgil cost him much time and labour; but they have existed near two thousand years universally admired, while the compositions of that poet, who boasted he could write two or three hundred verses while he stood on one leg, were lost perhaps in as short a space as that in which they were produced. (*EML*, 1:37–38)

The literary field may be crowded and cluttered, but deliberate composition can still produce works of quality, and these can be chosen, as Knox makes clear elsewhere, by discerning readers. This is an assessment of literary merit that differs in fundamental ways from later Romantic theories of inspiration and genius, but it shares with those accounts of literary value a sense of duration, for the works of Virgil have endured for nearly two thousand years. In a pattern typical of so many assessments of the later eighteenth-century literary field, we see the condemnation of proliferation and the "depraved taste of readers" (*EML*, 1:39) function as a source of eventual valuation. The field might be flooded with hasty mercenary productions of questionable quality, but buried within are works composed with care and deliberation, works that may not be most original nor most erudite but that remain deserving of their reputation by virtue of their "force, elegance, and correctness of style" (*EML*, 1:40). The problem here is to establish the standards to help readers recognize these works of quality. Who should do the selecting: better trained readers or periodicals themselves? Regardless of the answer, the question is pressing because Knox's model of the literary field is predicated on consumption and not production: "The depraved taste of readers is another cause of the degeneracy of writers" (*EML*, 1:39).

One contributor to the multiplicity of literature and the perceived "depraved taste of readers" in the later eighteenth century was, of course, the novel, and it is not surprising that the genre becomes the central villain in Knox's account of modern literature. In his essay "On Novel Reading," also in *Essays, Moral and Literary*, Knox insists that "If it is true, that the present age is more corrupt than the preceding, the great multiplication of Novels probably contributes to its degeneracy" (*EML*, 2:185). Knox is clearly wary of novels, but the claim for degeneracy is couched in the conditional, and other essays suggest that Knox does not share this view of the present age. The antidote to proliferation is selectivity. Knox here enlists Pliny to ground his argument against those that devour many books, the so-called *Helluo Librorum*, "who is more studious of quantity than quality" (*EML*, 1:167). Instead of reading more books less attentively, we should follow the great Roman and read "*non multa sed multum*"; we should, in other words, "be content with fewer books and study them perfectly" (*EML*, 1:168). Once again, an argument about quantity and proliferation produces a judgment of value, and as the essay develops, Knox encourages the choice of classical authors like Plato, Aristotle, and Epictetus over modern novelists like Richardson, Fielding, and Smollett. Distraction is here presented as one of the perils of modern literature that draw people away from value, in this case a narrow range of classical writing. Elsewhere, Knox's comments on style offer a similarly "classical" canon, though not one comprised strictly of antique writers. "Vivacity, spirit, fire are the ingredients which embalm writers for eternity" (*WE*, 2:281) and Knox singles out Virgil, Milton, Shakespeare, and, especially, Homer, for these qualities. Passages like this show not only the particular works that Knox values, helping to constitute a kind of canon of worthwhile (mostly) modern writing, but also, when combined with his comments elsewhere, the qualities for which he values it.

In addition to "vivacity," Knox values a plain style as that which can most effectively and efficiently convey moral truth: "perhaps the best method of conveying [instruction] is that which is plainly addressed to the understanding, without any quaint contrivance, or laborious attempt at novelty of form" (*WE*, 1:69). So while he denies the value of novels, Knox's modern canon has capacious space for the miscellany and the essay and for popular writing more generally. Knox praises the condensed moralism of authors like Montaigne, Collier, Addison, and Steele and their followers, and of essays like those found in the *Tatler*, the *Guardian*, and the *Spectator* and their later eighteenth-century heirs. Since "the real utility of literary labours is to be estimated by the extent of their influence on the national manners and understanding," writers need to address "the common reader who takes up a book for the amusement of a leisure hour" (*EML*, 2:4).

Modern commercial people, Knox repeatedly implies, are busy. They do not have time for the "painful attention" required by abstruse theories like those of Newton, especially "in a commercial country like our own, where only the short interval which the pursuit of gain, and the practice of mechanic arts affords, will be devoted to letters by the more numerous classes of the community" (*EML*, 2:4–5). Again, we have a sense of the speed of business and the accelerated pace of commercial time. For Knox, commercial time dictates informational time: because people have less time to read, but a "short interval," their reading must be focused. Commercial society demands brevity, plainness of style, and accessibility above all; rather than lament the decline of literature and the lack of taste, Knox accommodates his understanding of literary value to the values of commercial life with its pressing constraints on time.

Moments like this recall the previous chapter's discussion of William Playfair, who emphasizes similar qualities and whose charts were designed to impart information with maximum efficiency to men of business operating in a world of haste and temporal pressure. Note that Knox does not lament the situation and suggest that the hustle of the commercial world degrades the thirst for knowledge; instead, he makes a virtue of the situation and suggests that short, sharp essayistic writing conveyed in a plain style is ideally suited to capture the attention and develop the morals of those who have little time and much writing from which to choose. Knox's preference is for moral truth over mathematical truth in the context of what he repeatedly calls the "busy world" (*EML*, 1: 67; 2: 246). Consequently, "A hint of practical wisdom has often preserved a whole life from folly and misery, and thousands and ten thousands have benefitted as well as delighted by Addison, to every one who has read Malbranche [sic] and Locke" (*WE*, 2: 110). There may be too many books published, but the selective reader who chooses to spend his limited spare time with a good essayist like Addison will learn more not only than the novel reader, but also more than the more serious and often pedantic reader who seeks wisdom from difficult to unlock texts like Malebranche and Locke. Here we see as well Knox's attention to a different kind of quantity, for the selective reader is not part of a select group, but exists as part of a broad group of readers in a ratio of a thousand or ten thousand to one "philosophical reader."

A "busy world," "the amusement of a leisure hour," "the short interval," these phrases and others like them underscore the hustle and bustle of the new world of commerce, but Knox also uses them to suggest the suitability of certain kinds of writing for the temporal pressures that abound in this commercial world of getting and spending. Phrases like this suggest how informational time can be made to accommodate the precariousness and rush of commercial time. More, that very world of rapid change and accelerated mutability offers greater subject matter for the author, because "Political revolutions, religious reformations, the whims of fashion, and the changes in literature, enable the moral writer, when he travels even in a beaten road, to discover prospects hitherto unobserved" (*EML*, 2:12).

The plethora of new paths available to writers, combined with a greater number of outlets for publication and a rapidly increasing number of books being published, suggests a darker side as well, however, one in which the economy of books and time has become seriously out of balance: "While the objects of learning are encreased, the time to be spent in pursuit of it according to the modes of modern life, is greatly contracted." Faced with such choices, "The art of printing has multiplied books to such a degree, that it is a vain attempt either to collect or to read all that is excellent, much more all that has been published" (*WE*, 2:224). Here, since the sheer quantity of print media produces a sense that it is impossible to engage them all and thus contributes to a sense of hurry and time pressure, we see how the proliferation of print accentuates and intensifies the sense of hurry and acceleration understood as characteristic of commercial time. My suggestion, further, is that this sense of there never being enough time, of haste, of rush, as distinguishing characteristics of the present produces also a range of uneasy feelings – perhaps even akin to the kind of feelings that Sianne Ngai calls "ugly feelings," which she suggests are defined by "a flatness or ongoingness" and by "a remarkable capacity for duration"[18] – including perplexity, confusion, bewilderment, and disorder, that arise as people try to navigate an increasingly complex network of print media. For many, such feelings tend toward despair as they underscore the uncertainty and precariousness of print media as a system whose sheer proliferation comes to resist order and arrangement and whose fragility comes to be associated with an instability that can only result in decline.

This is the sort of apocalyptic panic that we see so frequently in the eighteenth century from early examples like Pope's *Dunciad* to later ones like James Ralph and Catharine Macaulay. Ralph, for example, complained about "the Glut of Writing which has cloy'd the present Age" in the form of "journals, chronicles, magazines, and other periodical and occasional productions," which he likens to "Pharoahs years of abundance" and in response to which he summons "a dearth as durable" to quell the overflow of print.[19] Macaulay meanwhile declared that "the literary market is overstocked, as those many warehouses which totter under the weight of immense piles of printed copies can very sufficiently evidence."[20] Indeed, what distinguishes Macaulay's complaint here is the vividness of her image, the manner in which both she and Ralph see the proliferation of books in apocalyptic terms. For Ralph, these productions are akin to a plague of biblical proportions, while, for Macaulay, the piles of printed papers are best understood through images of imbalance – like the tower of Babel, all that tottering weight of books threatens to unsettle the nation and bring everything and everyone crumbling down in the wake of all that paper. Political economy, with its shift in the basis of wealth from land to trade, made it possible to imagine a future of progress through commerce without war or the need to defend territory from invasion (the fantasy of *doux commerce*). Ralph and Macaulay, however, underscore a different kind of threat with a vision of print as a kind of contagion, one whose mass might be understood as an insidious invader from within and a problem that needs to be addressed directly. In the hands of Macaulay and Ralph, books and print generally are not marks of enlightenment, but rather forces of precariousness and confusion, forces moreover that threaten to invite decline as a kind of fifth column from within.

Macaulay's image of warehouses struggling under the weight of paper, of print run wild, offers an image suitable also for Knox's vision of print saturation, but Knox ultimately resists her apocalyptic tendencies. This is not to suggest, however, that Knox is complacent, as his review of different categories of books would indicate. Here, the effort to divide knowledge into a series of related areas recalls not only Enlightenment drives at indexing and categorization, but also the disciplinary moves of the nineteenth century, which similarly aspire to make knowledge more organized, more systematic, and hence more manageable. And yet the result of Knox's enumeration is precisely the opposite: the constant expansion of print produces only a sense of imbalance and futility. Knox observes that works related to travel – including "history, geography, botany" – are now "sufficiently numerous to fill a large musæum" (*WE*, 2:225); that advances in science "have multiplied the books necessary to be read by the general scholar to a wonderful extent" (*WE*, 2:225); and that the study of antiquities "has added greatly to the number of books. Politics, history and law, have crowded the library," while divinity "has been most indus-triously cultivated and the harvest has been rich" (*WE*, 2:226). Similar results are found in moral philosophy, philology, and in new genres like the novel. "Add to all this a vast quantity of poetry or verse of all kinds, and on all subjects; add tragedies and comedies; add pamphlets in all their variety, fugitive papers, publications of diurnal intelligence, and the sum becomes so great as to lead the student to a degree of despair" (*WE*, 2:227). There is now an "infinite number of books" and their proliferation produces not a contented survey of the advance in knowledge that such a plethora might provoke, but rather "despair" at how many books there are and how little time there is to read them in "modern life." Knox's survey shows clearly how what I have been calling commercial time and informational time feed off each other to produce a sense of acceleration, one that, for Knox, leads inevitably to despair and to concern that literature might be in decline and, more, that the decline of literature both reflects and exacerbates national decline.

To get a sense of what is distinctive about Knox's accounting, we might compare his reflections to earlier observations by Oliver Goldsmith in *The Citizen of the World* (1760). Writing in the voice of a Chinese visitor to London, Goldsmith also characterized England as a nation of books, and he, too, saw this as representative of something other than the spread of knowledge and enlightenment. Goldsmith was quick to note that many more books were being published than could ever be read by the population:

> Were we to estimate the learning of the English by the number of books that are every day published among them, perhaps no country, not even China itself, could equal them in this particular. I have reckoned not less than twenty-three new books published in one day; which upon computation, makes eight thousand three hundred and ninety-five in one year. Most of these are not confined to one single science, but embrace the whole circle. History, politics, poetry, mathematics, metaphysics, and the philosophy of nature, are all comprized in a manual not larger than that in which our

children are taught the letters. If then we suppose the learned of England to
read but an eighth part of the works which daily come from the press (and
sure none can pretend to learning upon less-easy terms,) at this rate every
scholar will read a thousand books in one year. From such a calculation, you
may conjecture what an amazing fund of literature a man must be possessed
of, who thus reads three new books every day, not one of which but contains
all the good things that ever were said or written.[21]

This passage is notable for its numeration, for the way that it offers an
efficient accounting of books on the basis of average daily publication
compounded over a year and then figures an average of daily reading.
It reads like the kind of calculation we would find in political economy, but
its effect is to show how books are unlike many other goods: their
proliferation exceeds their use value, and while this overproduction may
result in more consumer choice, this is not conceived as a benefit. In this,
Goldsmith resembles Knox, but while Goldsmith quickly whittles the mass
of books by an eighth, Knox succumbs to a sense of what he calls "despair"
at the sense of haste and time pressure that he sees as characteristic of
"modern life" nearly twenty years after Goldsmith. Goldsmith's cool
reckoning surveys the situation with an ironic eye attentive to the imbalance between the production of books and the resulting knowledge of the
populace; Knox focuses instead on the imbalance between books and the
time required to read them. Having too much to choose from does not
enhance knowledge. It overwhelms readers, creates intense pressure on
their time, and makes them feel rushed. More, it enables the kind of
panicked uncertainty and bewilderment, the confusion in the face of the
complexities of contemporary life, that for so many eighteenth-century
readers generated suspicions of inevitable decline, the very suspicions
whose prevalence and frequency both Knox and Goldsmith elsewhere
observe.

Knox's response to this problem of abundance is to pick out, "in the
classical sense of the word, LEGERE" (*WE*, 2:224). His solution implies
that proliferation is not a mark of decline but a challenge to be met in a new
commercial world of goods. But the way that he engages the problem with
a list and tally of all the many categories of publication and the vast increase
in the output of each clearly underscores the challenge of reading when the
book has become more than just a readily available commodity and has
instead become an object so prolific and so proliferating that it threatens to
occupy all available space. Indeed, Knox elsewhere recognizes the market
dimensions of the vast proliferation of books, for "A great quantity of any
thing valuable naturally depreciates it. A market overstocked reduces the

price of the commodity. . . . The public is distracted with the number of publications, and the ignorant and injudicious often purchase at a considerable price that which is of no value" (*WE*, 3:121). Both aspects of this proliferation – the saturation of every category of print that pressures time and makes one always in a rush to read more and the distraction of so very many worthless publications – threaten the decline of literature and must be remedied by selectivity and winnowing, by reducing the complexity of print saturation.

Decline, Proliferation, Selection, and the Temporality of Literature

My argument thus far focuses on Knox not because he presents a set of distinctive and unique claims but rather because his work is representative of two key factors in discussions of print proliferation in the later eighteenth century. These are, first, the tendency to discuss the decline of literature as a problem of numbers, but to shift from the quantitative to the qualitative in attempts to address the problem and, second, the increasingly common contiguity of anxieties about the expanding quantity of print and the decreasing quantity of time in which to read. The convergence of these two factors, I have been suggesting, generates the anxieties about the decline of literature that are so common in the later eighteenth century. This, in turn, has a series of implications for those thinking about the problem after Knox. From here, I want to address how the relationship between print saturation and time pressure shapes some of the most important claims about the value of literature in the Romantic period, from Wordsworth's "Preface" to Shelley's *Defence* to De Quincey's distinction between the literature of knowledge and the literature of power. My point will be that the sense of hurry and rush, the press for time exacerbated by the expansion of print and the correspondent need to use one's time selectively, contributes to the emphasis on time (and timing) in a number of Romantic arguments for the value of literature. This is not to suggest that concerns with immortality, the afterlife of writing, or permanence do not exist prior to the Romantic period, but rather to insist that these values come to have new significance in the face of the seeming ephemerality of so many products of the press.

Knox responds to print proliferation and correspondent pressures on time by advocating for a plain style and emphasizing the value of shorter pieces that can be more readily consumed in "the short interval which the pursuit of gain, and the practice of mechanic arts affords." Wordsworth's response is both similar and different. Considered in the context of the concerns discussed above, Wordsworth's famous claim that "The invaluable works of our elder writers, I had almost said the works of Shakespeare and Milton, are driven into neglect by frantic novels, sickly and stupid German Tragedies, and deluges of idle and extravagant stories in verse"[22] begins to look like another version of what was becoming, by the later eighteenth century, an increasingly common complaint. But embittered as the statement may be, it is not terminal, and Wordsworth, like Knox, aspires to intervene and remedy what he perceives as a lapse of taste. More specifically, he hopes that his "experiment" in lyrical balladry can correct the seemingly jaded tastes of the reading public, that their enthusiasm for reading can be redirected to an aesthetic of recollection in tranquility, one grounded in natural encounters that will affect not just the way that an increasingly urban population engages with nature but that also redirects their tastes and preferences toward work written in the "real language of men" (*LB*, 241). Poetry, in other words, helps its readers to discover "what is really important to men" (*LB*, 247n20) because in contrast to a craving for eventfulness, it develops "habits of mind" such that its reader "must necessarily be in some degree enlightened, his taste exalted, and his affections ameliorated" (*LB*, 247).[23] Central to this reengagement with nature via poetry, then, is the way that poetry, for Wordsworth, has the capacity to heighten attentiveness, to make its readers more aware generally of what is "really important" by virtue of its capacity to convey something elemental and enduring in contrast to the ephemerality of print. My introduction briefly mentioned this in connection with the literary absolute and we are now in a position better to understand why.

In contrast to Knox and others, Wordsworth's description of the problem does not catalog or quantify the increase in print, but Wordsworth is acutely aware of what he perceives to be the perils of the present. These are the "multitude of causes" that Wordsworth understands as making "the human mind" less "capable of excitement without the application of gross and violent stimulants" (*LB*, 249). These Wordsworth famously identifies as "the great national events which are daily taking place, and the increasing accumulation of men in cities where the uniformity of their occupations produces a craving for extraordinary incident, which the rapid communication of intelligence hourly gratifies" (*LB*, 249). The "great national events" to which Wordsworth refers here clearly indicate the French Revolution and its aftermath. It is curious, however, that Wordsworth is as much concerned with the response to these events as with the events themselves. The events are threatening because they create an impression of eventfulness, which generates a craving for news that is then gratified by the speed of the press. This shift of emphasis from the events of the French Revolution to the craving for eventfulness that they engender suggests that Wordsworth's argument for poetry, one of the cornerstones of Romanticism, can be read less as a response to the apparent rupture of the French Revolution, and more as continuous with those pre-Revolutionary, later eighteenth-century responses to the proliferation of print that were similarly concerned with the sense of haste and hurry promoted by an abundance of print and the perceived threat of daily and weekly news to faculties of attention and perception. Though Wordsworth does not use the term, this is the hurry of life in a commercial, media society, and for him it is dangerous because the literature and theater of the country conform themselves to it: as with Knox, consumption drives production. To Wordsworth's horror, Shakespeare and Milton are trumped by a "degrading thirst after outrageous stimulation" (*LB*, 249). The steady accumulation of daily and weekly newspapers answers this desire, and it is this cycle of a craving for eventfulness met by the recursive rhythms of print that according to Wordsworth so threatens faculties of attention and perception, that makes men overlook what is "really important" by making them incapable of "excitement" without "the application of gross and violent stimulants." This also helps to explain Wordsworth's emphasis on meter.

Although Wordsworth adds in 1802 that "there neither is, nor can be, any essential difference between the language of prose and metrical composition" (LB, 252), he nonetheless repeatedly refers to the value of metrical arrangement. Ultimately, he insists that given two equally well-executed passages, one in prose and the other in verse, "the verse will be read a hundred times where the prose is read once" (*LB*, 267). This is because while only "a very small part of the pleasure given by Poetry depends upon the meter" (*LB*, 263) meter makes the experience of reading "regular and uniform" because it "obeys certain laws" (*LB*, 262). Such regularity, according to Wordsworth, works to heighten the pleasure and excitement associated with poetry but it keeps these within "proper bounds." Meter, in other words, regularizes attention and contributes to those habits of mind that for Wordsworth help his reader to see what is really important. Only through such heightening of attention and through the development of a capacity for attentiveness can ordinary life come to seem unusual and interesting. In making reading regular and uniform, observation slows down and becomes more acute such that the unessential, distracting, or ephemeral precipitates out. Here, we should note that the terms of appetite through which Wordsworth describes the corruption of contemporary taste suggest his dismissal of such fashions as ephemeral, and his efforts to counteract it aspire to standards that he considers to be more lasting and, perhaps, even out of time.

But how do we get from the ephemeral to the timeless? Poetry has a technical capacity to model habits of attentiveness that induce "slow time" and through such slow, heightened attentiveness readers can recognize what is "really important." The restorative or curative role of meter, its capacity to vitiate the degraded sensibilities of readers through regularity and uniformity, works as a local, formal vehicle for the qualities of slowness that Wordsworth values. Such slow attentiveness, then, might be understood to mediate between an ephemeral eventfulness that Wordsworth associates with hurry, rush, and rapid communication and the qualities of timelessness, permanence, and immortality that Wordsworth underscores as aspects of his own poetic program.

Through the qualities of attentiveness produced by poetry its readers are linked to a sense of what is really important, ongoing, and permanent in ordinary life, for "the Poet binds together by passion and knowledge the vast empire of human society, as it is spread over the whole earth, and over all time" (*LB*, 259). Readers of poetry are linked, in other words, to that which is deathless and transhistorical, to futurity itself. But they are also linked to the distant past because in Wordsworth's account of poetic diction, the imagination associated with poetry links to an elemental quality of the human: "The earliest poets of all nations generally wrote from passion excited by real events; they wrote natural, and as men: feeling powerfully as they did, their language was daring, and figurative" (*LB*, 317), in other words, "the first poets, as I have said, spake a language which, though unusual, was still the language of men" (*LB*, 318). As Maureen McLane notes, comments like this align poetry, more than the general category of literature, with the origins of man as a species.[24] For my purposes, the untimeliness of poetry that Wordsworth continuously insists on shows how he understands poetry as a form of communication distinguished from something as base as the contemporary sea of print. It explains, then, why poetry can be understood as the literary absolute, as that which has an autonomy that carries the promise of totality and futurity and which consequently stands as the privileged mode of the literary as such.[25] It is so because it counters a craving for eventfulness and a related pressure on time by offering a sense of permanence and timelessness that transcends history and that resists historicism. Poetry does this specifically through technical qualities of meter and language that work to model habits of attentiveness that counter the speed of the contemporary with slow time through which readers achieve a communion with timelessness.

This emphasis on duration accounts for why Wordsworth values what he calls the "language really used by men" (*LB*, 244n11); it is because "such a language, arising out of repeated experience and regular feelings, is a more permanent, and a far more philosophical language" (*LB*, 245) than that used by more fanciful poets. Moreover, language of this sort appeals to "certain inherent and indestructible qualities of the human mind, and likewise of certain powers in the great and permanent objects that act upon it which are equally inherent and indestructible" (*LB*, 249–50). This repeated emphasis on the "permanent" and "indestructible" can now be more clearly understood as a response to later eighteenth-century anxieties about the proliferation of print, but more specifically to the kind of pressure on time with which such proliferation was increasingly associated. Wordsworth's argument is not about decline per se, but it is shadowed by the prospect of decline, by the craving for eventfulness and the profusion of print media that cater to it, and yet Wordsworth's response is to turn this craving, via a slow and deliberate attentiveness to the elemental qualities of ordinary life made regular and uniform through meter, into an appeal for permanent, timeless standards that he is confident will eventually triumph. Wordsworth's solution to the problem is selective like Knox, but it works generically. From the great mass of writing, Wordsworth selects poetry as that which has the most value and the greatest claim to one's limited time. Rather than squeeze an engagement with literature into a spare hour, as Knox suggests, Wordsworth insists that reading poetry written in the language really used by men can repair the harm done to sensitive faculties by that very sense of rush and hurry. Poetry achieves this by taking its readers out of time into a realm of permanence and a different sense and scale of time. Poetry, then, is restorative, reparative, medicinal even. The disease for which it acts as a cure is the contagion of print proliferation. More even than this, however, poetry achieves its curative function by moving its readers from the eventfulness and rapid communication that characterize contemporary life especially in its urban variety into a renewed and deliberate attentiveness, a slow and patient focus on the more ordinary and everyday that returns them to an awareness of its elemental aspects, to a sense of what is "really important." Readers of poetry thus pass via slow attentiveness out of time and into a realm of permanence and a different sense of the scale of time altogether.

Such an analysis might also shed new light on Shelley's *Defence of Poetry* (1821; published 1840). Like Wordsworth, Shelley selects poetry as an elevated form of expression distinct from the mass of print, and he, too, understands the utility of poetry as a function of time. In Shelley's account, the kind of ephemerality that Wordsworth associates with the excess of the press and the lapse in the taste of the reading public comes to be linked instead to the "calculating processes" and the "owl-winged faculty of calculation."[26] Though Shelley does not make this explicit, this, too, might be understood as an outgrowth of the rush of commerce because the utilitarian calculation that Shelley loathes repeatedly leads to transitory preferences. Poetry, in contrast, caters to a pleasure that is "durable, universal and permanent" and not to the "transitory and particular" pleasure that Shelley identifies with utilitarian thought and the "calculating faculty" (*SPP*, 528). Shelley does not comment specifically about the decline of literature here – indeed, he is fundamentally optimistic that he lives in great times for poetry – but we should not forget that he is writing in response to Thomas Love Peacock's attack on poetry, *The Four Ages of Poetry* (1820), which explicitly characterizes poetry as declined, as having completed a cycle of birth, growth, decay, and irrelevance.

Peacock's satire dismisses poetry as having outlived its use value and suggests that in the face of other intellectual pursuits like political economy the poet had become a "semi-barbarian in a civilized community."[27] Peacock believes in the progressive advance of knowledge and does not seem much bothered by the proliferation of print. He is content to dismiss the poet as a kind of drooling infant who looks on while "magazine critics. . . debate and promulgate" the significance of his work while others get on with the more serious business of cultivating the intellect, developing rational faculties, and advancing knowledge. Poetry, in contrast, satisfies only those "yawning for amusement, and gaping for novelty."[28] In this account, poetry itself is part of a cycle of news and the accelerated time of the present. It becomes one more item of ephemeral fashion, its readers looking for transitory values of amusement and novelty. For Shelley, in contrast, only poetry can stand out of the accelerated time of contemporary commercial life and be judged before future generations: "the jury which sits in judgment upon a poet, belonging as he does to all time, must be composed of his peers: it must be empanelled by Time from the selectest of the wise of many generations" (*SPP*, 516). This is what I have described in this book's introduction as a future perfect mode, a tendency to view the present from the projected vantage of some future time. I will discuss the future perfect more fully in Chapter 3, but for now, I want to note how

Shelley uses the imagined vantage of the future to construct a set of values that he understands as enduring and permanent. For my purposes, the emphasis is less on the values themselves and more on how they come to be constructed in response to the utilitarian calculation of political economy and other disciplines that Shelley considers transitory and ephemeral.

Both Shelley and Wordsworth, then, seek to rescue literature from its potential decline by distinguishing poetry as a special case among a mass of other kinds of writing, and they further seek to associate poetry with a timelessness and permanence that those other forms are understood to lack. My suggestion here is that these defenses of the value of poetry depend on a perceived decline for which they can act as a remedy and, further, that their emphasis on timelessness and permanence needs to be understood in the context of debates about the decline of literature and the proliferation of print. This is also the case for De Quincey's later distinction between the literature of knowledge and the literature of power in his essay on "The Poetry of Pope" (1848), in which De Quincey refines the category of literature and makes his famous distinction between a literature of knowledge and a literature of power. Not all books, he suggests, are literature, and, furthermore, literature itself can be divided into two categories. There is the literature of knowledge, whose function is to teach, and the literature of power, whose function is to move. The first might be associated with a cook book, while the second refers to works like *Paradise Lost*, which engage the moral capacities. The literature of knowledge builds upon itself such that even the works of a great thinker like Newton are superseded by those who come after as knowledge advances. Works of knowledge, then, are inherently transitory; their very success ultimately destroys them as its knowledge transmigrates into other forms. In contrast, examples of the literature of power like Greek epic and tragedy, Shakespeare and Milton, are "triumphant forever."[29]

De Quincey's division between knowledge and power recalls Knox's earlier distinction between the difficult wisdom of Malebranche and Locke and the practical wisdom of Addison, between mathematical truth and moral truth. Knox's point was that moral truth was not just more useful, in that it could save readers from "folly and misery," but also that it was more accessible because it was easier to unlock and could be consumed in a "leisure hour." De Quincey also emphasizes the time value of the literature of power, but as with Wordsworth and Shelley, it has worth not because it is quickly accessible and suited for what De Quincey calls the "chance and change" (*WDQ*, 337) of the world, but precisely because it is not suited for such transience. The literature of power keeps a different time. "At this hour, five hundred years since their creation" the works of Chaucer endure (*WDQ*, 339). "At this hour, one thousand eight hundred years since their creation" the works of Ovid are still read (*WDQ*, 339). In each case, the immediacy and fleeting quality of "this hour" contrasts with the long time span and carefully enumerated years associated with the literature of power, thus drawing into sharper relief the contrasting time-scales measured in each. The literature of power has no connection to hours, days, or weeks, to the "knowledge literature," which, "like the fashions of this world passeth away" (*WDQ*, 339). The timescale of power is, rather, that of centuries and millennia – the very timescales used to evaluate the longer term by Smith, Gibbon, and Playfair as discussed in Chapter 1 of this book. "This man's people and their monuments are dust," De Quincey notes of Ovid, "but *he* is alive; he has survived them... by a thousand years, 'and shall a thousand more.'" (*WDQ*, 339). For DeQuincey, power produces duration, it propels its readers into the *longue durée* and the scale of millennia; it is "so much more durable than the literature of knowledge" (*WDQ*, 339).

"That the Literature of This Country Has Declined and Is Declining": Decline to Value

My discussion of arguments regarding the decline of literature from the later eighteenth century forward has thus far been particularly attentive to the problem of time. What distinguishes accounts of print proliferation as the eighteenth century advances, I have been suggesting, is the increasing awareness that the profusion of print is multiplying in inverse proportion to the time available to engage with print media. Media time in this account often works in conjunction with the measured, incremental time of commerce that is parceled out into minutes and hours, days and weeks. This combination of a sensibility more attuned to the steady and incremental measurement of time's passing with what is frequently described as the hurry of commercial life produces an enhanced sense of temporal pressure, a sense that, for some, when turned to the increased offerings of the press, leads to a sense of despair and a correspondent forecast of the decline of literature. But others see the potential threat to literature as an opportunity to resist decline and to clarify particular aspects of literary value. For Vicesimus Knox, the temporal pressures of modern life required a literature of efficiency, a plain style and a short format that could accommodate itself to a leisure hour – to the interstices of commercial life and to a time that was increasingly carved up by the hour and sometimes by the minute. By contrast, Wordsworth, Shelley, and De Quincey are all dismissive of the perceived ephemerality of such forms. Their disdain for what they dismiss as the transience of so much contemporary writing leads them to select from the expanding mass of writing a portion perceived to have particular value. Though the emphasis differs for each, permanence and a capacity to endure through time repeatedly stand as the quality that distinguishes poetry for Wordsworth and Shelley and the literature of power valued by De Quincey. To an extent, this is not new – standards of immortality have repeatedly been invoked for literature from Homer onward and likely even before – but this renewed emphasis on poetry as operating within a longer timescale comes to have a distinct significance in its explicit contrast with the perceived speed and transience of contemporary commercial life and in the context of the new awareness of time that I have been describing.

I now want to close this chapter with a final example: John Stuart Mill's early nineteenth-century account of the literary field. Unlike most of those figures discussed above, Mill does not attend to the particular temporal pressures of print capitalism and his work thus underscores that what I have been characterizing as the repeated invocation of time in the face of print proliferation is not universal. But if the example of Mill exposes the messiness of my claims, this is intentional. My account is meant neither to be teleological nor comprehensive. No single narrative can accommodate the range of responses to the expansion of print in the eighteenth and nineteenth centuries and there will inevitably be exceptions and complications to my claims. Though he does not focus on time, Mill does share with all the thinkers I have discussed, including Knox, an awareness of proliferation and for him, as for the others, the threat of decline produces a renewed sense of value, value that is, moreover, articulated through a process of selecting particular kinds of work from the mass of writing. Furthermore, Mill responds explicitly to the question of whether British literature "has declined and is declining." He thus shows that the problem of literary decline extends from the eighteenth into the nineteenth century even as "literature" comes to be understood as a special category of expression within a larger field of writing. Moreover, Mill's account of the literary field returns us to some of the concerns of Chapter 1 of this book as he explicitly uses concepts from political economy to characterize literary production in 1827.

Asked to choose the question for a meeting of the London Debating Society in November 1827, Mill proposed "That the Literature of this Country has declined and is declining." Cognizant of the recently shifting usage of the term "literature" to distinguish poetry and novels in the most narrow sense from all written or spoken composition in the broadest sense, Mill proposed that his use of the term would cover all publications that "address themselves to the general reader."[30] This focus on the expanded and still expanding reading public offers a clue as to Mill's position that "The literature of any country may be properly said to have deteriorated, if its tendency, in regard to the opinions and sentiments which it inculcates, has grown worse, and if it is less distinguished than formerly by the beauties of composition and style. In both these respects I am inclined to think, that our literature has declined and is declining" (*MCW*, 410). Mill, like Knox, understands the literary field as driven by demand and not supply and, for Mill, it is the masses, the expanding reading public that are responsible for literary decline. The problem turns on the concept with which Mill remains associated, the spirit of the age. Individual writers can act on the masses of readers, but so, too, the masses can act on individuals and to "a prodigious extent" (*MCW*, 410). This is how the spirit of the age works: its peculiar modes of thinking instill it through a series of early impressions before one begins to write and it colors literary expression. While such effects are, for Mill, inescapable, the problem begins when writers "studiously endeavour to resemble" the spirit of the age, "and not only imitate but are apt to caricature its leading peculiarities" (*MCW*, 411). Most writers, in other words, inevitably pander to the spirit of their age – to their readers – in an effort to achieve success.

Mill's account, then, frames the production of literature as a problem of political economy: "It is the demand, in literature as in most other things, which calls forth the supply" and therefore "the writers of every age are for the most part what the readers make them" (*MCW*, 411). The problem of the reading public in turn is a problem of numbers. "The present age is very remarkably distinguished from all other ages by the number of persons who can read" (*MCW*, 411). But reading is not thinking and, for Mill, "it is to the immense multiplication in the present day of those who read but do not think, that I should be disposed to ascribe what I view as the degeneracy of our literature" (*MCW*, 412). Mill's reference to "degeneracy" recalls Knox, but unlike Knox, who proved largely tolerant of popular periodical writing as a source for imparting morals quickly and painlessly for a busy commercial reading public, Mill has no patience for popularity. There are more readers than ever before, but because of such multiplication, there are more *bad* readers: "Reading has become one of the most approved and fashionable methods of killing time, and the number of persons who have skimmed the surface of literature is far greater than at any previous period of our history"

(*MCW*, 412). Here, in one of the few instances where Mill links the problem of print proliferation to time, the issue shifts from Knox's concern with *filling* time to Mill's concern with *killing* time, from a problem of haste and speed to one of boredom and leisure as bad readers struggle to dispense with a time that now seems marked by something like Wordsworth's "craving for extraordinary incident." The degraded, popular tastes of these half-instructed readers bring down the level of writers who inevitably pander to their judgments and literature sinks accordingly. In his longer explanation of the problem, Mill characterizes the negative results on content and style produced by the tendency to pander to this public. He reserves his greatest scorn for periodical publications and his analysis returns to the terms of political economy.

Periodicals, Mill complains, deliver too much return. They are too good an investment for minor intellects because they tempt emergent writers to turn "a small capital of intellect" to too good of an account and prevent them from making "that capital larger" (*MCW*, 416). The result is what Mill terms a "heavier charge": that periodicals have "made literature a trade" by turning it into an act done "for the mere sake of pecu[nia]ry profit" (*MCW*, 417). Older writers, like Pope and other satirists, wrote out of "fondness for the occupation" in contrast to Mill's early nineteenth-century contemporaries "who chose authorship as an advantageous investment of their labour and capital in a commercial point of view, contracted for a stipulated quantity of eloquence and wit, to be delivered on a certain day, were inspired punctually by 12 o'clock in order to be in time for the printer's boy at one, sold a burst of passion at so much per line, and gave way to a movement of virtuous indignation as per order received" (*MCW*, 417). Mill here emphasizes the idea of literary inspiration in his insistence that eloquence, wit, passion, and indignation cannot be called up on cue like a commercial stock of butter and salt, but in his analysis such inspiration no longer motivates most contemporary writers who work for profit instead of pleasure, and "What is carried on as a trade, soon comes to be carried on upon mere trading principles of profit and loss" (*MCW*, 417). The problem with contemporary literature, then, the reason that it has declined and is declining, is economic. Literature has become a trade, a commodity, an intellectual labor subject to the same kind of calculation and maximization of return as any kind of bodily labor or physical commodity. We have come a long way from Knox's earlier esteem for periodical literature with its benign capacity to impart moral value succinctly for consumption in a "short interval."

Smith may have been keen to point out that, by his terms, writing is unproductive labor since it does not add value to the materials that it works upon.[31] Mill, however, clarifies how in an information economy literature might more readily be understood as productive labor and as capital. This is both because the book, periodical, and newspaper are tangible commodities that can be traded at a profit and in some cases exchanged for more liquid capital (as Smith previously acknowledged), and because writing has now become accepted as an activity that is performed for money – a profession – and certain authors, styles, and subjects can command more money than others, because, to Mill's distaste, they pander to the degraded taste of the public. But still, such preferred topics, writers, and styles have the capacity to add more value to the raw materials – paper and ink – out of which their work is fashioned. In part, this reflects a familiar anxiety about literary professionalism that was largely resolved by the mid-eighteenth century.[32] Mill is quick to point out that "a literary man should receive remuneration for his labour is no more than just," but he then qualifies this concession with a more gentlemanly antifinancial ethos when he adds "provided that he writes in every respect as he would have done if he had no remuneration to expect" (*MCW*, 417). It is okay to write for money, in other words, so long as one pretends that one is not writing for money.

Mill's sensitivity about the relationship between literature and money, a sensitivity that allows for literary professionalism but that remains profoundly discomfited by the idea of writing for money, reaches a predictable crescendo near the very end of his manuscript when he declares:

> The hack author who considers not what sentiments the subject ought to inspire, but only what are the sentiments which are expected of him, and who after having on due enquiry and examination settled to the satisfaction of his own mind which side of the question will be the marketable side, proceeds thereupon to brandish his mercenary thunders, and burst forth into the artificial transports of a bought enthusiasm; the occupation of a street walking prostitute is surely far more respectable. The present times have brought forth a plentiful harvest of this kind of handicrafts. (*MCW*, 417)

Such comments echo the terms and anxieties of John Brown's *Estimate of the Manners and Principles of the Times* (1757) in which Brown, too, harangued his audience about the imminent decline of the nation on the grounds that an emergent preference for fashionable literature and other supposedly effeminate leisure activities were ruining the English character.

The connection between literature, economics, and gender here underscores how arguments about print proliferation continue to pick up moral concerns with luxury carried over from the eighteenth century and how, even after literature became more widely accepted as a source of national pride and strength, such associations persist. The final line about a plentiful harvest is also telling: even as Mill compares most professional authors to practitioners of the oldest profession, and hence as a kind of unproductive labor, his metaphor slides and he likens mercenary literary production that caters to public taste through a large network of periodicals, the supposed source of the decline of literature, to the two main examples that Smith uses to define productive labor: agriculture and manufacturing, a "harvest" of "handicrafts." The terms further recall other such pronouncements that liken literature to activities Smith classes as productive labor like agriculture and manufacture, as when *The Retrospective* referred to the "fertile and luxurious crop of modern literature."[33]

Such persistent resurfacing of value, even if unwitting, suggests the overall impact of Mill's argument, which works to excoriate the present age on account of the greater achievements of past ages. All of Mill's anxiety about the great quantity of literature and the sheer size of the reading public, the "immense multiplication" of those "who read but do not think," and the consequent proliferation of periodicals, works to establish not only the "degradation" or decline of the present age, but the superiority of "other ages." Mill is explicit about the authors that he has in mind, including Richardson, Addison and Goldsmith, Fielding, Swift, Sterne, Hume, Bolingbroke, Mandeville, Berkeley, and Bacon. These writers, Mill insists, exemplify "the superiority... of other ages to our own" (*MCW*, 415). But even a quick perusal of the list reveals that, with the exception of Bacon, by "other ages" Mill means the eighteenth century. And an argument from quantity, one that objects to the unchecked proliferation of both readers and writers, a form of literary mass culture, shifts from a problem of quantity to a standard for quality. The complaint about quantity turns into an exaltation of a particular kind of quality. Mill uses his anxiety about multiplication to narrow the literary field and to assign value to a particular kind of work, one that prioritizes a range of eighteenth-century sensibilities.

Mill's list of valuable writers constitutes what we might describe as a canon, and suggests how the responses to the perceived decline of literature that I have been tracking in this chapter have implications for how we understand canon formation. Prescriptive responses to the decline of literature and perceived failures in the literary field – like those of Knox,

Wordsworth, Shelley, De Quincey, and Mill – commonly insist that because so much is being published, the value of literature must be declining. Their response is to restore perceived value by, in a sense, reducing supply, by selecting a small category of merit from the larger field of print. Selection, distinction, or what we would now call canon formation, might then be recognized as a response to the problem of quantity and the related problem of literature's perceived decline. My argument here might thus be understood as related to that of William St. Clair, who understands later eighteenth-century canon formation as a response to price and quantity generally, but more specifically as an outcome of developments in copyright law like *Donaldson v Beckett* (1774), which made it cheaper to publish "classic" works that had come out of copyright and hence helped to constitute a literary canon.[34] I depart, however, from what might be understood as the economic determinism of St. Clair's account because it is my suggestion that the problem of quantity in the literary field produces an account of qualitative value, a process of selection, narrowing, and simplification that can be understood as drawing upon the quantification of political economy but nonetheless departing from it toward a more qualitative standard.

Numerous other accounts of canon formation locate their key developments in the eighteenth century and in relationship to the development of print capitalism.[35] I concur with these accounts in my suggestion that canon formation is a response to the proliferation of print; more, I follow their suggestion that canonicity is therefore not a property of the work but of its transmission. In my account, however, canon formation is not a singular event, but an ongoing one, one that can accommodate constant readjustments and reassessments of value and, further, one that cannot be accounted for through a singular cause. Canon formation may be a product of the eighteenth century but the association of timeless qualities with certain canonical works attains new significance in the Romantic period. Accounts of the decline of literature are critical for the development of canon because, as I have suggested, they respond to the time pressures exacerbated by the proliferation of print with a renewed emphasis on the timelessness of great works of literature, on the enduring value of certain works especially for their ability to bring readers out of time, out of the hustle and rush of commercial and media time.

Ultimately, my point is that anxieties about the decline of literature are used to emphasize the need for selection from among an increasingly confusing and complex mass of writing. This bears on the idea of canon formation, but it also echoes my larger point, seen also in Chapter 1 of this book, that concerns about decline are commonly a source of value, that concerns about decline can be reordered into a projected future of progress. It seems fitting, then, to close with a passage from Hazlitt, whose essay, "On the Influence of Books," offers one of the most terrifying and apocalyptic images of print proliferation, "the whole world converted into waste paper."[36] We should recall, however, that Hazlitt is not immediately concerned about this prospect, and that he sees the spread of print and the growth of literacy as a positive good, as part of the progress of reason. Hazlitt is the democratic inverse to Mill's antidemocratic skepticism over the expansion of the reading public. It is striking, then, that the image through which Hazlitt articulates such progress is one of slow and gradual ruination:

> So slow and difficult is the progress of reason! So gradual the approach to common sense and humanity through that mass of prejudice and folly, which power and bigotry have been for ages raising on the foundation of barbarous ignorance! A few quaint devices (a devil or cherub's head) are one by one chipped off; a crack, a weather-flaw is now and then discovered. . . anon a huge fragment falls, undermined by the engineers, or tottering from its own disproportioned weight;—it is not even now. . . a regular, entire, and well-cemented building, but has many gaps and mouldering capitals and prostrate columns to show, and will, ere long tumble an unsightly building to the ground with hideous crash and outcry, and mingle with the common dust, hated, forgotten, or a by-word.[37]

In the crumbling building of despotism and unreason, we have an image of ruin as progress, of certain kinds of decline as ultimately productive and not disabling. It is a fitting image for the many complaints about the decline of literature discussed above, but also for the focus of Chapter 3, Anna Barbauld's vision of London in ruins.

CHAPTER 3

The Politics of Prediction: Anna Barbauld and the Ruins of London

Ideas about the future rest upon a structural repeatability derived from the past.

– Reinhart Koselleck, *"The Unknown Future and the Art of Prognosis"*

Introduction

In the last essay that he wrote, "The Letter Bell," William Hazlitt surveys the memories of his adult life, from the execution of Louis XVI to the July Revolution of 1830. Toward the end of the essay, he quotes from William Cowper's *The Task* and laments the advent of the telegraph through a melancholic longing for the Post-Boy:

> [T]he Mail-Coach is an improvement on the Post-Boy; but I fear it will hardly bear so poetical a description. The picturesque and dramatic do not keep pace with the useful and mechanical. The telegraphs that lately communicated the intelligence of the new revolution to all France within a few hours, are a wonderful contrivance; but they are less striking and appalling than the beacon-fires (mentioned by Aeschylus), which, lighted from hill-top to hill-top, announced the taking of Troy and the return of Agamemnon.[1]

Hazlitt's description of the mechanization and acceleration of communication echoes complaints about the speed of commercial society discussed previously in Chapter 2, which also demonstrated the link between the time pressures produced by processes of acceleration and arguments for the value of certain genres and forms of writing. For Vicesimus Knox, the enhanced speed of modern commercial society meant less time in which to read and thus placed a premium on shorter, morally enriching works like the essay. For later Romantic authors like Wordsworth, Shelley, and De Quincey, the effect of acceleration was to make most writing ephemeral and of little importance; in opposition to this, these authors argued for poetry as a special case, as a particularly valuable form of writing on account of its timelessness. Such emphasis on the enduring value of poetry, in turn, implied something about the time that one should spend reading it in a busy, accelerating society: certain poetry, because it was for all time, was worth the investment of one's time. This is one way that we can understand how lyric poetry became for Romantic writers the literary absolute. It is also how we can understand canon formation both as something more than a response to copyright and new market conditions as William St. Clair would have it, and as more than the new economy of prestige that in John Guillory's account reflects the asymmetric distribution of cultural capital.[2] Canon becomes also a response to new temporal pressures and constraints that accompany commercial society, the same pressures and constraints that contributed to the forecast of literary decline.

But Hazlitt's preference for the Post-Boy and the beacon-fires of Aeschylus over the mail coach and the telegraph says something also about the disenchantment of modernity. Hazlitt associates slowness with the picturesque and the dramatic and he prefers the slow to the fast. The progress and speed accompanying modern forms of communication may make them more useful, but they also become less interesting. The contrast that Hazlitt invokes here between the slowness of the past and the speed of the present, moreover, underscores an uneven quality in the experience of time as the rate of change in the "picturesque and dramatic" fails to keep pace with that of the mechanical. Progress may be irreversible but not all experiences advance at the same rate or pace. Such unevenness recalls also the Romantic preference for poetry in Chapter 2 where the longer timescale ascribed to the best poetry attains distinct significance in its contrast to the speed and ephemerality of contemporary commercial life. At bottom, though, Hazlitt's focus on the increased speed of communication technologies highlights the problem of acceleration. As Hartmut Rosa argues, "*the experience of modernization is an experience of acceleration*" (21, italics original)., and we can see this starkly in Hazlitt's account of the transition from the beacon-fires of Aeschylus and the Post-Boy to the mail coach and telegraph. In Rosa's account of acceleration, the technological component of speed is but one of three features. Complementing technological acceleration are an acceleration in the tempo of life and an acceleration of the social and cultural rate of change. It is not just that things are speeding up, but also that they are speeding up more quickly than previously – the rates of change are themselves accelerating. The combination of these three factors produces a crisis of time that also serves to indicate a time of crisis, all of which we can extrapolate from Hazlitt's melancholy over the lapse of the Post-Boy.

This time of crisis produced by acceleration bears also on new understandings of the future as a space of progress. The Enlightenment understanding of progress brings the possibility that the future will be fundamentally different from the past because new ways of understanding the world create future possibilities that are conceived as new in ways that cannot be entirely derived from previous experience.[3] What I am suggesting, in other words, is that the way that historical actors relate to time shifts from the later eighteenth century and forwards such that past experience becomes less of a guide for future possibilities. As François Hartog puts it, "The lesser the experience, the greater the expectation."[4] From this perspective, the future is at once approaching more quickly than previously and it is also more uncertain, more unknown. This is what Reinhart Koselleck calls an "open future," which he characterizes by a newly unpredictable quality that distinguishes the sense of futurity itself from the eighteenth century forwards.

This chapter asks what happens to the meaning of decline in the context of both an uneven, accelerating experience of time and the emergent understanding of an open future. Its focus is on Anna Barbauld's poem *Eighteen Hundred and Eleven* (1812), in which Barbauld predicts that the continuation of the Napoleonic Wars will bring not only the choking of British commerce that she sees already in place but also "Ruin" itself to British shores. Barbauld's account of decline is distinctive because while she imagines national and imperial ruin instigated by the negative economic impact of war, her sense of decline does not extend to culture and literature. Rather in the face of national and imperial decline, culture and literature are what will persist. Like Wordsworth, Shelley, and De Quincey, Barbauld sees British literature as having made a permanent contribution to the cultural field, one that will continue to be appreciated elsewhere when British power is no more. Unlike them, she does not need to distinguish this contribution from more ephemeral kinds of writing; she does not distinguish poetry from literature. Instead of a distinction between ephemeral and permanent forms of writing, Barbauld differentiates between the transience of worldly power and the possibility of culture, and especially literature, as a category that can transcend such limitations. Barbauld even suggests that tourists will come from the new world to visit a ruined London much like her contemporary beneficiaries of empire revisit the ruins of Rome and Greece on the Grand Tour. The current British Empire – Barbauld's modernity – will become the antiquity of the future, one dominated by the empires of the new world as the course of empire follows the sun from east to west.[5]

In thinking about Barbauld's poem, I seek to work through the complex temporality of her prediction. In this sense, this chapter extends the book's argument as developed over the previous two chapters that decline is an index of new Enlightenment and post-Enlightenment ways of experiencing time, especially the experience of conflicting timescales and heterochronicity more generally. In Barbauld's case, to look at the present and to the future and see decline might be understood as a way to contain an open future by making it knowable. The future will be a repetition of past decline. Given this increasing sense of uncertainty surrounding the future, it is thus not surprising that many would project the repetition of past decline onto that unknown future. For reactive (and reactionary) as anxieties of decline often appear to be, the way in which they imagine what will remain of the present in the future has a productive function as well: Imagining future decline serves to constitute a canon of value against which present lapses are judged and often works to enhance the prestige of such categories of experience as "culture" and "literature." This, I would suggest, is because many Romantic attempts to imagine the contours of future decline project the continuity of the present into the future on the model of classical antiquity. Because classical ruins form the quintessential example of ruin and a memento mori that civilizations can decline, to invoke ruin as the fate of an existing civilization can be threatening; but because the remnants of classical civilization were commonly understood as the basis of European civilization, there was also a potential recompense in the repetition of classical decline. Fantasies of decline thus produce a structure in which the continuity and persistence of culture comes to stand in a compensatory relation to the loss of economic and political predominance, a structure that paradoxically enables the fantasy of loss and decline to stand also as one of continuity and permanence.[6]

But in addition to indexing new ways of experiencing time, decline, like contemporary concerns about climate change, also represents a problem of temporal prediction: How can one be in a position to predict or forecast the onset of decline? What sort of relationship to time, to narrative, to historical events allows one to say with confidence when decline will occur? How can a prediction of decline organize experience and generate value? These questions, especially the last one, framed my discussion of the decline of literature in Chapter 2. Here I offer an extended reading of Barbauld's poem as a case study of similar issues, but one that leads me to speculate more about the sense of time and the anticipation of the future in Britain circa 1800. Barbauld's poem offers a prediction, but because it intends this as a warning, it might also be understood, like Playfair's charts, as invested in preservation, in the possibility of changes that will avoid ruin and produce an alternative future. Read this way, the fantasy of a ruined empire provides Barbauld with an occasion to construct a detailed commemoration of that empire's achievements and accomplishments. The poem thus works in the present to celebrate the past while simultaneously imagining multiple futures – one explicit, of ruin, and the other, implicit, of ruin avoided. None of these possibilities are mutually exclusive. They all exist simultaneously, and I argue that, while the poem can be understood in connection with a historicist emphasis on dating and the date, such a date – especially when combined with the implied future perfect tense of a poem that offers a richly detailed sense of what Barbauld's present will look like from a future vantage when all that is will have been – also serves as a marker to call our attention to a more complex, layered, and heterochronic understanding of temporality that we might understand as an affective history of the present moment.

Ruins and the Temporalization of Space

The ruin that Barbauld describes in *Eighteen Hundred and Eleven* will come about through the potential of war to inflict financial catastrophe. Barbauld's anxiety about ruin and the traumas of debt and credit in a commercial economy thus underscores the broader relationship between decline and political economy. In *Eighteen Hundred and Eleven*, Barbauld's bitter lament about the effects of the war is always linked to the manner in which war inhibits commerce. For Barbauld, trade and commercial prosperity are valuable because it is through prosperity that the arts and sciences prosper. "Art plies his tools, and Commerce spreads her sail,/And wealth is wafted in each shifting gale" (273–74). [7] The problem with the war is that it inhibits commerce – the Thames, as she puts it, is "choked no more with fleets" (175) – and with commerce grinding to a halt, the only future that Barbauld can foresee is one of decline.

In the context of cultural pessimism and widespread anxiety about decline discussed in the previous two chapters, one distinguishing feature of Barbauld's account is the explicit detail of her vision of London in ruins. The poem describes youths "from the Blue Mountains or Ontario's lake" (130) making a pilgrimage with "duteous zeal" (129) to visit England's ruins, but Barbauld is at her most graphic when describing a deserted and weed-strewn London:

> Pensive and thoughtful shall the wanderers greet
> Each splendid square, and still, untrodden street;
> Or of some crumbling turret, mined by time,
> The broken stairs with perilous step shall climb,
> Thence stretch their view the wide horizon round,
> By scattered hamlets trace its antient bound,
> And, choked no more with fleets, fair Thames survey
> Through reeds and sedge pursue his idle way.
>
> (169–76)

In this passage, the combination of the soft and the hard reflects the contrast between the natural ("reeds and sedge") and the man-made (the "crumbling turret" and "broken stairs"), in a series of images that broadly suggest the ruins of classical antiquity and the weed-strewn, overgrown Coliseum in particular. The passage might also be read as an allegory of cultural progress itself, as it describes the movement through ruin as a "perilous" but profitable "climb" that enables enlightenment through a view of the "wide horizon round," thus offering the mastery of complete perspective and a view of the future that functions as a means to inscribe and perpetuate the value of the present.

The uncertain timing of the passage – just when, in relation to the 1811 of the title will these travelers walk through the ruins of London? – also suggests a contingency and an uncertainty that push against the firm and fixed date of the poem's title. Barbauld, writing in the thick of wartime, has a contingent view of the future. The annual calendar time of the title indicates a rationalizing and ordering impulse, but the poem itself offers a competing sense of time at odds with its measurement, a more experiential, affective sense of time to be found in its use of verb tenses like the future perfect, in its use of noise and interference as marks of discomfort and disturbance, and in its representation of instruments of timekeeping, like calendars and clocks and newspapers. Such instances confirm that the time of Barbauld's poem is what Mary Favret calls "meantime," a time of waiting upon an uncertain and unknown future while living through a present whose meaning will be determined only by its unknowable outcome. Such a meantime, in other words, works as "an affective zone, a *sense* of time that, caught in the most unsettled sort of present, without knowledge of its outcome, cannot know its own borders."[8] Against the confident, measured certainty of the dated title of Barbauld's poem, such unsettled and barely articulate feeling preserves a sense of future uncertainty and contingency, and its affective response works as what Favret calls "a cure to the arithmetical eye" (36) that confidently announces its moment in time – its *year* – while agonizing over what that year will mean to future years. *Eighteen Hundred and Eleven*, then, is a wartime poem, but in my reading, the firmness of its date seeks to mark and contain more than the anxiety of wartime but also an anxiety about time itself produced by war along with a sense of dizzily proliferating media in tension with an increasing awareness of geological slowness and what we have come to call "deep time."

Barbauld's sense of the future as I have hinted is at once pessimistic and optimistic: the deprivations of the war disrupt commerce and will bring ruin to Britain, but when empire translates westward to North America, those inhabiting the new seats of empire will make cultural pilgrimages to its old seat in Britain, much as eighteenth-century Britons duly visited Rome and sometimes Greece. Furthermore, British literature will become the new "classics" and form the basis of education for those new empires. Ruin in this case is culturally productive.

Moreover, the ruin foretold by the poem when combined with the model of linearity and periodicity implied by the poem's dated title provides a kind of certainty – a negative certainty, admittedly – that stands in contrast to, and that might be understood to offer compensation for, the more unsettled temporal experiences described by the poem. Because this is a poem whose temporality is refracted across a series of different moments originating in the contrast between the poem's present as marked by its title and the poem's imagined future of a ruined London, it might be understood as a poem that draws its force from the "future perfect," that verb tense used to describe an action that will have been completed before some reference point in the future, as in the rather arch and ironic sentiment of the poem, which might be summed up as: "We will have understood the meaning of this current war, and this current year, when London is ruined." This is why the poem's repeated use of various future tenses works as an index of disturbance and a marker of the speaker's deep uncertainty and confusion when contemplating future prospects.

Though the poem begins with a sustained use of the present tense, that present soon slides to contain an anticipation of the future as one in which "low murmurs spread, / And whispered fears, creating what they dread" (47–48). Such uneasy feelings of fear and dread that are broadcast, as it were, below the surface of normal conversation register as a mark of disturbance that is then picked up by the "sad" merchants whose "anxious" (59) dispositions anticipate only a "tempest blackening" (60). This moment might be understood as a microcosm of Barbauld's poem itself, as the fears articulated in the poem – that war will so drain the nation's resources as to stop commerce and lead to ruin – then create what they dread as the poem continues to describe both the material ruins of Britain, but also the cultural legacy left behind. Here and elsewhere in the poem to look forward, to anticipate the future, is to cultivate fear, anxiety, dread, sadness, and various other inflections of uncomfortable affect that float through the poem. The collective effect of such feeling registers as temporal disturbance as "imaged woes" produce "untimely tears" (114).

Such disturbances, as we might expect from Favret's account of wartime and war at a distance, contrast with the predictable dailyness with which news of war is distributed. Barbauld describes women left behind by war poring over newspapers: "Oft o'er the daily page some soft-one bends / To learn the fate of husband, brothers, friends" (33–34). The repetitive and daily quality of this newspaper reading recalls, of course, the dated specificity produced by the poem's title, but the affect produced by the reading, the "anxious eye" (35) that fears "wrecked... bliss" (37) threatens to encompass such predictability with the more mute and shapeless feelings of anticipated loss and dread.

But time in the poem is marked not only by a dailyness whose aggregation produces the year 1811, but also by a less specific manner of marking time through stone and rock. We have an initial sense of this in the "georgic time" invoked when the poem notes how European armies frustrate agricultural production as "The tramp of marching hosts disturbs the plough" (17). The reference recalls Virgil's plowman, and his turning up the battlefield resting places of ancient heroes with their moldering javelins and giant bones, as Virgil, like Barbauld later, stops to imagine his own present as the future's past in Book I of the *Georgics*. Such sentiments are then borne out later in the poem's description of future ruin. Here no dates are given and the temporal specificity of the poem's present moment stands in contrast both to its uncertain future and to the uncertain time of that future, a time marked not by years and the regular predictability of annual dates, but by less precise and more visual decay. Britain, in this uncertain future, will come to be known only by "the grey ruin and the mouldering stone" (124), when its "crumbling" turrets will have been "mined by time" (170). Rocks and stones tell time. The time they tell is slow and, as the reference to mining would indicate, deep. Barbauld's initial reference to the "gradual progress" (85) of the arts and sciences has now become the lesson inscribed "[b]y Time's slow finger written in the dust" (214). Such slowness stands in contrast to the regularity and frequently perceived acceleration of the daily time marked by newspapers and the news of war, and the clash between the two helps to explain the connection between unsettled feelings of disturbance and the affective response they elicit, "untimely tears."

Furthermore, though it might at first seem a stretch, such a reference to stone "mined by time" might also be understood in connection with a different kind of mining than that of the poem's later reference to "the ponderous ore" (227) that when drawn from its bed serves to initiate the motor force of commerce. It might be linked, especially given the way that Barbauld's plow recalls the uncovering of weapons and bones in Virgil's *Georgics*, to the digging up of bones and fossils and to the slow time that these objects come to represent in the later eighteenth century and into the nineteenth. While the poem does not explicitly refer to new developments and disputes in natural history, the time of ruin in the poem is itself a kind of slow, or deep time, a time that in its intentional incomprehensibility and confusion – can London really fall into ruin in the manner of Rome? – stands for the closest regular human time can come to the vast and incomprehensible timescales of earthly change, to a timescale where the earth itself might be understood as "mined by time."

The care with which Barbauld sketches her image of London in ruins further recalls related fantasies in the visual arts, particularly the work of the French painter Hubert Robert and the English draftsman Joseph Gandy (see Figure 0.1). In contrast to the anxious futurity evoked by Robert's images, which frequently depict scenes of catastrophe like *The Decentering of the Pont de Neuilly* (1772) or *Burning of the Opera in the Palais-Royal* (1781), Gandy's images consistently draw upon tropes of the picturesque. Even though they show the projected ruins of Sir John Soane's designs – buildings that, it should be noted, were only just finished or in the process of being constructed – Gandy's fantasies suggest a prolonged and indefinite futurity for Soane's work, work that, even when ruined, will have a permanence that comes to stand for a new set of classical standards, making Soane's Regency neoclassicism a replacement for classicism itself. Considered thus, Gandy's images might serve as a visual counterpart to Barbauld's poem.

Like the images of Robert and Gandy, *Eighteen Hundred and Eleven* evokes a temporality with three distinct layers: the material ruins (like those of Rome) extant in Barbauld's present moment imply that they were once completed buildings at some point in the (largely antique) past. Looking at them, then, projects the structural relationship between present ruin and past wholeness forward into the future so that the present comes to be imagined as the future's past, or, more concretely, as the classical standard for new, future empires. As this combination of temporal change with the spatial movement of *translatio imperii* would imply, the transposition between times suggested by Barbauld's poem has its spatial correlatives in what we might describe as the "temporalization of space."[9] The poem suggests a future elsewhere, somewhere in North America, or even South America as its final lines indicate. Such a process might appear frightening in the detail with which it predicts Britain's ruin (even if it is not clear about exactly where in North or South America succeeding empires will arise), but one advantage of imagining the unknown future as the repetition of the known past in a different location is that through such a process the present and the future are always experienced as a repetition of the past and hence as potentially knowable. The fantasy of ruins in the classical model makes recognizable an increasingly unfamiliar modernity.

This is why, I would suggest, the example of classical antiquity remains so important for Romantic thinking about decline. Antiquity represents a completed time horizon in that what was, at some point in the past, about to happen has now transpired and can be known in its entirety. The epochal understanding of history that is emerging at this time – Antiquity, Middle Ages, Renaissance, Reformation, etc. – seeks to keep the past contained and knowable.[10] In contrast, the present stands as an uncompleted time horizon. To forecast decline on the model of antiquity suggests how an uncompleted time horizon will be completed. It helps to make the future knowable. It is in this context that I now want to turn to the function of the date in Barbauld's poem.

Ruins and Value

The ruin imagined in *Eighteen Hundred and Eleven* may stand as a cultural prospect to be met with apprehension and alarm, but it also offers the possibility of making an unknown future known and imaginable. This is, moreover, not the only more positive effect produced by the fantasy of future ruin. To imagine modern buildings not just as future ruins, but as *classical* ruins modeled on Greece and Rome, serves as a kind of national validation: it works to equate the value of Britain with the values and permanent example of the classical past. In Shelley's sonnet "Ozymandias" (1818), the forgotten ruin – the "colossal wreck" that stands "boundless and bare" as the "lone and level sands stretch far away" – represents an ironic monument to the hubris of power, much like Marx's later assertion that all that is solid melts into air.[11] Barbauld, in contrast, uses a fantasy of ruin to imagine something else entirely: that the destroyed remains of Britain's national monuments will attract pilgrims from a future empire who seek to model their own potential accomplishments after Britain's example in literature, science, politics, and the arts. Just as the British Empire was modeled on classical antiquity, the "classics" of a future empire will be recognizably British.

Barbauld may have been inspired to this insight by the *Vindication of the Rights of Men* (1790), in which Mary Wollstonecraft imagines the British Empire as heir to the Roman Empire. There, Wollstonecraft noted that, "The time may come when the traveler may ask where proud London stood? When its temples, its laws, and its trade, may be buried in one common ruin, and only serve as a byword to point a moral, or furnish senators... on the other side of the Atlantic, with tropes to swell their thundering bursts of eloquence."[12] Wollstonecraft, like Barbauld after her, emphasizes the ephemerality of Britain's temples, laws, and trade; but, even as she seems to denigrate the practice of classical citation, she implies that British literature broadly understood will persist and form tropes for senators in the Americas.

Barbauld's poem stages a similar trade-off. *Eighteen Hundred and Eleven* is undoubtedly critical of British imperial ambitions and sees the war with France as a source of national ruin. Her critique is especially powerful because it repeats familiar material and topoi for unfamiliar ends and thus represents, in Suvir Kaul's words, a "reversal of the aspiration of national expansion, doubly effective in that she reiterates and works within the comparative historical schemas and the poetic idiom constitutive of the poetry of empire."[13] Nonetheless, the place occupied by British literature and learning in Barbauld's poem – the canon of British classics – suggests that Barbauld is also celebrating aspects of empire. Telling, here, is Barbauld's reluctance to name historical protagonists or events (Napoleon, for example, is referred to only as "The Despot" in line 9), which contrasts with her eagerness to announce the names of British national heroes like Samuel Johnson, William Pitt, Charles James Fox, David Garrick, General John Moore, Humphrey Davy, Joshua Reynolds, and Joseph Priestley in lines 185–204.

Robert, Gandy, and Wollstonecraft had all previously imagined their present architectural landscape as the ruins of the future, and so, too, would Shelley in the dedication to *Peter Bell the Third* (1819, published 1839).[14] One distinctive feature of *Eighteen Hundred and Eleven*, however, is the way that it uses projected ruin to elaborate an explicit canon of British political, scientific, and cultural achievement. Even as Barbauld describes her pilgrims visiting the remains of Westminster Abbey with its "long isle and vaulted dome / Where Genius and where Valour find a home" (lines 179–80), she constructs her own version of the Abbey's commemoration of the vaunted "silent dead." In this way, the poem constructs a pantheon of British accomplishment, one that ranges from statesmen and orators (Chatham, Fox) to stage actors (Garrick) to military leaders (Nelson, Moore), scientists (Davy, Priestley) and painters (Reynolds). Most telling here is the literary canon that Barbauld establishes. Just as "British tongues the fading fame prolong / Of Tully's eloquence and Maro's song" (lines 287–88), so, too, "new states shall know" British "stores of knowledge" (line 87). Their youth will be instructed by Locke and Paley and enthralled by Milton, Thomson, Shakespeare, and Joanna Baillie. British literature and learning will become the new "classics."

Passages like this show that Barbauld is not just criticizing empire but also celebrating it, as the fantasy of future ruin here works to consolidate a present canon of value. This clear concern with the present in relation to an anticipated future calls our attention to the most prominent feature of Barbauld's poem, the feature that firmly distinguishes Barbauld's fantasy of ruin from those of Robert and Gandy and also from Shelley, whose dedication to *Peter Bell the Third* also imagines London as a tourist destination from a future whose center is elsewhere.[15] I am thinking here of Barbauld's title: *Eighteen Hundred and Eleven*. In assigning a title that joins an anticipated decline with a precise historical year, Barbauld encourages us to think about decline as part of a datable historical process, one whose developments can be traced through a precise series of events whose relationship to each other can be codified in regular historical units, years.

For this reason, *Eighteen Hundred and Eleven* has often been discussed as an index of Romanticism's historicist preoccupations. James Chandler, for example, suggests that Barbauld's engagement with history helps to clarify "the complex terms of the new Romantic-historicist configuration" and is one of a number of texts that reveal the Romantic period as "the age of the spirit of the age."[16] For Chandler, "what makes Romantic historicism distinctive... is the quality and extent of its interest in what might be called 'comparative contemporaneities.'"[17] Barbauld, in particular, combines a preoccupation with time, as manifest in her dated title, with a description of the spatial movement of empire, *translatio imperii*. She thus serves for Chandler as an early and prominent example of Romantic historicism's comparativist tendencies, its desire to think about different geographical places at the same time, in a way that enables the concept of "uneven development" and, further, its insistence that to understand the state of the world we must also understand "the transnational simultaneity that makes national-cultural specificity imaginable."[18]

Barbauld's title certainly calls attention to its particular moment within a trajectory of even, equal temporal units – years. The precise year 1811, in turn, helps us to recognize that when Barbauld was composing the poem, the outcome of the Napoleonic Wars remained unknown and the economy was near collapse.[19] Clearly, the date of the poem itself is meant to serve as a sign of these times; it is a marker for the concrete set of events that surround the poem's composition and a clue to the anxieties about national ruin unfolded within.[20] Turning from the title to the poem proper, however, one cannot help but be struck by the near total absence of any explicit sense of historical time and the omission of any concrete event to which one might assign the date 1811. Anne Grant's much more celebratory poem, *Eighteen Hundred and Thirteen*, which is often mentioned as a response to Barbauld, while not explicitly a narrative of recent events, still offers, in the words of its author, a "retrospective sketch" of them.[21] Barbauld, in contrast, glosses over current events. This point was not lost on reviewers, especially John Wilson Croker in his devastating attack on the poem for the *Quarterly Review*:

> The poem, for so out of courtesy we shall call it, is entitled Eighteen Hundred and Eleven, we suppose, because it was written in the year 1811; but this is mere conjecture, founded rather on our inability to assign any other reason for the name, than in any particular relation which the poem has to the events of last year. We do not, we confess, very satisfactorily comprehend the meaning of all the verses which this fatidical spinster has drawn from her poetical distaff; but of what we do understand we very confidently assert that there is not a topic in "Eighteen Hundred and Eleven" which is not quite as applicable to 1810 or 1812.[22]

With its dismissal of Barbauld as a "fatidical spinster," comments like this suggest, as scholars like Chandler, Lucy Newlyn, and others have observed, that part of the poem's power comes from its mismatch of gender and genre: Barbauld, a woman, dares to write Juvenalian satire in formal couplet verse that offers a critique of the present and seeks actively to intervene in contemporary history.[23] We need to recognize, however, that whatever his motivations for the attack, Croker is right: The poem has no particular relation to "the events of last year." But this, in turn, is a very narrow way of thinking about the force of prediction and the meaning of a date.

Certainly, the poem manages, as William Keach suggests, to provide a structural and material explanation for Britain's woes, and the first sixty-six lines can be read as a damning account of the effects of eighteen years of nearly continuous war.[24] Barbauld is clear about the war's effects on civilians at home, but she understands Britain to be culpable. When ruin comes, it is with "an earthquake shock" and "baseless wealth dissolves in air away, / Like mists that melt before the morning ray" (53–54). The metaphors here, as Mary Favret argues, are meteorological, but I would add that the effects of war are financial.[25] War produces the loss of wealth because it reveals the airy basis of speculative finance and disrupts commerce. In one of Barbauld's more damning lines, she suggests that,

> thy Midas dream is o'er;
> The golden tide of Commerce leaves thy shore,
> Leaves thee to prove the alternate ills that haunt
> Enfeebling Luxury and ghastly Want;   (61–64)

Decline begins with the disruption of commerce, which Barbauld locates as the source of British prosperity and the basis of its modern condition. The slowing of commerce and the end of the "Midas dream" leave Britain open to potential invasion and the infliction of violent physical catastrophe. For Barbauld, then, ruin will be twofold: it will result both from the disruption of commerce, which she locates as the source of British prosperity and the basis of its modern condition, and from the "earthquake shock," which will ensue when the war can no longer be contained on the Continent. Barbauld must have intended something with her date as title, but the date in question is not connected to a concrete temporal process or, as Croker pointed out, to the particular events of 1811.

One effect of this omission, of course, is to shift focus away from the present onto her prediction for the future. From this perspective, the date of the poem works within a traditional historicist framework to ground a place in time and in space. Consistent with its vision of ruin, the title invites a future historian using the concepts and categories of Romantic historicism to explain that in Britain at this moment, the situation was one that evoked despair and anger at the present and a correspondent fear of the future, while those in the Americas, say, were experiencing a different state of feeling. Here, the date is transferable to other places and it is what makes potential future comparisons possible.

The use of the date also forces us to ask about the relationship between the date in the title and the time of decline described in the poem. The poem is clear on the rough contours of some of the events and individuals that have helped Britain achieve empire, but what is missing is any sense of *when* the forecast decline will occur and of *how* the process will play out in time – of how we get from the "now" of the present to the "then" of the future ruin. Such absence of temporality as a process, in turn, puts pressure on the status of Barbauld's vision of ruin as a concrete prediction and has at least two further effects. First, time is transposed into space. Movement in the poem is developed not through a temporal axis, but through a spatial axis and change is thus represented not through a causal link of events that culminates in ruin as an outcome, but rather as a geographical movement westward as the Spirit of progress repeatedly relocates the seat of empire. Second, the relative absence of dated events and developed temporality in the poem suggests that Barbauld constitutes her prophecy through the juxtaposition of two large epochs of time: antiquity and modernity. Barbauld shapes her entire prophecy of England's ruin around her understanding of the example provided for modernity by antiquity, and she suggests that the example of antiquity will be repeated and can hence be forecast into the future.

I suggested earlier that Barbauld's omission of the particular events of 1811 places emphasis on the future and the predictive aspect of her poem. From another perspective, however, the date serves *not* to call attention to a temporal trajectory projected into the future, but rather to the present and to what we might call an affective history of the present moment. Here, the tenses Barbauld chooses are significant. We might expect a poem that looks from a concrete present to a projected future to make use of the future perfect or future anterior tense: "will have been."[26] Most of *Eighteen Hundred and Eleven*, however, is written in the simple present, with the simple future framed within a conditional "if" and reserved for Barbauld's description of the Grand Tourists from the Americas. In this way, we can look past Croker's petty critique and read the poem as providing a robust and immediate sense of what it felt like to live in 1811. The ruin that Barbauld foresees in the future may not have come to pass as she imagines it, and certainly not as quickly as she imagines it,[27] but that does not mean that it was not acutely feared as a very real possibility in 1811. And in this sense, the anxieties of 1811 can be seen as different from the anxieties of 1810, which are in turn different from the anxieties of 1812, especially after Napoleon's disastrous invasion of Moscow, or the anxieties of 1815 or 1819. This is the problem of the time horizon. In the open future of our modernity, we know less than ever before where we stand in the narrative arc through which we seek to comprehend our relation to historical process. What seems like decline might actually be part of a larger pattern of progress, while what seems like progress might be understood only as part of a longer process of decline. As a result, very different temporal arcs, or time horizons, are experienced simultaneously.

The "Cassandra of the State"

On the basis of his essay on "The Unknown Future and the Art of Prognosis," Koselleck would suggest that prediction works when historical experience and awareness of past precedent allow one to perceive structural patterns in events beyond their apparent singularity and uniqueness, and hence to recognize the contours of a time horizon and anticipate future developments.[28] But he further argues that modernity has made this possibility suspect because what he calls the "space of experience" no longer matches the "horizon of expectation."[29] It might thus come as no surprise that Barbauld predicts ruin and gets it wrong. But this, as I have been suggesting in my analysis of the predictive qualities of Barbauld's poem, is to miss the point. One way of thinking about the status of Barbauld's poem is that it ventures a prediction in order to get it wrong, in order to produce a different possible future. This, in turn, has a bearing on our understanding of Romantic historicism. The date "1819" has come to serve, especially since Chandler's *England in 1819*, as a sign of that historicism, as a mark of the way that an even chronology allows for comparative contemporaneity and the recognition of "uneven development" across space and, further, of the way that our ongoing confrontation with an open future owes a debt to the Romantic past. In my reading of *Eighteen Hundred and Eleven*, in contrast, this is but one of the temporal layers in which Barbauld's prediction operates; in projecting her modernity as the antiquity of the future – and hence as a repetition of the past – and in evoking the felt anxiety that comes from the anticipation of that repetition, Barbauld also allows us to recognize in the date "1811" not just the future time of her prediction and the historicist time of progression and comparison, but also the present time of her title and the way that predicted and imagined futures reveal the more felt and conflicted experience of temporal simultaneity and heterochronicity. Read this way, Barbauld's prediction of national decline positions her as the "Cassandra of the state,"[30] as one critic labeled her, but also in a different sense than intended. Here, state is not a synonym for nation, but rather a reference to the state – or condition – of that nation-state, and also to the state of feeling, to the condition of unsettled temporal experience that comes from weighing the balance between the known and the unknown, the ruins of the classical past and our open, insecure future.

CHAPTER 4

On Ruins: Contingency, Time Parallax, and "The Ruined Cottage"

> She is dead,
> The worm is on her cheek, and this poor hut,
> Stripped of its outward garb of household flowers,
> Of rose and sweetbriar, offers to the wind
> A cold bare wall whose earthly top is tricked
> With weeds and the rank speargrass.[1]   (103–108)

It is a powerful image. A poor, ruined hut, its bare wall overgrown with weeds and speargrass, that stands as a sad reminder of culture's prior (and transitory) check on nature. It is also a familiar image. The combination of building and weed recalls an experience of ruin associated most prominently with the vegetation sprouting through the stones of the Coliseum in Rome and visualized through the conventions of the picturesque. Here, the narrator of the passage, Armytage, Wordsworth's Peddlar, notes that he often muses on the scene "as on a picture" (118), and he takes from the ruin a rather conventional lesson.

The experience of ruins has been described as "a dialogue between an incomplete reality and the imagination of the spectator."[2] If this is the case, "The Ruined Cottage" might be seen as atypical because so little is left to the imagination of the spectator. The ruin around which the poem builds is surrounded by Armytage's narrative and the Poet's reception of that story. Perhaps this is why most critical discussions of the poem have tended to focus on the poetics of suffering represented by Margaret's story and only more tangentially on the ruin at the poem's center. Despite this lack of critical attention, I want to suggest that because the process of the ruin's mediated reception is so richly described in the poem, it provides an excellent place for thinking about the eighteenth century and Romantic fascination with ruins.

In connection with the concerns about decline that this book has been tracking, ruins themselves offer a powerful icon of decline made visible. Their representation in poetry – as we saw in Chapter 3 with Barbauld's fantasy of Britain's future ruin – commonly articulates a reaction to ruin that works simultaneously as a sentimental image of decline and as a discursive counterweight to it. The disconnection implied by ruins, in other words, can indicate a break with the past, but, as we saw in Chapter 3 and will see again, in a society moving with apparent speed into an unknown commercial future, ruins can also offer a mark of the continuity between time past and time present. This is because ruins like those of Margaret's cottage can be thought of in connection with slow time, a sense of time that, as the following chapters will further develop, offers a riposte to the speed of commercial society. The ruin thus serves to index a series of new relationships to the future that emerge in the later eighteenth century in connection with decline. As Chapter 3 showed, Anna Barbauld's *Eighteen Hundred and Eleven* deploys the fantasy of England's future ruin through the mode of the future perfect so that its present, marked so clearly by its dated title, can be understood as that which will have been. But this future projection is framed by a title that calls emphatic attention to its present moment, and one effect of this, I suggested, is that it under-scores the relation between the particulars of Barbauld's imagined future and the present time of her title in a manner that allows later readers like us to recognize the felt and conflicted experience of temporal simultaneity, of the heterochronic sense of time revealed by ruins. This is why we cannot properly consider the popularity of ruins and indeed the obsession with them circa 1800 without understanding ruins in connection with the temporal issues that arise from the concerns with decline that this book has been tracking.

In a century that witnessed the Lisbon earthquake of 1755, the discovery of Herculaneum and Pompeii, and later the French Revolution, writers and visual artists alike were keen to exploit the aesthetic potential of natural and man-made catastrophe. In the British tradition, there is Thomas Littleton's "The State of England in the Year 2199" (1780) or more well-known fantasies of future ruin like Barbauld's *Eighteen Hundred and Eleven* (1812) or Mary Shelley's *The Last Man* (1826). Further evidence can be found in the prominence given to sculptural fragments and ruined build-ings in Shelley's "Ozymandias" (1818) and Peacock's poems on Palmyra (1806, 1812), or in the way ruins create the shadow of immanent disaster in the Gothic novel. But the fascination with ruins was not solely an oppor-tunity to brood over real and imagined catastrophe, as the less sudden transitions in Wordsworth's "The Ruined Cottage" would indicate. Ruins and fragments could also be conventional reminders of mortality as in Keats's "On Seeing the Elgin Marbles" (1817) or an opportunity to construct connections between past and present as in Scott's *The Antiquary* (1816). Nor was the fascination with ruins limited to print: the Elgin Marbles were brought to Britain in this period (1810–1812), King George IV built a sham ruin from fragments imported from North Africa on the grounds of Virginia Water (1826), while the end of the Napoleonic Wars eventually made the ruins of Rome again accessible to travelers. In the spirit of Littleton and Barbauld, John Soane even commissioned his draftsman, Joseph Gandy, to paint an image of what the rotunda of his newly renovated Bank of England would look like in ruin (Figure 0.1). Ruins – sham and real, projected and present, imagined and concrete – were omnipresent in Romantic culture.

But what did this fascination with ruins imply? For Diderot, writing of Hubert Robert's paintings at the Salon of 1767, the meaning of what he called a "poetics of ruin" was clear: "we contemplate the ravages of time, and in our imagination we scatter the rubble of the very buildings in which we live over the ground; in that moment, solitude and silence prevail around us, we are the sole survivors of an entire nation that is no more."[3] In Diderot's account, today's built environment becomes the future's ruins. He reads ruins as an invitation to speculate about future catastrophe in the mode of the future perfect, the tense used to articulate an action that will have been completed at some future moment. This mode, as I elaborated in the introduction, might serve as indicative of a range of eighteenth-century concerns about the future generally, and Diderot's anticipation of ruin stands accordingly as a mark of the uncertainty of the future, an attempt to race through time and look back upon the present with projected retrospection and the privilege of historical distance. But, as the plenitude of material referred to above would indicate, Diderot does not have the final word. Ruins are well-trodden critical territory, and a range of distinct but complementary theories have been put forward seeking to explain their fascination. This should not be at all surprising because the abundance of signification represented in ruins makes them readily available to a breadth of interpretations. Like any iconic image, ruins have the capacity to exceed reference.

Thomas McFarland, in one of the earliest and most influential arguments about the Romantic fascination with ruin, clarifies a phenomenology of incompleteness, fragmentation and ruin in Romanticism, which he explains as "diasparactive" (after the Greek *diasparaktos*, torn to pieces) and which he sees, following Heidegger, as central to all human endeavor.[4] For Anne Janowitz, in contrast, this in itself is a Romantic reading of fragmentation and ruin, one that neglects the historical circumstances in which such an interpretation emerges. Janowitz's is one of the most compelling readings of the English cult of ruins. Drawing upon Laurence Goldstein's previous linking of ruins and empire, Janowitz suggests that one of the paradoxes of eighteenth-century ruin was that the image of decay lent the authority of antiquity to the construction of the nation and hence came to authorize England's autonomy as a world power.[5] Eager to push this reading to help explain the history of poetic form, Janowitz sketches a genealogy of ruin poetry whereby the genre moves "away from narrative forms and toward lyric forms conceived in spatial terms."[6] We see, in other words, a shift in emphasis from the object of ruin and the violent events that produced them (the ruined castle poem) and toward the observing subjectivity that recounts the story. This same privatizing impulse, according to Janowitz, can also be located in the emergence of the Romantic fragment poem, which substitutes spatial incompletion on the page for the ruin poem's central category of decline over time.

Sophie Thomas shares Janowitz's concern about the relationship between ruin and history. For Thomas, ruins, which "float between past and present," exhibit a particular "double temporal identity" such that they are neither past nor present, but both simultaneously: "Ruins thus represent the historical relation, rather than history 'itself.'"[7] Thomas is particularly interested in the sham ruin and the Romantic fragment, whose traces encourage viewers and readers to extrapolate the whole from the part, but whose imagined reconstruction produces an object or experience that was in fact never whole. In this way, "Desire for the full apprehension of the historical whole arises from the *lack* of it, its irretrievable loss, and this state of affairs impels the creation of imaginary or fantasized 'histories' that in their own (particularized) way tell us a great deal about the construction of 'history' in general."[8] Thomas's approach, in other words, shifts emphasis away from the perceived pastness of the past and toward an emphasis on the place occupied by ruins in the present.

Most recently, in an account that works predominantly with the visual tradition and the painting of Hubert Robert in particular, Nina Dubin links the conjectural relation between past and future associated with ruins to the uncertainties and instabilities of an eighteenth-century credit economy. For Dubin, it is not an accident that the cult of ruins coincides with the emergence of modern market structures because "market forces appear to have catalyzed an awareness of contingency that eighteenth-century artists and aesthetes brought to bear on their apprehension of ruins."[9] Credit, Dubin suggests, "injected uncertainty into the present, and disrupted the linear passage of time by conflating yesterday's debts and tomorrow's earnings." In this sense, credit sits perched "between plenitude and mere potentiality, between past value and future returns," a position that for Dubin exhibits precisely the condition that is the hallmark of the ruin. Drawing upon J. G. A. Pocock's description of the "unpredictable contingencies and emergencies" of what he calls "fortune," Dubin further explains that it was in the eighteenth century that ruins came to be understood as unstable sites of temporal fluctuation: "just as credit existed only on the order of opinion and belief... so was the ruin an object of wonder for its symbiotic relationship with nature and exigency."[10]

What all these approaches share – and not surprisingly – is a tendency to read ruins as indexing a particular relationship between past, present, and future. They are all, in other words, arguments about Romantic temporality, but they are incongruous with each other as to the significance of what this time represents. Each seeks to assign a particular meaning to changes in temporal understandings, whether that is the constructed time of empire and a literary-historical transposition from time to space as Janowitz would have it; or the way that, for Sophie Thomas, ruins set historical actors in relation to time and reveal the constructed nature of historical experience in the present; or, finally, how ruins reflect for Dubin the insecurity of credit and produce a new sense of futurity stemming from the eighteenth-century financial revolution. While each of these accounts is cogent and compelling, none are fully satisfactory. Instead, this chapter will suggest that the Romantic cult of ruins is not about assigning a specific meaning to the temporality of ruin, nor is it about insisting that the ruin reveals a specific relationship to time. Instead, the Romantic ruin is about experiencing the incommensurability of multiple temporalities. The ruin reveals a series of new relationships to the future that emerge in the later eighteenth century, a series that includes the accounts of those discussed above but is not limited to either one.

The concerns about decline in various guises that we have seen repeatedly over the previous chapters serve as an index of this new relationship to the future. Such worries inevitably raise questions about when the projected or imagined decline will occur. Drawing upon Smith's insistence on evaluating the significance of economic data over the course of a century, Playfair's time-series line graphs, for example, invite speculation about the projection of past patterns into the future. Concerns about the decline of literature also look toward the future as they appeal to a selection of works or types of work that they hope will become the cornerstones of future reading. Inevitably such attempts to constitute a canon of value confront the seeming transience of so many products of the press and thus seek both to constitute new possibilities of permanence and timelessness and to imagine an engagement with literature that takes readers out of a sense of time understood as increasingly preoccupied by a need to manage time efficiently in the face of information overload. Anna Barbauld's fantasy of the ruins of London, in turn, combines both trajectories in its imagination of a civilization ruined by the economic effects of warfare but whose great works and historical examples continue to inspire future empires located elsewhere. All these examples underscore the connection between concerns over decline and changes in how Romantic subjects perceived their relationship to time and, especially, to the future.

In this context, ruin might be understood as a particular form of decline that also foregrounds temporal problems. My suggestion here is that these kind of temporal concerns – and especially the changing understanding of futurity developed in connection with my discussion of various aspects of decline in the previous chapters – allow us to think about the temporality of ruin in new ways. The range of concerns about decline detailed in the previous chapters relate closely to new and developing senses of time and attitudes toward the future in the eighteenth century, especially a sense of the transient and ephemeral nature of print and of time experienced as accelerated and documented in the many concerns about the hurry, rush, and bustle of modern life. As this chapter suggests, the ruin also shares a sense of transience, but its time is not the accelerated time of the press. Nonetheless, it stands as a representation in space of the new types of temporal concerns that this book details in connection with decline.

In an essay on ruins and bones, Andrew Piper draws upon Matthais Schöning's argument that the ruin is where Romantic individuals came to sense time in two particular forms: "time giving time" and "time consuming time." In the first instance, the ruin represents a sense of duration ("time giving time"), while in the second, ruin represents a sense of decline ("time consuming time").[11] But in Piper's reading of Goethe's *Italian Journey*, and in my reading of the ruin more generally, the ruin is that which disrupts a stable sense of spatiotemporality, or scale. This is why, in one of the original episodes of the eighteenth-century critical reception of ruins – the episode that initiates a concept of "the poetics of ruin" – Diderot constantly calls attention to the scalar confusion produced by Hubert Robert's ruins paintings. Looking, for example, at a "Small, Very Small Ruin," Diderot notes that "there isn't anyone who wouldn't ascribe several square meters to its little ruin, though it's really no larger than my hand."[12] Earlier, inspecting an image of a ruined bridge, Diderot says "I won't tell you about the effect of this picture, I'll simply ask you on what size canvas you think it's painted. It's on a very small one, roughly two-thirds of a meter wide by less than half a meter high."[13] Such confusions of spatial scale recur throughout Diderot's comments on Robert.

In my reading, ruins disrupt not only spatial, but also temporal scale. Ruins come to index the plurality of emergent and competing timescales that characterize the experience of modernity, the particular combination of a sense both of acceleration, as technologies of communication and transportation appear to make modern life faster than earlier temporal moments (time consuming time), and a sense of duration, of slow or deep time as discoveries in natural history and geology begin to deliver ever longer estimates for the age of the earth (time giving time). Ruins point to different and competing orders of time, to a past and a future that transpire on a scale of time that individual human experience struggles to recognize; more even than this, however, they disrupt the perceived continuity between these now multiple scales of time. Indeed, these two senses of time, I would suggest, are closely related because the recognition of a sense of speeding up can lead to a compensatory reach for a competing sense of slow time, while to grasp the slowness of time one needs an accelerated or condensed point of view – a point that I have developed elsewhere in connection with my reading of book 3 of Adam Smith's *Wealth of Nations*.[14] Ruins reveal both the presence and the incommensurability of these multiple time frames. To illustrate this point, I turn now to a close analysis of the representation of time and temporal process in Wordsworth's "The Ruined Cottage."

"The Ruined Cottage"

Wordsworth's "The Ruined Cottage" has been described as "the longest and most complex of Wordsworth's ruined nature poems" and it is one of Wordsworth's most frequently discussed works.[15] It has been a particularly rich (those familiar with Alan Liu's discussion of the poem will recognize that I choose this term with care) source of discussion especially for new historicist critics like Jerome McGann, Marjorie Levinson, Alan Liu, Anne Janowitz, Karen Swann, Celeste Langan, and, most recently, David Simpson.[16] All of these readings highlight the complex layers of mediation that surround the poem, a device whose narrative effect is to create distance between the reader and the story of suffering and to turn attention to the construction of the narrative itself.

What I am calling mediation refers to how the poem establishes its narrative indirectly by passing it along to readers at one degree removed, as the representation of Armytage to the poet, who then passes it along to us, its readers. The process of telling the reader in the voice of the poet a story that the poet has heard from Armytage while also recreating the immediacy of Armytage's telling might more conventionally be termed framing. I choose the term mediation, however, to indicate a more complex sense of framing: to underscore, first, how the poet's reception of Armytage's narration models an attentiveness that can be understood in connection with Wordsworth's quarrel with the culture of eventfulness promoted by later eighteenth-century print media; and, second, to emphasize a more acute self-consciousness about the process of transmission and especially of the potential and perhaps inevitable sense of interference that accompanies such processes. Part of what motivates my insistence on mediation over framing is Wordsworth's perception of the impact of contemporary media on the faculties of understanding and feeling, his quarrel with "the rapid communication of intelligence" that is "hourly gratified" by later eighteenth-century print and its culture of news. The deliberate telling of the story of the ruined cottage and its recreation in writing of an oral event become in this account an alternative to the "rapidity" associated with print media. In "The Ruined Cottage," in other words, the oral transmission of the Pedlar's story, and its passage to us in the form of metrical poetry, stands as an alternative form of communication, slower perhaps than the kinds of print transmission that Wordsworth associates with the craving for eventfulness generated by print media, and more deliberate certainly.

But as with any form of transmission, mediation is susceptible also to disturbance and interference. In Chapter 2, we saw how the proliferation of print was understood as a threat to temporal order, as creating a sense of time pressure and hurry initiated by the ever-increasing difficulty of keeping up with the output of the press. For Kevis Goodman, print culture and the emergent technologies of the new science "occasion a concern about sensory over-extension, perceived initially perhaps as an influx of opportunity, but increasingly, and more negatively, sustained as a wounding of perception."[17] If the recounting in print of an oral event like the Pedlar's story might work to protect readers against the aggressive rapidity of certain forms of print communication and against the sensory overextension that such communications foster, then, such a narrative might also function, according to Goodman, as an aperture, one that discloses "the pressures it might seek to cover." In my reading of Wordsworth, the focus on how the mediation of the poem shapes its handling of time is precisely such an aperture. While Wordsworth may be sensitive to the disturbance and interference of mediation, there nonetheless remains a sense of cognitive dissonance, an unaccounted for remainder in his representation of time and times mediated through narrative and this disturbance is what allows us to register the critical stakes in the poem's handling of time.

I earlier mentioned that Armytage draws a rather conventional lesson from the ruin of Margaret's cottage. Reading the view through the traditional memento mori associated with ruin, he tells the narrator that

> We die, my friend,
> Nor we alone, but that which each man loved
> And prized in his peculiar nook of earth
> Dies with him, or is changed, and very soon
> Even of the good is no memorial left.   (68–72)

Armytage's subsequent description of the cottage in ruin as a "cold bare wall" (107) here recalls the narrator's earlier description of the cottage as "four naked walls / That stand upon each other" (31–32). Such humanizing descriptions of the ruined building suggest that the cottage works as an objective correlative for Margaret, who, in turn, might be understood as being monumentalized by the poem. This connection underscores Wordsworth's innovation. Despite Armytage's efforts to see the ruin through the picturesque and to take from it a conventional moral, the layers of mediation between Armytage's description, the narrator's response, and the reader's further interpretation of the interplay between the two indicate a more complex process.

Janowitz, for example, uses her understanding of the mediated responses to Margaret's story to demonstrate how the subject of rural decline marks a rift between nature and nation, which is then mended through an act of poetic reparation. Cultural effects like war and unemployment are naturalized and then repaired as the poem suggests that monumentalizing can repair suffering. For Janowitz and others, the meaning of the poem turns around the relationship between the ruins as a reminder of human suffering and loss and the resulting question of what possible compensation could be drawn from such suffering. As it plays out across the various levels of mediation, the contrast between suffering and the attempt to mend or repair it in the poem forces readers to recognize the poem's staging of mediation as a technics, a deliberate exposure for critical reflection on a process of suffering that might otherwise be brushed off as part of the natural order. While the poem's layers of narrative mediation make its meaning far from straightforward, they are at least clearly and deliberately marked: we always know who is speaking and where we are for all of the episode's mediated layers.

This, however, is not the case for the temporal mediation that is also put into play by the poem's sequence of events and distinct narrative voices. David Simpson locates Wordsworth's value in offering "a place of not knowing, a space of disturbance and concern."[18] In "The Ruined Cottage," I would suggest, a key aspect of this not knowing arises from the temporal disturbance the poem produces for its reader, a temporal disturbance that might be likened to the experience of Robert, Margaret's husband, when after his illness, he loses track of seasonal distinctions and no longer knows, in the broadest sense, what time it is. Place and voice, in other words, may be clear, but this kind of clarity does not map onto a similarly precise sense of the temporal frame of events. This is because throughout "The Ruined Cottage" time is marked through a series of different scales and temporalities, ranging from the daily movement of the sun that frames the poem, to seasonal change and natural cycles of growth and decay, to what have now become the more conventional markers of modern, capitalist time like clock time, monthly time, and annual time. In "The Ruined Cottage," then, we can recognize both the kind of rigid, structured, commercial time that E. P. Thompson encourages us to associate with industrial work and the growth of capitalist production; but also, in the interference between these various forms of keeping time, we can distinguish a form of temporal asymmetry akin to what Mark Turner calls "periodical time," as a way of referring to the combination of confusion and cohesion that marks periodical culture, the way that the regular, insistent, and steady movement of publication – in dailies, weeklies, and Sundays, in monthlies, quarterlies, and annuals – produces both regularity through its repetition of cycles but also the way that the same hurried periodicities cannot be contained by a single cycle and therefore can be out of sync as well as in sync.[19]

We can now look closely at how this works in "The Ruined Cottage." The poem opens with the summer sun ("'Twas summer and the sun was mounted high") leaving us with a sense of daytime and seasonal time but no sense of exactly when the events recounted transpire. James Chandler has called our attention to the influence of James Thomson's *Seasons* on Wordsworth's poem, an influence so marked that Wordsworth seems to be "cribbing" from Thomson's "Summer."[20] This connection underscores the link between the narrator's centrality and the observing consciousness, the "I" and the "eye," in what Chandler describes as an accrual of detail "enumerated with a vividness that is unsurpassed in Wordsworth's mature poetry."[21] The effect of this influence, however, works as a kind of trick, with the intensity of the observation presenting a setup that is brought to an abrupt and ironic halt with the unexpected transition to the Pedlar, a transition that shifts from a vivid first-person experience to the second-order experience of listening to another voice. For Chandler, the shift from first-order observation to second-order listening clarifies how both reader and speaker are being taught to read "by being made to listen" to the extent that the poem works as a programmatic statement of Wordsworth's argument that writing "can only succeed by aspiring to the condition of speech."[22] For my purposes, the link to Thomson and the seasonal time of the poem reinforces the operation of seasonal time in Wordsworth's poem, but the abrupt cut away from the first-order observation that underwrites the introduction of seasonal time works to call into question the singularity of seasonal time itself as it gives way to other temporal modes and other ways of marking temporal passage. This is especially important in my reading because seasonal cycles work throughout the poem to distinguish the thematics of decay, which can produce rebirth as the seasonal cycle continues (as Shelley's "Ode to the West Wind" would later acknowledge even more emphatically), while temporalities of decline tend to unfold in a more singularly downward and unredeemable direction.

Soon after the poem's opening in the midday summer's heat, we learn that Armytage, a friend as dear to the narrator "as is the setting sun" (40) – note here how the temporal sense pervades even the poem's figurative field – was last seen "Two days before" (40). I want to pause over this detail. It is the first of many concrete markers of relational time in the poem, but it does not seem material to the story in any way. The events of those two days before are never told, and it seems unimportant to establish the precise amount of time that has passed between the "now" of the poem and the "then" that immediately precedes it. As a result, such markers commonly serve not temporal clarification, but rather allude to the temporal confusion that the poem will develop. On the basis of temporal markers like this, we become unsure of which aspects of time we are meant to take as significant just as we become attuned to distinctions between the time of decline and the time of decay.

The next subtle marker of time is purely natural. Armytage points the narrator in the direction of a spring, and he sees:

> . . . a plot
> Of garden ground now wild, its matted weeds
> Marked with the steps of those whom as they passed,
> The gooseberry-trees that shot in long lank slips,
> Or currants hanging from their leafless stems
> In scanty strings, had tempted to o'erleap

> The broken wall. Within that cheerless spot,
> Where two tall hedgerows of thick willow boughs
> Joined in a damp cold nook, I found a well
> Half covered up with willow-flowers and weeds.
>
> (54–63)

Alan Liu uses this moment to emphasize how "in some of the most luxuriant still lifes, vegetation tropes persons."[23] In my reading, this description of the cottage garden as wild and overgrown indicates additionally the passage of time, of natural unmeasured time as vegetation intercedes on what had been human cultivation. Nature here is that which makes time and that which makes time material, *but that which cannot measure it in any precise sense*. Looking at an overgrown garden does not tell us when or how it fell into neglect, only that some abstract time has passed. And in the ruin of the garden, we can see more generally how ruin operates as the visualization of temporal process, as the articulation in space of something that happens over time.

It is, of course, Armytage's narrative that clarifies this vague overgrown past and turns it into a story whose episodes make narrative sense. Armytage combines calendar time and natural time in recounting Margaret's demise. It begins "some ten years gone" (133) when two bad harvests and war create "sorrow and distress" (138) across the countryside. Before the "second autumn" (148) Margaret's husband, Robert, is seized by a fever. In her discussion of how the poem represents economic crisis and the alienated aesthetics of sensation, Karen Swann describes Robert's fever as "the urban disease" of modernity, which produces some of the very symptoms that Wordsworth disdainfully describes in the "Preface," a dissociation of sensibility and a craving for incident.[24] To this I would add a further aspect of modernity, its temporal dissociation, what we might recognize as a particular contrast between the fast and the slow seen, for example, in the "Preface" where the "rapid communication" that produces this craving for "extraordinary incident" brings with it also "an almost savage torpor."[25] For Robert, such temporal confusion appears in the disregard of seasonal time, for when his strength returns,

> He blended where he might the various tasks
> Of summer, autumn, winter, and of spring.
>
> (170–71)

Here, the signs of Robert's distress work as a sign of temporal confusion more broadly as Robert, whose peasant labor would have been conditioned by seasonal time, can no longer read its signs. Spatially, he knows where he stands, but temporally he is lost. This, I would emphasize, is the sort of condition typified by ruin.

At the start of the second part, the narrator of the poem explains how "the things of which he spake / Seemed present" (211–12) and Armytage describes how the ruin produces tranquility and "a power to virtue friendly" (229). At this point, Armytage resumes his tale and time becomes most out of joint. As things fall apart for Margaret and Robert, the time sequence of the poem also starts to read like interference across competing frequencies. Armytage travels to a "country far remote" (240) but we are never told where or for how long. We know that we are still within the ten years marked by Armytage as the span of Margaret's demise but we do not quite know where we are within that time period. Armytage returns in "early spring" (282) to hear of Robert's enlistment in the army, whose temporal particulars are clearly marked: it happened two months before, and after two days, Margaret found "a purse of gold" (265) on the morning of the third. Armytage then travels again, with "heat and cold" (290) indicating the change of season before he returns "towards the wane of summer" (299) and begins to see the signs of ruin and neglect in Margaret's garden. We have a sense of time passing, but we do not know how much; we do not know which spring or which autumn, or, for that matter, how many of each season have passed.

Here, natural, seasonal times converge and temporal change is shown in the overgrowth that takes back Margaret's garden – a hint of what will become nature's more full reclamation in the passage I cited earlier. As the sun sinks in the west, Armytage stands contemplating the change:

> . . . looking round I saw the corner-stones,
> Till then unmarked, on either side the door
> With dull red stains discoloured, and stuck o'er
> With tufts and hairs of wool, as if the sheep
> That fed upon the commons thither came
> Familiarly, and found a couching-place
> Even at her threshold.   (330–36)

Amid this stillness and reflection, something unusual happens: "The house-clock struck eight" (336) and Armytage turns to see Margaret. It is (literally) a striking moment both for the way Margaret now wears time as the dissolution of her body, but also for the disruptive quality of the time. This is the first and only mention of clock time in the poem and its disjunctive quality disorders our experience as readers just as the sound of the clock startles Armytage. Such precision in the hour of day contrasts with the poem's other timescales, most notably with Armytage's consistent marking of time through seasonal change. As Armytage's story continues, "many seasons pass" (444) as Margaret continues to decline. For Margaret, time is linear, one protracted process of decay and decline presented to others both in her personal appearance and in the steady neglect and ruin of her cottage. For Armytage, however, time is cyclical, just one damned season after another. Eventually, the Pedlar specifies that she lingered for "five tedious years" and we again recall the original frame of the story as "some ten years gone." By the time we reach the poem's ending as the "sun declining shot / A slant and mellow radiance," the arc of the day aligns clearly with the ruined cottage around which the narrative of the poem turns, but the temporal experience surrounding the space of the ruin has become multiplied and fragmented.

In Armytage's recounting of the story of Margaret and the narrator's rendering of that account, then, we recognize the intermixing of the various times of nature and of culture: clock time and annual time, seasonal time and sun time. One question, then, becomes most generally how are we to read the relationship between these various times? What does time do in this poem and what might that tell us about the time of ruin or the ruin of time?

To begin with the obvious, the marking of time allows us to compre-hend Margaret's story and the narrator's account of it *as a story*, and even as a history, whose originality and distinctive nature, as Lévi-Strauss reminds us, depend upon "apprehending the relation between *before* and *after*."[26] Perhaps this is why the poem has had such appeal to new historicist criticism, which has used the poem to query the relations between Margaret's decline and the particular historical circumstances that surround it. Jerome McGann's reading, for example, emphasizes the concrete historical determinants that produce Margaret's pain. The displacement of such factors as the American war, a system of impressment, and the decline of cottage industries in favor of an empha-sis on the compensatory reparation offered by ruins, all become, for McGann, part of the Romantic ideology, the grand illusion "that poetry, or even consciousness, can set one free of the ruins of history and culture."[27] Alan Liu similarly insists that "*The Ruined Cottage* is one of the strongest cases of the denial, the over-determined and precise absence, that is the poet's sense of history."[28]

In keeping with new historicism's emphasis on the relation between the poem and the historical circumstances that frame it – whether conceived in McGann's case as a denial, or understood as the fundamentally economic nature of the poem's topic and its coming into being as for Liu, or the close connection between problems of surplus and distress and the divided liberal subject as for Langan and Simpson – I want to suggest that a further dimension of the poem's historical significance can be found in its handling of the very problem of time. If, as Karen Swann suggests, Wordsworth's "poetic practices, instead of working consistently to naturalize the social, tend to acknowledge as a technics – as a captivating representational economy – phenomena that socially powerful narratives seek to naturalize,"[29] then this insight might extend also to the poem's handling of an economy of time. Rather than naturalize cultural time, "The Ruined Cottage" seeks, through the figure of the ruin, to call attention to the technics of timekeeping and to the contrasts and incommensurability between natural and cultural time. In this context, it is instructive to compare the poem to another, slightly earlier Wordsworth poem that also treats temporal experience and that also takes its title from a ruin.

Wordsworth's "Tintern Abbey" – or, to call the poem by its full title, "Lines Composed a Few Miles above Tintern Abbey, On Revisiting the Banks of the Wye during a Tour. July 13, 1798" – closes its very title with a calendrical date. The dated precision of the poem's title is then picked up in the time span of the opening lines, "Five years have passed; five summers, with the length / Of five long winters!"[30] The interplay between the date of the title and the five years whose passage give the poem its occasion allow readers to locate the poem in time and to locate also the passage of time within the poem as part of a readily understood continuum. "July 13, 1798," in other words, not only calls attention to the poem's setting on the eve of the anniversary of the French Revolution, but the date more generally locates the poem in the grid of measured time shaped by the calendar and allows us to calibrate the events described within the poem as part of a temporally precise series of events with a distinct before and after.

As the poem continues, the explicit markers of this precisely dated, even, homogeneous time fall away and the speaker's reflections place us in the more personal time of memory and recollection. We learn of the significance of the first visit, the one five years prior, and the frequency with which the speaker has revisited and recollected his experience there. The discrepancy between the memory and the experience as renewed in the poem's lyric present of 1798 reveals the "sad perplexity" (61) that generates the poem's account of the imagination. Ultimately, the capacity of imagination to create in retrospect – the way that for Wordsworth experience itself is constituted in retrospect – helps to explain the discrepancies between the first visit of 1793 and the later one of 1798 but also the less precisely dated but earlier set of experiences where "nature was to me all in all" and the anticipation of future experiences, the food "for future years" of line 66 and the "after years" of line 138. What I want to emphasize here is how the use of a precise date in the poem's title gives order to all of these less precisely calibrated experiences, and how the poem thus shows that the temporal blurring and blending of lived experience can be shaped by the cultural grid of the calendar.

"The Ruined Cottage," with its temporal span of ten years, also references this grid of time, but unlike "Tintern Abbey" with its dated specificity, temporal shifts in the poem render its readers simultaneously placed and lost. Cultural time often comes bursting through the time of nature and tempts readers to calibrate between the gridded time of the calendar and the seasonal time of the poem, but ultimately this is to no avail. Time in "The Ruined Cottage" allows us to assemble and order the narrative of Margaret and the cottage, but it also comes to resemble the process of ruination that the poem describes. It begins, indeed, to resemble Lévi-Strauss's account of the historian's code.

Recall that, for Lévi-Strauss, chronological coding works on a series of levels: there is the ordinal and linear that establishes before and after. But, he adds "each date is also a cardinal number and, as such, expresses a *distance* in relation to the dates nearest to it."[31] Finally, then, each date is also a member of a class "definable by the meaningful character each date has within the class in relation to other dates which also belong to it, and by the absence of this meaningful character with respect to dates appertaining to a different class," what James Chandler calls the date's "exponential function."[32] The years 1789, 1815, and 1819, in other words, are members of a certain class of dates that have no meaning in relation to other classes of higher order dates like the first, second, or third millennium or to lower order dates like January 23 or August 17. Lévi-Strauss's point, then, is that the myth of history is that all of these different orders of dates cohere as part of a series. On the contrary, he insists that "the dates appropriate to each class are irrational in relation to all those of other classes," and, further, "All these dates do not form a series: They are of different species."[33] At the highest, millennial or epochal level of explanation, the most famous episodes in modern and contemporary history cease to be pertinent, while, we might add after Chandler's assessment of this argument, at the lowest explanatory level, say, that of a year, the events that are significant at the level of the millennium are equally irrelevant.[34] What we take to be a continuum or a coherent system is revealed instead to resemble a rectangular matrix of points.

At its base, then, the historian's code described by Lévi-Strauss is about scale. Scale as a principle is what establishes the meaningful relationships between dates within a particular class and allows for the comprehension of the distance between them. Ultimately, however, the perceived movement between scales, between different orders of time is impossible, and Lévi-Strauss's exposure of the historian's code emphasizes the problem of scalar incommensurability. This, in turn, is a problem exposed previously by the ruin, for in my account ruins generally and the particular ruin at the center of "The Ruined Cottage" similarly underscore the problem of establishing the commensurability of different orders of time. What for Lévi-Strauss is a problem particular to the date is for Wordsworth a problem of the various ways that time is measured by and sensed on the body. These timescales ultimately fail to correlate and the ruined cottage at the center of the poem then marks an interference in the order of time and reveals the lack of calibration between competing orders and scales of time. In this way, I would suggest, one important – and overlooked – aspect of the poem is the manner in which the ruined cottage around which the episode is framed comes to stand not only for an ambivalent but humanized experience of suffering, what the poet describes as "that secret spirit of humanity" (503), but also for the confusion produced by multiple and competing modes of temporality. It is as if Wordsworth opens a series of parentheses to indicate temporal layers, but because he then rarely closes them, we are left with a series of temporal levels whose relationship to each other is never clarified.

Again, to see this point more clearly, it helps to compare "The Ruined Cottage" with another poem composed around the same time. Published in the second edition of *Lyrical Ballads* (1800), "Michael, a Pastoral Poem" tells the story of a shepherd who, after a lifetime of hard work, is forced to send his beloved son, Luke, into trade to discharge a forfeiture on his property. On the eve of Luke's departure, a despondent Michael takes Luke to lay the cornerstone for a sheepfold that the two would have built together. Luke soon loses himself in the dissolute ways of the city – Swann's "urban disease" comes to mind again – and is forced to hide overseas. He never returns. For Michael, the unfinished sheepfold then stands as an objective correlative for Luke's loss and he is frequently seen sitting by it with his faithful dog. Seven years after Luke's departure, Michael dies brokenhearted, leaving the sheepfold unfinished.

As with the ruined cottage, the sheepfold of "Michael" comes to signify both a person and a narrative about that person's loss and suffering. Both poems, furthermore, play themselves out across a landscape that is changing with urbanization and the spread of manufacture, thus creating the conditions for the kind of alienation that Wordsworth describes in connection with Margaret and Michael. And, finally, the sheepfold and the ruined cottage both serve as monuments (though perhaps not enduring ones) in contrast to The Evening Star, the colloquial name for Michael's cottage, which by the end of the poem has been destroyed and plowed under as part of the "great changes" (487) wrought in the neighborhood. The sheepfold of Michael, however, represents a different kind of monument than Margaret's ruined cottage, since, unlike the cottage, the construction of the sheepfold is never completed. But we can imagine that both would look similar, and this similar state of incompletion between a structure in ruin and a structure in the process of being constructed, the "struggling heap of unhewn stones" (17), calls attention to the proximity of the two states. It is tempting to say that the cottage of Margaret represents a domestic happiness that is lost, while the sheepfold of Michael stands for the completion of a domesticity and an inheritance passed from father to son that can never come to be. But in the case of Michael, we have seen evidence of that very domesticity and so it, too, is lost in a manner related to that of Margaret. But if a comparison of the two poems thus underscores the proximity of the ruined and the unbuilt as sites of lost potentiality, the handling of time in each puts the temporal confusion of "The Ruined Cottage" into further relief.

The loss in both poems spans ten years: that is the time Armytage identifies between the start of Margaret's demise and the narrative of it that he offers the poet, and that is the total time from the departure of Luke until the death of Michael after seven years and his wife after a further three. But if "The Ruined Cottage" focuses on this ten-year span and unfolds what I have described above as the temporal contradictions within it, the ten years of the sheepfold in "Michael" are relatively uncomplicated. The years leading up to the sheepfold, however, are more interesting with respect to the poem's temporality. In the story of Michael, time moves steadily on, guided by a routine of natural work that proceeds "from year to year" (121) "through a length of years" (147) as many months pass on, day by day. Years are used especially to mark age as we are repeatedly told of Michael's eighty years and we watch Luke grow from five years to ten years to eighteen years. This is the time of the calendar used to mark the time of the body, that also serves to indicate the passage of specific, measured time.

But as a mark of distinction from "The Ruined Cottage," the emphasis in "Michael" is not on the kind of remarkable events and setbacks that produce the gradual dissolution of Margaret and her cottage. "Michael" is rather a poem "ungarnish'd with events" (19) and it focuses instead on the routines of rural domestic industriousness that characterize Michael's life both before Luke's birth and after. It is a poem of continuity. When that continuity is eventually interrupted, the poem turns most closely to a kind of relational dating marked not by a calendar date as in "Tintern Abbey" but by the moment of Michael's forfeiture.

Michael ponders this news for two days, his wife works on Luke's things for a further "five days," and ultimately three weeks pass between the forfeiture and Luke's departure. This time is all carefully and clearly marked; its minute details work to divide the poem between the continuous routines that precede the news and the ten years that follow it. Further, in the first 39 lines that frame the poem, the significance of the episode also conveys the more conventional time of ruin, especially as the poet suggests that, though he recounts "a history / Homely and rude" (34–35), he does so "for the sake / Of youthful Poets, who among these Hills / Will be my second self when I am gone" (37–39). The poem, then, functions as a legacy to its poetic inheritors as a reparation for Michael's failure to pass his land on to Luke. This transmission works through what I have described as the conventional time of ruin, the future perfect tense, as it imagines a time when the poet is gone. It works also as an inverse of Diderot's poetics of ruin, for instead of imagining our own continuity after the built environment has been destroyed, as the "sole survivors of an entire nation that is no more," the poet here foresees his own demise and the continuity of his poetry. "Michael," then, seems secure about its place in time and its future. Even if its subject has failed to transmit his legacy to Luke, as part of a poem, his story, his history, will continue. In this secure confidence in its transmission, of its place in time and its continuity through time, the poem is missing the temporal confusion of "The Ruined Cottage," what I have described as a sense of parentheses opening never to be closed or reconciled.

The thematics of both "The Ruined Cottage" and "Michael" seek a reconciliation between nature and culture of the sort that Georg Simmel sees in more monumental ruins, where the ruin combines in a delicate balance the upward striving of culture and the downward pull of nature. Wordsworth thus succeeds in turning this from the grand stone monuments of Simmel to the quotidian worker's cottage and the unfinished sheepfold.[35] But the temporality of "The Ruined Cottage," though working toward establishing a coherent frame for that moral, shows instead how ruin undermines temporal order and disrupts temporal scale. In this sense, Reinhart Koselleck, one of the most perceptive analysts of eighteenth-century *Neuzeit*, again provides a useful model for thinking about the kind of temporal effects I have been describing. For Koselleck, the particular combination of Copernican revolution and changes in science, the development of new technologies of communication and transportation, the increasing discovery of the globe and the so-called "uneven development" of its peoples, and the dissolution of long-standing social orders with the impact of industry and capital – what we might characterize as "modernity" – exposes "the contemporaneity of the noncontemporaneous, or, perhaps, rather, of the nonsimultaneous occurring simultaneously."[36] Koselleck cites the German publisher Friedrich Perthes to clarify this explosion of experience and perceived sense of acceleration characteristic of the later eighteenth century. For Perthes, "Our time has... united in three contemporary, existing generations, the completely incommensurable. The monstrous contrasts of the years 1750, 1789, and 1815 dispense with all interim and appear in men now living not as a sequence but as coexistence, according to whether they are grandfather, father, or grandson." In the later eighteenth century, then, "The one process of time became a dynamic of a coexisting plurality of times," a process that I have been repeatedly referring to as heterochrony.[37]

Koselleck explains these changes through a felt sense of acceleration, which makes it more difficult for those living in the eighteenth century to imagine the future because what he calls the "space of experience" (the way people relate to their present) no longer matches the "horizon of expectation" (their imagination of a potential future). I would suggest that the emergence of this temporal plurality or heterochrony is perhaps even more complicated because alongside the sense of temporal acceleration so amply described by Koselleck, we must also consider the simultaneous development of natural history and geology, which produces a dialectic of slowness and speed, a problematic of time, that marks virtually every aspect of Wordsworth's poetry. We have seen portions of this in my discussion of "The Ruined Cottage," and I will develop the point in Chapter 6 by eliciting the contrast between the accelerated time of the "Preface" and the speed of poems like "Expostulation and Reply" and "The Idiot Boy" and the slowness of figures like the old man traveling and the old Cumberland beggar (or, to gesture toward another example that I will not discuss, the hunger-bitten girl of *The Prelude*, book 9).

Similar to these ruined figures that slowly make their way across Wordsworthian landscapes, physical ruins like the ruined cottage also reveal the slow and gradual. They thus work to renounce suddenness, a repudiation that works to stir an acute awareness of what Nina Dubin calls "the sublime vastness of time."[38] Contrasting this element of slowness to accounts of modernity like those of Koselleck and Hartmut Rosa after him that conjoin the experience of modernization with acceleration, suggests that the temporality of ruins might be characterized through the idea of parallax. Derived from the Greek παράλλαξις (*parallaxis*), meaning "change" or "alteration," parallax was initially used figuratively to indicate seeing wrongly or in a distorted way, but has come to refer to "the difference or change in the apparent position or the direction of an object as seen from two different points" (Shorter OED). The term is predominantly spatial and is the principle used by astronomers to measure the distances to celestial objects, but I think that it can be applied to time as well. Accordingly, I want to propose the concept of what I call "time parallax" as a way of indicating the difference and disturbance – the distortion – that stems from the felt experience of a coexisting plurality of times of the sort that we see in "The Ruined Cottage" and elsewhere in Wordsworth's poetry. Such distortion or time parallax might more generally be understood to characterize the temporality of Romantic ruins.

In a typical demonstration of spatial parallax, an object set against a distant background will appear to align directly with the left side of a visual field when viewed from the right, but the same object will appear to align directly with the right side of the same field when viewed from the left. While calibrating the two perspectives allows for the accurate measure of distance, each single point perspective makes the same background appear as different or distorted. Similar visual effects occur when we illustrate parallax effects in three dimensions instead of two. When scanning a visual field in which objects are placed at varying distances from a single point, the objects closer to the point appear to move more quickly than objects in the distance. This, of course, is the key to depth perception and it helps humans and other beings with two eyes locate themselves in space. What I am calling "time parallax," while partaking of the general idea of perspective, is most closely akin to the movement effects of parallax in a three-dimensional field, but with one caveat: the perspectives and distance effects do not properly align. In a unified field of vision, one may see distant points differently but because the scale of such differences is consistent, seeming distortion can be properly calibrated by adjusting one's measurements from multiple points. But in the distorted temporal parallax that I am trying to characterize, and that I am suggesting can be seen in characteristic ways in Wordsworth's poem, distinct senses of time do not correlate. They cannot be made to correspond to a unified or nested sense of time, where different points within a temporal horizon can reliably be made to correspond to each other. It is as if the scale too adjusts with changes in perspective, and the various temporal scales at play fail to correlate. Or, to return to the example of a three-dimensional visual field, it is as if one were to scan a visual field in which objects placed at varying distances near and far all move at similar speed. Such distortion would make it ultimately impossible to locate the point of perspective in a three-dimensional field, impossible in other words to map one's position in space and consequently impossible not to feel lost and astray. Though described through a visual metaphor, this is the temporal experience conveyed by Wordsworth's poem and by time parallax more generally.

Central to the concept of time parallax, I want to suggest, is the perspective from which we view changes in time and consequently how we feel time's passage. In connection with "The Ruined Cottage," this effect is achieved by Wordsworth's close attention to a series of temporal markers from natural time to calendrical time, from the time of the sun and seasons to the quick flash of clock time that signals Margaret's demise. Here, time is both linear, as in the demise of Margaret's cottage, and cyclical, in the movements of Armytage and the rotation of the seasons. There is, of course, nothing extraordinary about this: we generally experience time as a mix of divergent and convergent rhythms. What is distinctive about time in "The Ruined Cottage," however, is that, as I have suggested above, this effect is so consistently rendered as disorientating or distorted because the different scales of time markedly do not correlate. Just as Robert, Margaret's husband, can locate himself in space but not in time, the manner in which the poem handles its interleaved scales of time works to produce a similar effect upon its readers. We too never quite know what time it is. The temporal disturbance or time parallax that I associate with ruin, in turn, is compounded by the experience of reading Margaret's time through the even, regular time kept by the meter of Wordsworth's iambic pentameter lines. Such regularity, in turn, works to bring into relief the irregular experience of time that it is used to describe.

Such effects of temporal distortion are distinctive of ruins more generally because ruins can be easily located in space, but the time that they tell cannot be placed. Instead, the ruin implies temporal process – something after all had to happen to produce ruin – but the ruin itself cannot provide an account of time's movement. We cannot know from looking at a ruined object when the ruin occurred, how long it took, what caused it, and this confusion produces an effect of knowing one's place but not one's time. It thus underscores, in my account, an experience of temporal confusion more generally, one produced by the meeting of processes of social acceleration keyed to the emergent rhythms of print media and the business cycles of commercial society with slower experiences of time commonly associated with the emergence of geology, with longer estimates for the age of the earth, and with nature generally. Romantic nature, I'm suggesting, is the same earth being theorized in geology. Poetry's printed media thus becomes a key locus for working out the intersection of the accelerated time of print capitalism and the slower, more recursive rhythms of nature. The figure of the ruin sits at precisely this intersection, calling our attention to the problem of time parallax.

If the effects that I am here calling time parallax are characteristic of Romantic ruins, this does not mean that all forms of time are distorted, or that it is impossible ever to measure or calibrate different senses of time into a coherent historical sense. While the ruin calls our attention to the distinctive difficulty of such reconciliation, Samuel Taylor Coleridge's account of the French Revolution invokes a tendency for temporal comparison and layering similar to that of the Romantic ruin. In Coleridge's attempt to calibrate distinct temporal processes between events in France and the Roman empire, however, comparison creates confidence and perhaps even precision rather than confusion, as we will see in Chapter 5.

CHAPTER 5

Coleridge's Slow Time

Chapter 4 introduced the concept of time parallax to indicate the difference and disturbance that stem from the felt experience of a coexisting plurality of times, something that this book has alternately referred to as heterochrony or more generally as temporal conflict. My suggestion in Chapter 4 was that this mode of experiencing the tensions between different ways of measuring and marking time that are so persistent in Wordsworth's "The Ruined Cottage" – daytime and nighttime, calendar time and seasonal time, clock time and bodily time – might be understood to characterize the temporality of Romantic ruins, which frequently suggest oblique and unmarked relations between past and present that can be interpreted alternately as a sentimental icon of distorted, disrupted time or as a mark of the continuity between time past and time present. More commonly, ruins combine both a sense of continuity and disruption, a sense of how slow time connects past with present, but also of how the ruin itself preserves dormant possibilities of the past for possible reactivation in the present. This is what Peter Fritzsche describes as the "half-life of the past" to characterize how new structures of temporality reveal the past as a source of latent and buried possibilities. Ruins, then, come to serve as a sign for the kind of broad speculations about the relationship between the past, the present, and, especially, the future that this book has suggested can be indexed through concerns about decline.

In this chapter, I want to associate heterochrony not with ruins per se or with the distorting effects that I call temporal parallax, but rather with the divided temporality that Samuel Taylor Coleridge uses to project the possible future of France under Napoleon. In a remarkable series of essays written for the *Morning Post* in 1802, Coleridge suggested that the situation in Napoleonic France was not just parallel to that of Rome under the Caesars but a precise repetition of that earlier historical moment, except that events in France unfolded much more quickly than in Rome. By contrasting the movement of time between antiquity and his present,

Coleridge enlarges the sense of temporal acceleration that this book argues is central to the experience of decline circa 1800, but he also develops an alternative in the slower movement of time that characterizes political transition in Roman antiquity. Such slow time is one of the latent possibilities from the past that are given new force and urgency in the present, as we will see especially in my reading of Wordsworth's poetry in Chapter 6. But slow time and accelerated time are not simply opposites, and problems of acceleration cannot be solved by slowness. Rather, as Coleridge's use of Rome underscores, slowness and acceleration are mutually imbricated, interpellated even. They emerge concurrently as part of a similar pattern of intensification and each divergent pace can be understood to contain the other, much as in Chapter 1, the acceleration associated with the development of commercial society was based on slow and gradual change, change that was "not sensible" in Adam Smith's term.

In his insistence that France under Bonaparte was a precise repetition of the transition from republic to empire in ancient Rome, Coleridge maintained that the only difference was "the degrees of rapidity with which the same processes have been accomplished." As he insists, "The reigns of the first three Caesars have been crowded into the three first years of the reign of Bonaparte."[1] Speed, then, is what distinguishes the present from the past. As Coleridge seeks to anticipate the outcome of Napoleon's rule, however, the legacy of imperial Rome, that earlier and slower historical moment, remains relevant as Coleridge uses the parallel between Napoleonic France and Rome under the Caesars to predict that Napoleon's decline will be as swift as his rise. Coleridge's argument here echoes a common understanding of the modern world as the heir to the ancient, an issue of continuity that turned, through much of the eighteenth century, on whether Europe might repeat the ancient cycle of decline and fall under the conditions of modern debt-financed warfare. As Michael Sonenscher suggests, in linking the classical past with the European present what came to matter in the eighteenth century was whether new mechanisms for financing warfare through national debt would produce a repetition of the ancient cycles of decline and fall. The threat to political stability and economic prosperity, in other words, "was not so much the inequality and luxury that, according to a long-standing tradition of political and historical analysis, had been responsible for earlier cycles of decline and fall, but the new financial instruments and fiscal resources that had accompanied the transformation of warfare during the seventeenth and eighteenth centuries."[2] Coleridge also links patterns of decline and fall in antiquity to his present moment, and he too moves away from an analysis of the link built around inequality and luxury, but for Coleridge the problem is not one of debt and credit. Rather, Coleridge adds to the issue of historical repetition and parallel the problem of historical speed or pace. Present events may repeat past events, but what distinguishes them is their "rapidity," the speed or pace at which they unfold.

In this reading, "Rome" functions as the sign for a series of events that form a complete set and whose outcome is known; it stands in contrast to the uncertain position in which Coleridge and his contemporaries find themselves in relation to their own present, but it can for them be used to shed light on that present and it can help to imagine the potential futures that might flow from it. In this sense, Coleridge's use of Rome might be seen as an extension of exemplary history, or what Cicero calls *historia magistra vitae*, a type of argument that had long characterized European thinking in which perceived parallels between events or individuals in the past and the present were used to offer contemporary models of political and moral prudence. Reinhart Koselleck has suggested that while this topos varies greatly its very longevity indicates its elasticity and its usefulness. Whatever doctrines *historia magistra vitae* could be made to support, however, the topos works only as long as certain assumptions and conditions are upheld, namely the constancy of human nature and the constancy of circumstances that admitted the introduction of the initial parallel. Any social change that occurred would have to unfold "so slowly and at such a pace that the utility of past examples was maintained."[3] According to Koselleck, "The temporal structure of past history bounded a continuous space of potential experience."[4] He argues, however, that this tradition of understanding the relationship between past and future breaks apart at the end of the eighteenth century as a result of the French Revolution and a corresponding new sense of time, *Neuzeit*. This new time is predicated on a rupture between past and future as the experience of the past ceases to correspond with horizons of future expectation. Such a modern conception of time makes the future less and less knowable, less and less related to that which precedes it. It is precisely this sense of rupture that Coleridge pressures as he links France and Rome.

Coleridge, then, might be understood as an anomaly within the broad trajectory of Koselleck's account of *Neuzeit* and the changing significance of the past. For a start, Coleridge refuses to recognize a sundering of the present from the past, and he continues to assert that "As human nature is the same in all ages, similar events will of course take place under similar circumstances" (*CW*, 3:312). This is the very constancy of circumstances that Koselleck suggests is requisite for exemplary thinking, and we should therefore not be surprised when Coleridge's analysis of the French under Napoleon uses Rome in an exemplary fashion. That analysis, however, also acknowledges the sense of temporal acceleration and the corresponding new time that Koselleck sees as formalized with the French Revolution and its aftermath. In Coleridge's account, analogies can be struck between Rome and contemporary European events, but those analogies must recognize one central distinction between the two, namely that the contemporary experience of time is different because things happen faster.

Coleridge, as we might expect, was not the only one to acknowledge the seemingly increased pace at which events unfolded. These kinds of claims for historical compression or intensification and a corresponding sense of temporal acceleration become commonplace by the end of the eighteenth century. William Eden, for example, when writing about the relationship between a particular point in time and a larger event that frames that moment, set out to characterize an "eventful period of history, in which a few years have given the experience of whole centuries."[5] Similarly, Byron's "Epistle to Augusta" suggests that he

> had the share
> Of life which might have filled a century
> Before its fourth in time had passed me
> by.   (stanza 14, lines 110–12)

For Coleridge, Eden, Byron and others the present moment is an accelerated present. Time is speeding up and history produces more experiences in a shorter time than one might have at other times. Coleridge's account of this process is distinctive, however, because it seeks simultaneously to insist on the exemplary parallel between present and past while also recognizing the present as fundamentally distinct from the past, primarily on account of the rapidity at which events now unfold. Within this context, Rome stands for Coleridge as the standard of time against which the present is measured. If, as Coleridge suggests, events happen faster, they happen faster in comparison to the events of Roman history.

As this chapter will argue, Rome particularly important for Coleridge as he developed his ideas about the aftermath of the French Revolution, but it was also central to Coleridge's understanding of time and his historical situation in the broader sense. We can thus understand Coleridge's reflections on the links between Napoleonic France and imperial Rome as part of the effort to understand the initiation of "revolutionary time," that new sense of time thought by many at the turn of the nineteenth century to be a product of the French Revolution. In the

context of revolutionary time, the possibility of change is both instantaneous and radically transformative because it produces a rupture between
past and present. Coleridge, I will show, uses Roman history to clarify his
present situation and to speculate about the future, and in this way we
might wonder about the perhaps paradoxical situation whereby ancient
events were used to articulate a fundamentally modern conception of time,
one grounded in the radical contingency and unknowability of a future
divorced from a ready connection to past precedent, one seemingly cut free
from the past. In this context antiquity, as we will see, serves as a stable
anchor, a period of time that because it has finished can be known. More,
for Coleridge Roman antiquity – and the transition from republic to
empire most pointedly – comes to be associated with a particular pace
and rate of change, and with slowness generally, a slowness that serves as
a marked contrast to the apparent speed of his present moment. But the
knowledge offered by the comparison of Roman antiquity with the
European present comes at a cost, for by invoking the Roman parallel
and using it to work out his prognostication of how events in France will
turn out, Coleridge also undermines the potential applicability of an earlier
historical trajectory (Roman antiquity) to the present because the two
historical trajectories transpire at fundamentally different paces. What
can be gained by comparison between two such temporally uneven durations of time? Is it even possible to link two series of events that are
understood to unfold at different speeds? In developing his comparison
between ancient Rome and revolutionary France, in other words,
Coleridge understands his present moment as at once joined to the past
and fundamentally sundered from it.

The argument of this chapter, then, focuses on the reception of Roman
antiquity by one of the central figures of Anglo-American romanticism,
but it offers a way of thinking about reception that is different from the
approach taken by many whose work fits into what has become the
burgeoning field of Classical Reception Studies. In keeping with
Reception Studies, this chapter generates its argument from techniques
of close reading, but its focus is not on the afterlife of particular ancient
texts, nor is it particularly concerned with models of influence and the
transmission of the corpus of an author or authors.[6] Instead, I am more
invested in tracing how Roman history, and the transition from republic to
empire specifically – more than a classical text, author, or set of authors –
functions as a sign of the classical more generally and on the subsequent
uses to which that sign is put in an effort to comprehend an unfamiliar
present and an uncertain future. "Rome" and "Roman history" in this

context function less as part of a textual reception history and more as what Simon Goldhill has described as "a horizon of recognition, a more diffuse sense of antiquity, or a more general sign of the classical,"[7] one commonly overlooked by the specificity and particularity of other more text-based approaches to the reception of antiquity.

The French Revolution has commonly been understood to initiate a new, modern sense of time. With their self-conscious and deliberate attempts to destroy the symbols and traditions of the past and their reorganization and renaming of the months and weeks by which time is "kept" and understood, the revolutionaries sought to initiate a new chronology originating retroactively with the Year One.[8] As Lynn Hunt argues, "A new relationship to time was the most significant change, and perhaps the defining development, of the French Revolution."[9] Most significantly for Hunt, the attempt of the revolutionaries to manage and control time signals a rupture, a break in secular time and a separation from the past. Like Hunt, Peter Fritzsche also sees a break in the understanding of time around the French Revolution, which is similarly understood as a rupture between past and present. For Fritzsche, "One of the distinguishing characteristics of the nineteenth-century sense of time . . . is the dramatization of change as the restless iteration of the new, and also the insistence that the experience of this change is unique and foundational to the idea of modernity."[10] Modernity, then, comes into being in conjunction with novelty, specifically with the "restless iteration of the new." As the claims of Hunt and Fritzsche indicate, "revolutionary time," with its interpretation of change as sudden and transformative, is a concept whose meaning and implications scholars continue to try to reconstruct today.

Whether this "restless iteration of the new" is a product of the French Revolution, however, is an open question, and one that, as we will see, Coleridge's essays on France and the Caesars help to complicate. Either way, one effect of being freed from the contingencies of the past is that elements of the past can be invoked as part of the present selectively and without the burden of historical continuity. In brief, the topos of *historia magistra vitae* has ended and the future becomes a more open and unpredictable problem.[11] The past, in turn, becomes available in a new way. It can be summoned no longer on the basis of a certain and secure parallel between a past and a present conceived as contiguous on the model of exemplarity, but rather more indiscriminately as a means to make an unfamiliar present seem familiar. This is something of what Marx was after when he described the French Revolution as being carried out through the precedents of the Roman republic. For Marx, the point here is that the invocation of Rome appears to be a summons to the past, but it is really a form of bringing a new future into being under the guise of repeating the past. As Marx explains:

> unheroic as bourgeois society is, it nevertheless took heroism, sacrifice, terror, civil war and battles of peoples to bring it into being. And in the classically austere traditions of the Roman republic its gladiators found the ideals and the art forms, the self-deceptions that they needed in order to conceal from themselves the bourgeois limitations of the content of their struggles and to keep their enthusiasm on the high plane of great historical tragedy."[12]

The instantiation of Rome here functions as a kind of false consciousness: it uses the familiarity of past precedent and the glory of the Roman past to hide the limitations of a present struggle. But it is emphatically not a parody of the Roman past it invokes: "the awakening of the dead in those revolutions served the purpose of glorifying the new struggles, not of parodying the old; of magnifying the given task in imagination, not of fleeing from its solution in reality; of finding once more the spirit of revolution, not of making its ghost walk about again."[13] Invoking the past, for Marx, does not provide a model to constrain present possibilities; instead, it is the very invocation of the past that brings the future into being.

The particularity of the French use of Rome has now been amply documented by scholars,[14] but for my purposes here, the point is that Marx's interpretation of the French cult of antiquity insists on how the classical past can be used, intentionally or not, to forge new and previously unimaginable futures. But invoking the past to bring a new and previously unimagined future into being is, of course, not the only way of reading the French use of Rome or the particular processes of temporal acceleration and renewal in which it is enmeshed. In the context of a new sense of time marked by its seeming rupture from the past with all of the uncertainty about the future that this brings, Coleridge's voice stands out in the absolute confidence with which he nonetheless ventures a future prediction, and that confidence is based on a combination of difference and continuity and an assertion that time is not singular, that time is filled with the presence of the now that can explode out of the continuum of history.

We find this most clearly in the series of three essays by Coleridge written for the *Morning Post* in 1802 in which he compares the present state of France with that of Rome under the Caesars. Like Marx after him who insisted that "all facts and personages of great importance in world history occur, as it were, twice,"[15] Coleridge was obviously aware of those many French patriots, those Brutuses and Gracchis and Publicolas, who dressed the novelty of their revolutionary activities in the borrowed clothing and tongue of the Roman past. His implicit purpose in the essays was to deflect attention away from France's claim to be a "new Roman Republic" by suggesting instead that if France resembled any period of Roman history it was not the Republic, but the period "when Rome ceased to be a Republic" (*CW*, 3: 314).

Having introduced the shift from republic to empire, Coleridge must work out the accuracy of the resemblance. Is it total, or only partial, he asks? Will it produce the same effects or have "the same duration" (*CW*, 3: 314)? In response, Coleridge argues that the parallel is total, and over the course of his three essays he develops a sustained comparison between the conditions of the late Roman republic and Europe at the turn from the eighteenth to the nineteenth century. Enlightenment skepticism, in Coleridge's account, is akin to Epicurean metaphysics and ethics; the Roman agrarian laws are the equivalent of the nationalization of Church lands in France; the granting of universal suffrage matches the effects in Rome of extending full citizenship to the Italian states, and so on. The results of this general pattern are the same as their initial occurrence in Roman precedent: a weakening of what Coleridge calls the "natural aristocracy" through the internal dissolution of luxury and skepticism and a correspondent strengthening of the "mad tyranny of the multitude," all of which produce a power vacuum filled by the military and their generals.

In the case of Coleridge, the acknowledgment of the deep parallels between Napoleonic France and imperial Rome might be understood as problematic since, even if we associate the Roman Empire with precariousness and tyranny, it did last over four hundred years. This, however, is why intensification and acceleration are so central to Coleridge's claims. Rapidity is the quality that Coleridge most associates with the French Revolution. Bonaparte, for example, as Coleridge notes in another set of *Morning Post* essays, "Affairs of France. II," should fear "the rapid spread of Royalism in France" (*CW*, 3:351). When France changes constitutions, it is a "rapid change of constitutions" that Coleridge describes in "On the Circumstances that Appear to Especially Favour the Return of the Bourbons at this Present Time" (*CW*, 3: 360), and, in "Our Future Prospects," when the French armies triumph it is in a "chain of rapid successes" (*CW*, 3: 421). Coleridge's invocation of historical parallel allows him to suggest that the future will unfold along predictable patterns gleaned from the classical past, but here and elsewhere, Coleridge's association of the French Revolution with rapidity means also that he can turn the increased speed at which events unfold in modernity to Britain's advantage in his prediction of the future. An emphasis on "degrees of rapidity" and related concepts like acceleration and intensification become the crucial distinctions around which Coleridge establishes the salient dissimilarity between imperial France and imperial Rome. According to Coleridge, the greater rapidity, the acceleration and intensification, with which the French empire has established itself under Bonaparte presages a shorter duration, "a duration as brief as its rise has been rapid" (*CW*, 3:324). This question of speed is central to Coleridge's analysis and it becomes the basis of the most significant differences he discerns between France and Rome.

Speed works in two ways in Coleridge's argument. First, he suggests that the establishment of the institutions of the Roman Empire was slow and deliberate. Augustus acted with "the utmost caution, slowness, and decency" (*CW*, 3:335). Popular liberties were not wiped out "at a blow" (*CW*, 3:336) and Augustan despotism, which maintained the forms of republican institutions, was "well concealed." Napoleon, in contrast, acted quickly and rashly in a manner that left his power like "an isthmus of Darien" by alienating both royalists and republicans. In the rapid establishment of his despotism, the French "are permitted to see what the Romans saw only after a lapse of forty-seven Augustan years" (*CW*, 3:336). Coleridge thus establishes the acceleration of contemporary historical processes through the prominent contrast between the speed of the present and the perceived slowness of the classical past. In characterizing the speed of events in France, Coleridge privileges the slowness of Augustus, which he associates with caution and decency. But it is the rapidity of Napoleon's rise that offers comfort and potential future security.

In this way, fast and slow can be understood to contain each other, and the process can be compared to a similar contrast in Wordsworth's "Preface" to the *Lyrical Ballads*, which was revised the same year that Coleridge's remarks were published. There, Wordsworth also expressed concern over the speed of contemporary life with his disdain for popular cravings after "extraordinary incident" that the "rapid communication of intelligence hourly gratifies."[16] For Wordsworth, as we saw in Chapter 2, such rapid communication and craving after incident produce a concomitant slowness, the "savage torpor" that blunts the discriminating powers of the mind. Coleridge privileges Augustan slowness but his perceived speeding up of contemporary time offers consolation because it augurs a more rapid end to the French regime; for Wordsworth the outlook is more ambivalent and, consistent with Fritzsche's emphasis on the "restless iteration of the new" as the distinguishing feature of the nineteenth-century sense of time, the increased speed of modernity serves only to gratify a craving for novel incident or event. For both Wordsworth and Coleridge, however, acceleration and slowness exist in a complicated interrelation in which the perception of speed enables the recognition of slowness and vice versa. The difference here is that while both characterize speed through its interrelationship with slowness, for Coleridge slowness is explicitly associated with antiquity. Indeed, slowness functions for Coleridge as the sign of the classical, a point to which I will return.

The second aspect of speed in Coleridge's argument, one that might also be linked to Wordsworth's emphasis on "rapid communication," concerns Coleridge's awareness of how the very speed with which Napoleon established his dictatorship exposes him to a further kind of acceleration: specifically, the more rapid speed of communications technologies, especially the newspaper. Of course the hand press in 1800 was no faster than it was in 1500, but Coleridge perceives communication as quicker because of the late eighteenth-century proliferation of print wherein more presses produced more writing. We can sense this as early as Coleridge's extended lyric from 1798, "Fears in Solitude," which opens with the calm retreat to "A green and silent spot, amid the hills, / A small and silent dell!" (lines 1–2) The stillness of this space then contrasts with the perilous world of events that surround it, a world brought to bear by the reading of a newspaper, "The best amusement for our morning meal!" But even here, the world of events is not simply one of speed that contrasts with the slowness of retreat. The vices that produce war work with "slow perdition," while the terms of war, in a further reference to slow, uneven movement, "trundle smoothly o'er our tongues," – where "trundle" suggests slow, heavy, and uneven movement – in a manner to which "no form" can be attached. Here it is processes of slowness and not speed that resist form, while with "quickened footsteps" the speaker of the poem returns home from his silent spot, rounding the poem back to where it began while bringing form rapidly from a moment of slow retreat. A lyric like this suggests the complicated temporalities that attach to such seemingly obvious distinctions between speed and slowness in Coleridge's work and also underscores how processes of speed and slowness work to contain each other in Coleridge's thought and indeed in Romanticism generally.

In his *Morning Post* essays, Coleridge has a more positive sense of the press and its powers. The French government, Coleridge insists, is "insecure," because "The very newspaper, which our reader has now in his hand, and which, in a few hours hence, he may probably rumple up for 'vile uses,' is so powerful an agent as to constitute an essential difference between the probable duration of a despot's reign in the present age, and that which it often was in the time of Imperial Rome" (*CW*, 3:330). Coleridge describes the printing press as "the only 'infernal machine'" that is truly formidable to a modern despot. It is the means for acquiring and perpetuating freedom, and need only be feared by the enemies of freedom. Furthermore, for Coleridge the press is so formidable and threatening precisely because of its speed, because of "the rapid intercommunication of thoughts and discoveries, the amiable social vanity, that is the result of this free intellectual commerce ..." (*CW*, 3:330). The point here is that like Wordsworth, Coleridge also associates acceleration with changes in communications technology, with what we would today describe as an explosion of print and with what Rolf Engelsing, in a much debated claim, calls a "reading revolution."[17] Romantic readers very much understood themselves to be living through a media as well as a political revolution, one that saw the creation of what Andrew Piper has described as "a new media reality" characterized by proliferation and excess, by the "imminent sense of too-muchness that surrounded the printed book."[18]

This raises an important question about Coleridge's analysis: is this modern sense of accelerated time, this increased rapidity of events, the result of the seeming eventfulness of the French Revolution, with its new calendar and its initiation of a corresponding new time, or is it rather a result of the seemingly increased speed of communications technologies and other processes of what we would today call mediation? The two explanations, of course, are not mutually exclusive. We have seen how Coleridge associates rapidity with the French Revolution, but, in addition to the analysis of the role of newspapers and media in Napoleonic France discussed above, a similar sense of rapidity also shapes Coleridge's understanding of communication generally. In his essay on Bonaparte from March 1800, Coleridge notes, "Yesterday we again received French Papers, and up to the 12th inst. The spring of the year approaching, in which nature begins to re-produce, and man re-commences the work of destruction, each successive communication, however undecisive the facts communicated may be, cannot but rise in interest. It is, therefore, a pleasing superstition, not wholly unworthy of momentary indulgence in a generous mind, to regard the late unwonted rapidity of intercourse as an happy omen."[19] Similarly, in an essay on peace from January 1800,

Coleridge suggests that "No rapidity of mutual communication can be expected from different armies of different nations, equal to that which the armies of a single nation, acting under one plan, will easily realize."[20] In both instances, communication is evaluated on the basis of its speed.

And yet despite the fact that Coleridge associates rapidity with both the development of the French Revolution and with communications technologies, it is not events in France but rather, issues associated with an emergent print media apparatus, specifically the problem of what Coleridge calls "publicity," that provoke one of his most explicit assertions that there has been no rupture; that past and present are not discontinuous; and that the only way to see through the fog produced by the craving after incident and the novel "wonders of the day," is to look to the past and to recognize its relevance for the present. As he explains in *The Statesman's Manual*:

> If there be any antidote to that restless craving for the wonders of the day, which in conjunction with the appetite for publicity is spreading like an efflorescence on the surface of our national character; if there exist means for deriving resignation from general discontent, means of building up with the very materials of political gloom that stedfast frame of hope which affords the only certain shelter from the throng of self-realizing alarms, at the same time that it is the natural home and workshop of all the active virtues; that antidote and these means must be sought for in the collation of the present with the past, in the habit of thoughtfully assimilating the events of our own age to those of the time before us.[21]

With the term "collation" – the action of comparing the sheets of a document or a printed book – Coleridge uses a bibliographical metaphor to understand historical parallelism. Such a move underscores Coleridge's shift in emphasis from the fear associated with dissemination and the rapid circulation of print, here associated with publicity, to a different kind of print, one associated with bibliography in which books are engines of slowness and the kind of media technology that allow for the "thoughtful" collation of present with past. The contrast between slow and fast media forms brings to mind Chapter 2's discussion of Vicesimus Knox in which Knox imagines books struggling to counteract the effects of newspapers. Moreover, with its emphasis on the linking of present and past as a means to transcend the craving for novelty and its corresponding alarmism, the passage further underscores this process of collation as offering renewed grounds for hope in a context of "political gloom." In this way, it might serve as a blueprint for Coleridge's earlier comparison of Napoleon and the first three Caesars, which develops the analogy precisely as a means to broadcast hope through its ultimate prediction of Napoleon's rapid fall. In working out the particularities of his more general claim, Coleridge reinforces the connection between imperial Rome and the European present, but his analysis is surprising because he uses the classical past to ground his analysis of temporal acceleration, which he perceives to be a most contemporary phenomenon. Coleridge's reading of the increased speed and eventfulness of the present can be compared to related accounts of speed in more recent theorists of modernity,[22] but his argument is distinguished by its long reach back to the classical past and by its related account of speed and acceleration as enmeshed with patterns of slowness, especially the slowness that stands for Coleridge throughout the essays as a general sign of the classical.

Like Marx, Coleridge insists on the parallel between France and Rome. For Marx, the significance of that parallel hinges not on exemplary thinking but rather, on a temporal rupture that enables the invocation of the past as the means to bring a new, bourgeois society into being. For Coleridge, in contrast, the link between France and Rome is genuinely backward looking where the outcome of past events constrains future possibilities. But this constraint on future possibilities, in turn, makes the future more not less knowable because the present situation in France is understood as being not just parallel to that of Rome under the Caesars, but a precise reduplication of that earlier series of events. History repeats itself.

We might even suggest that in Coleridge's account, past time gathers as water in a reservoir, to be reused and recycled as part of later present moments. In this way, Coleridge offers us an example of nonsynchronous time prior to that of Walter Benjamin in the twentieth century. Benjamin repeatedly distinguishes different senses of time as he introduces procedures of repetition and what he calls "the presence of the now" (*Jetztzeit*) in contrast to "the homogenous course of history." For Benjamin, significance is to be found not in "the concept of the historical progress of mankind" that stands inseparable from "the concept of its progression through a homogenous, empty time,"[23] but rather in those moments that manage to rupture the stasis associated with continuity. In testament to the potential violence of temporal change and the shift of temporal expectations, Benjamin continuously associates such interruptions of homogenous time with an explosive blasting: they "blast open the continuum of history" (262) or "blast a specific era out of the homogenous course of history – blasting a specific life out of the era or a specific work out of the lifework" (263). Such "blasting," which stands in marked contrast to Coleridge's gentler and less violent metaphor of collation, is especially marked in

Benjamin's discussion of the French use of Rome, in which he introduces the concept of "now time": "History is the subject of a structure whose site is not homogenous, empty time, but time filled by the presence of the now [*Jetztzeit*]. Thus, to Robespierre ancient Rome was a past charged with the time of the now which he blasted out of the continuum of history" (261). In Benjamin's account, historical experience does not pass but instead accumulates; it can be recalled and reintroduced in new circumstances. Time is at once always moving and always stopped, always available, but the means through which what Benjamin calls *Jetztzeit*, or what I have been calling revolutionary time, can be claimed by the present are always violent.

For Coleridge also, we might venture, time is neither synchronous nor homogenous, though his understanding of temporal repetition and of historical lives and works shifting out of the continuum of time is less mystical, less messianic, and less violent than that of Benjamin. Repetition is possible, but it is understood in much less explosive terms than for Benjamin. If Napoleon appears to repeat almost verbatim the historical structure and outcomes of the first three Caesars, it is not because the Caesars have been "blasted" out of time to interrupt the continuity of history, but rather precisely because they have not broken that continuity, have not blasted through anything. Repetition provides not the enhanced awareness of the now and the uncertainty of a future ripe with new messianic possibilities, but the return of the past. History repeats itself. The future is not open and unknown but rather, closed by the past. The future can be known, and this is why Coleridge can be so confident and so hopeful in his prediction of Napoleon's imminent decline.

Coleridge's understanding of historical repetition might also be likened to that of Giovanni Arrighi, the twentieth-century historian for whom later forms of capital accumulation are conceived as replicas or repetitions of earlier forms that recur within a structure of accelerated time and increased speed. Focusing on the shift of capitalist centers of production, Arrighi locates the origin of capitalist accumulation in a fifteenth-century Genoese-dominated model and traces its transition from the Italian states to seventeenth-century Amsterdam, nineteenth-century London, and twentieth-century New York. At each spatial shift, the later instantiation copies the forms of the earlier one. In Arrighi's account, however, the process is far more complex than simple imitation because the growth and spread of capital (what Arrighi calls "systematic processes of accumulation") is accompanied by vast changes in the size, scale, and complexity of each successive regime. The process also develops more quickly at each successive stage in what Arrighi describes repeatedly as "the speed up in the pace of capitalist history" such that "as we move from the earlier to the later stages of capitalist development, it has taken less and less time for systemic regimes of accumulation to rise, develop fully, and be superseded."[24] For Arrighi, then, the growth of capitalism – like the parallel between France and imperial Rome in Coleridge's analysis – is a prolonged process of imitation and repetition but under conditions of increasing speed and complexity. Though he does not describe it in these terms, the present that results from this process becomes, therefore, marked by a sense of time that is not singular but plural. Such non-singular time for Arrighi is uneven and driven by a theory of repetition in which each subsequent phase of capitalist accumulation repeats and intensifies that of the prior formation. The past, in other words, persists in the present and any one particular moment in the process functions as what Ian Baucom calls "an uncanny moment," a moment in which "present time finds stored and accumulated within itself a nonsynchronous array of past times."[25]

   If Coleridge's understanding of the intensification and non-synchronous character of historical change can thus be likened to both Benjamin and Arrighi, the salient distinction is that Coleridge rejects the language of violent rupture that Benjamin uses to characterize the re-emergence of the past in the present, with his language of blasting and exploding, in favor of a more bibliographically inspired language of inter-leaving and collation that produces a more predictable process of accelera-tion and intensification along the lines later modeled by Arrighi. The past is continuous with the present; it just unfolds at a more rapid pace. As Coleridge notes, France has been changed into an empire "by the same steps as the Roman Republic was, and under the same titles and phrases: only as before, differing in the degrees of rapidity with which the same processes have been accomplished. The reigns of the first three Caesars have been crowded into the three first years of the reign of Bonaparte" (CW, 3:316–17). For both Coleridge and Arrighi, the present moment is one whose "conditions of possibility have not waned but intensified, a present in which that 'past' survives not as a sedimented or attenuated residue but in which the emergent logics of this past find themselves enthroned as the dominant protocols of [a] 'nonsynchronous' contemporaneity."[26]

   For Coleridge, furthermore, the seemingly increased speed of the pre-sent is not a product of the French Revolution but is instead associated with a longer trajectory of print media and rapid communication. The French Revolution, in other words, does not set the inevitable condi-tions of Coleridge's modernity; rather it is modernity as a product of the

increased speed of communications technology and the specific rapidity of
print that constrains the French Revolution and shapes the conditions of
possibility for its future outcomes. Within this context, Coleridge defines
his media-saturated present through its processes of acceleration and
intensification, but the meaning of these processes is brought into relief
by their contrast with the slowness of imperial Rome. Rome and "the
classical" more broadly then come to stand as a general sign for a slowness
whose significance is elicited through its comparison with an accelerated
present. Indeed, we might even venture to suggest that the reason that
slowness is possible in Rome is because it provides an example of the full
imperial cycle of rise, growth, decline, and fall in the absence of a network
of mass media. In this sense, there are crowds and public opinion in
imperial Rome, but what Rome lacks are the media communications
networks, increasingly associated with print and with newspapers in particular by the time of Coleridge's writing in the early nineteenth century,
that turn public opinion into publicity and make the times, in Coleridge's
description, "crowded," with news, with novelty and with "the wonders of
the day."

The analysis can be compared to another more famous Romantic
touchstone in which the classical also serves as a mark of the slow.
The speaker of Keats's "Ode on a Grecian Urn" begins his address to the
urn by describing it as

> Thou still unravished bride of quietness,
> Thou foster-child of silence and slow time . . .

Keats here associates the urn with the absence of sound, with quietness and
silence. With his initial pun on the word "still" the absence of movement is
likened to undisturbed continuity through time, to a quality of being pure
and "unravished." As the poem continues, it is this lack of movement and
sound that most distinguish the scene depicted on the urn. It is a scene that
is explicitly visual and not verbal, expressing its "flowery tale more sweetly
than our rhyme," and while the speaker calls deliberate attention to the
material and visual qualities of the urn, the longing of the "Ode" might also
be understood as a longing to achieve a purity of representation akin to
what Winkelmann described as the "edle Einfalt und stille Größe" (noble
simplicity and grandeur) of classical material culture. In Keats's account,
such purity of representation ultimately becomes so transcendent as to
escape both the noise of mediation, those processes that come "in between"
and transmit ideas through their materiality, and the noise of history, the
realm in which things happen. It might even be argued that this quality of

directness and purity associated with the lack of sound and the lack of movement come to stand in Keats's urn for a particular kind of classicism more generally, one whose origins extend back to Winkelmann's influence on eighteenth-century aesthetics. Neither the "Ode" nor the urn, of course, can achieve the unmediated qualities for which they long, and like the lovers who can "never, never" kiss, though "winning near the goal," the transparency to which they appear to aspire to will never be reached. But like the lovers also, this failure has its compensations, in this case the reflections that the poem develops about the unavoidable quality of mediation and the rich potentialities of silence (those "unheard melodies"), stillness, and lack.

The contrasts through which these reflections are achieved and the manner in which the "Ode" constructs the classical are comparable to Coleridge's reflections on Rome. For Coleridge, as for Keats, the classical is marked by slowness, a slowness that acquires its full meaning through its contrast with the apparent speed of a newly mediated present, one driven by the "rapid inter-communication of thoughts and discoveries" made possible by the technologies of mediation like print. Print technology is understood to speed time; the classical, in contrast, stands as a space in which such technologies are absent, and in their absence a deliberate slowness emerges in Coleridge's account, while for Keats greater emphasis is placed on the stillness and silence that might nonetheless be associated with the slow. This is not to suggest that classical antiquity was any more slow or quiet than the present for Keats or Coleridge, but rather, that they use the perceived slowness and stillness that they associate with antiquity to mark the present as a time of increased speed and noise.

It is tempting to stop there, but there is something else in Keats's introduction of the urn. In addition to the urn's unspoiled quality, its stillness and quietness, and despite attempts to locate the scene on the "leaf-fringed legend" with a moment out of time, the poem cannot avoid acknowledging the movement of time, just as it cannot avoid acknowledging the inevitability of mediation. For the urn is a "foster-child" not only of "silence" but also of "slow time." It is a "sylvan historian" that keeps record of the deeds contained on its surface. Echoing the earlier description of the urn's "leaf-fringed legend" Keats's use of "sylvan" here contains a pun that, like Coleridge's use of "collation," represents the slow time of antiquity through the bookish metaphor of the leaf. This characterization of the urn as an historian, and one explicitly associated with the book, works as a reminder of its timekeeping qualities, a reminder that the urn is a material remnant of the classical past. The time kept by the urn, though, is "slow time" and, just as in Coleridge's representation of imperial Rome, this works to further the association of the classical with slowness.

Slow time can also serve as a reminder, though, of a different kind of time, a time that we might today call "deep time" and that we would associate with geology, the earth sciences, and other emerging disciplines that, among other concerns, expanded estimates of the age of the earth and introduced the possibility of species adaptation and extinction. The temporal emphasis of this kind of thinking moves not towards the intensification described by Coleridge and others, but rather, towards the expansion of time found in the work of Buffon, Saussure, de Luc, Hutton, Blumenbach, Desmarest, Lamarck, Cuvier, and others. What this means is that the perceived acceleration of modernity that marks Coleridge's account of Napoleonic France can be understood to develop in relationship to the longer timescales of natural or geological history. Perceptions of speed are inherently related to perceptions of slowness, and with the increasing awareness of the vastness of the timescale needed to grapple with the age of the earth and processes of species adaptation and extinction, the comparative eventfulness and speed of the present become clearer.

While Coleridge's reading of the seemingly increased speed and eventfulness of the present can, as this chapter has shown, be compared to related accounts of acceleration in Marx, Benjamin, Koselleck, Arrighi, and other more recent theorists of modernity, his argument differs from their diverse accounts. It is distinguished by the manner in which it uses its long reach back to the classical past and its invocation of a classical exemplar, imperial Rome, and a particular form of mediation, the arboreally inspired book, to imagine a more complex temporal framework. In Coleridge's account, imperial Rome stands as a general sign of the classical, one that comes to mark forms of slowness more generally. But Coleridge does not simply contrast the slowness that he associates with antiquity with the speed and rapidity that he recognizes to be a fundamental, and fundamentally new, quality of the present. Instead, Coleridge understands speed and acceleration as enmeshed with patterns of slowness, especially the slowness that stands for Coleridge as a general sign of the classical. Coleridge's account, in other words, is motivated by a more dialectical incorporation of speed and slowness, antiquity and modernity, in which each quality is seen to contain the other. Coleridge thus represents time, and the complex layering of time that he understands as central to the interpellation of past and present, not as layers of different periods of time that can be sharply distinguished as "eras" or "ages" and understood as part of a movement in the direction of present and future progress, but rather as layers of different time frames that can be analogized and understood in relation to one another despite the different speeds at which they unfold. Coleridge's Rome thus offers an opportunity to think about how "Rome" enabled new ways of thinking about both the future and the past, which simultaneously encouraged a sense of compression and expansion, disrupting progressivist historical assumptions and altering perceptions of the pace and scale of time.

CHAPTER 6

Fast Time, Slow Time, Deep Time: Decline, Extinction, and the Pace of Romanticism

You can see the wheels turning. A young Charles Darwin, recently graduated from Cambridge, sets out late in 1831 with Captain Robert Fitzroy on the HMS *Beagle*. Having met gauchos, learned to hunt exotic birds, and escaped from a violent revolution in Buenos Aires, Darwin makes a base in what is now Uruguay, where he collects fossils of giant armadillos, ground sloths, and other extinct mammals. The contrast between the sudden violence of human revolution and the slow, less obviously violent change of the earth's surface must have been telling. In Darwin's *Journal* of these years (published 1839; 2nd ed., 1845) we can see the raw material of what would eventually become his theory of evolution. Perched at the tip of South America, Darwin considers the long pebbled coastline and reflects, "When we consider that all these pebbles, countless as the grains of sand in the desert, have been derived from the slow falling of masses of rock on the old coast-lines and banks of rivers; and that these fragments have been dashed into smaller pieces, and that each of them has since been slowly *rolled, rounded*, and far transported, the mind is stupefied in thinking over the long, absolutely necessary lapse of years."[1]

Within the frame of this long, almost incomprehensible lapse of years, Darwin began to reflect not so much on the origin of species but on their extinction. Doing so allowed him to offer a corrective to the view, expressed in Buffon's *Natural History* (1749–1788), that nature in the Americas was less vigorous than in Europe and a product not of adaptation but of degeneration and diminution: "If Buffon had known of the gigantic sloth and armadillo-like animals, and of the lost Pachydermata, he might have said with a greater semblance of truth that the creative force in America had lost its power, rather than that it had never possessed great vigour" (*EW*, 12). What, the question becomes, could have exterminated so many species and genera, so many flora and fauna? Darwin suggests that our first instinct is to imagine "some great catastrophe" (*EW*, 12). But the geological record will not support this conclusion: the larger, now extinct quadrupeds are recent enough – and I emphasize the relativity of the term recent – that their disappearance could not have resulted from climactic or geographic change. Reaching for his Malthus, Darwin proposed an alternative: that the supply of food is constant, but all animals tend to reproduce geometrically. Something, then, must check a great increase in numbers. The precise nature of this check, while generally inappreciable, is unlikely to be sudden. There is, Darwin concluded, an economy of nature, and within this economy adjustments are made slowly. Rarity precedes extinction, and although the slow process through which the adjustment is made makes it impossible to see, we should not therefore simply assume some sudden violence: "To admit that species become rare before they become extinct – to feel no surprise at the comparative rarity of one species with another, and yet to call in some extraordinary agent and to marvel greatly when a species ceases to exist, appears to me much the same as to admit that sickness in the individual is the prelude to death – to feel no surprise at sickness – but when the sick man dies, to wonder, and to believe that he died through violence" (*EW*, 14).[2]

The inappreciable check on species growth, however, is never specified. Ultimately, in *On the Origin of Species* (1859), Darwin would call this the struggle for existence, and he is led eventually to his theory of evolution. In place of the catastrophe that Darwin rejected, we get a motor force of change that is no less violent, but whose violence is slower, more constant, sustained, and often hidden from view. In an oft-cited passage, Darwin observes, "We behold the face of nature bright with gladness, we often see the superabundance of food; we do not see, or we forget, that the birds which are idly singing round us mostly live on insects or seeds, and are thus constantly destroying life; or we forget how largely these songsters, or their eggs, or their nestlings, are destroyed by birds and beasts of prey" (*EW*, 133).

I dwell on these reflections in particular detail in order to emphasize Darwin's interest in extinction and decline, death and disappearance, and, more importantly, his fascination with slowness – what I have been calling in this book "slow time." What makes possible this protracted, slow understanding of time as something that is glacial and stony, characterized by rocks more than trees, gray rather than green, incomprehensibly prolonged and yet not infinite? The conditions of possibility for Darwin's theory are of course overdetermined. Darwin's writings show a clear awareness of debates about timescale like those between Cuvier and Lamarck in the early nineteenth century, while explicitly acknowledging the influence of Malthus and Charles Lyell, among others. Scholars have largely taken these sources at face value. My claim here, however, is that Darwin's recognition of invisible violence, slow time, and the related mental wrangling with the unimaginably long periods of time that frustrate human comprehension (what we now call "deep time") might also be understood as an outgrowth of changes in the understanding of time that this book has shown developing in the later eighteenth century.

To talk about virtually any aspect of Darwin's theory requires an awareness of the plenitude of time and the consequent slowness of its movement. Such a fundamental reconfiguring of time grows most often out of the increasingly large estimates for the age of the earth and its development from Buffon forwards. Time, of course, has only one speed, but the ways that humans imagine time are extremely variable, both culturally and historically. Long time therefore is not necessarily slow time, but the longer model of time introduced by Buffon and others and taken up later by Darwin understands change differently than the sudden change favored by the catastrophic model that Darwin rejects. Evolutionary change takes longer because it occurs slowly, and the length of time required for change is made possible by the increasing recognition of longer time spans more generally. A new appreciation for slowness becomes a byproduct of these extended spans of time. We can thus understand Darwin's appreciation for the slow in connection with the slow time that this book has observed developing from the rejection of decline jeremiads by Adam Smith; in the depiction of slow, gradual processes that are "not sensible" in Playfair's graphs; in Coleridge's comparison of ancient Rome with modern France; in Keats's urn; and, now, in the poetry of Wordsworth. But such refiguring also raises representational and formal problems: how can humans imagine and grasp the slowness of time and the presence of temporal processes that operate below the level of the visual? The recognition of long timespans made by Buffon and his contemporaries, as Martin Rudwick has shown, requires above all a leap of the imagination.[3] And if we are to judge from the historical record, it also requires poetry, or at least the poetry produced in the decades we associate with the Romantic period.

Poetry helps here because in light of new ideas about time in the later eighteenth century, it served as an important source not just for representing slow time, but also for working out its imaginative and formal implications. In my argument, therefore, Romantic poetry stands as an unacknowledged, potent source for Darwin's thinking about slowness. Further, I contend that the temporal problems confronted by Darwin and his Romantic precursors have never fully disappeared; they continue to shadow current thinking about slow time and invisible violence. Considering the dialogue between

Romantic verse and slow time, I believe, can help to explain change in a range of timescales, from the simple past, to the antique past to things ever more deep and remote. After Wai Chee Dimock and Mark McGurl, "deep time," though contested, has become an important new term in the literary critical toolbox.[4] The term refers to a geological scale of events that require a vastness of time unimaginably longer than the timescale of human history. Deep time in this sense is conventionally more closely aligned with the long timespans required for Darwin's theories. Slow time by contrast refers to human attempts to grasp imaginatively a pace of change that cannot be seen and that leaves few if any visible traces. In this way, slow time gives us a way into grasping the near-infinite plenitude of deep time, that deeper past of the earth's history itself. Put another way, slow time mediates temporal experience and, in the process of this mediation, enables us to see the emergence of the longer timeframes associated with deep time by providing a bridge between human history and natural history.[5]

Slowness is not a quality that we traditionally associate with modernity, which is more generally characterized by a perceived acceleration or speeding up, one commonly instigated by advances in technologies of communication and mobility like print and the railway.[6] But feelings of speed and acceleration associated with print saturation and a later eighteenth-century media shift also produced new understandings of slowness like those eventually developed by Darwin and exemplified in Chapter 5 by Coleridge's analysis of Napoleonic France and in this chapter by Wordsworth's poetry of unspectacular time. In suggesting that a recalibration of the relationship between perceived acceleration and slowness helps to shape Darwin's theory, I am not insisting on a model of direct influence but rather a threshold of emergence more akin to a Foucauldian archaeology of discourse.[7]

This might seem to take us far from my ostensible subject of decline, but my suggestion is that concepts like extinction for Darwin and the bodily decay seen in so many of Wordsworth's marginal figures are proximate to the discussion of decline developed over the previous chapters. Such concepts are linked by the manner in which they work to index a new relationship to time and a new sense of history that this book has suggested is a central feature of concerns about decline across a range of discourses.

Though the historical period we call "Romantic" has been distinguished by the revival of romance, by the flourishing of philosophical aesthetics, by Revolution and reaction, and by the experience of war, my suggestion is that one of the defining features of this period is a sense of discordant temporality that responds to innovations within the conception of time, and more specifically, to a new sense of slowness perceived beneath but in close relation to the more commonly acknowledged sense of the acceleration or speeding up of contemporary life. This new sense of time produces "disturbance or unease," and a "particular type of tension," related to what Raymond Williams calls a "structure of feeling," that can be grasped by looking at the formal and representational problems shared by Wordsworth's and Darwin's writings.[8] This structure of feeling persists: When I claim that Darwin's recognition of slowness is part of a structure of feeling that can be linked to the adjustment between entangled senses of acceleration and slowness that make their relation felt fully in the later eighteenth century, therefore, I intend to suggest the later eighteenth-century qualities of other related and more recent attempts to rethink slowness and to grapple with our own current temporal confusions.

Ursula Heise, for example, has coined the term "chronoschisms" to characterize a "sense of time that in its discontinuity, its fragmentation into multiple temporal itineraries and its collisions of incommensurable time scales highlights and hyperbolizes certain characteristics of a culture of time," one that she locates as beginning in the 1960s.[9] My suggestion, however, is that this supposedly postmodern sense of time might more accurately be traced not to the 1960s but rather to the later eighteenth century. More recently, in his manifesto on "slow violence," Rob Nixon has called for a project of redefining speed, a redefinition that recognizes the formal, representational challenges of showing effects delayed over long stretches of time and that emphasizes the particular difficulty of such formal problems in the context of turbo-capitalism and what Nixon calls "an era of enclaved time wherein for many speed has become a self-justifying, propulsive ethic that renders 'uneventful' violence... a weak claimant on our time."[10] In response, Nixon proposes a recasting of the glacial as "a rousing, iconic image of unacceptably fast loss."[11] It's an arresting image, and while I am sympathetic to both the urgency and the aims of Nixon's intervention, it overlooks how an earlier, eighteenth-century awareness of the increased speed and acceleration of contemporary life is already interpellated with the recognition of a concomitant slowness. Speed, slowness, and the collision of incommensurable timescales do create formal problems, as Heise and Nixon insist, but these formal problems are not new. They might better be understood as later eighteenth-century problems whose terms and contours, whose representational experiments, we can recognize especially in what I will characterize as a Wordsworthian – and even a more broadly Romantic – poetics of slowness.

Acceleration

In the "Preface" to the *Lyrical Ballads*, Wordsworth declares that,

> a multitude of causes, unknown to former times, are now acting with
> a combined force to blunt the discriminating powers of the mind, and,
> unfitting it for all voluntary exertion, to reduce it to a state of almost savage
> torpor. The most effective of these causes are the great national events which
> are daily taking place, and the increasing accumulation of men in cities,
> where the uniformity of their occupations produces a craving for extra-
> ordinary incident, which the rapid communication of intelligence hourly
> gratifies.[12]

This oft-quoted passage describes Wordsworth's understanding of his
contemporary moment. The present is for Wordsworth what Lévi-
Strauss would call a "hot chronology,"[13] a moment marked by a seeming
plenitude of happenings: "great national events," urbanization, and rapid
communication, all of which, for Wordsworth, have literary and aesthetic
impact. They blunt the discriminating powers of the mind and cause the
best works of British literature – Shakespeare and Milton – to be neglected
in favor of "sickly and stupid German Tragedies, and deluges of idle and
extravagant stories in verse." Though I have previously read this passage in
connection with the proliferation of print and Wordsworth's related
suspicion of eventfulness,[14] here, the relation between the fast and the
slow is of particular interest. As we saw previously, Wordsworth associates
his present with both an eventfulness (more things seem to be happening)
and a speeding up in which the communication of this eventfulness is
"rapid." But such an intensification and acceleration also produces
a slowing down in most of those who experience it, what Wordsworth
describes as the "almost savage torpor" of the audience for poetry circa
1800, where "torpor" describes not only insensibility, but also inactivity
and even the unmoving state of a hibernating animal.[15] This is an initial
indication of how fast and slow begin to contain one another in
Wordsworth's writing.

Wordsworth's sense of acceleration and eventfulness arising from the
rapid communication of information as characteristic of his contemporary
moment aligns him with more recent theorists like Paul Virilio, Jürgen
Habermas, Reinhart Koselleck, Hartmut Rosa, and Giovanni Arrighi (to
name a few) who also insist that such quickening is one, perhaps even *the*,
defining quality of modernity.[16] Virilio, for example, argues that speed is
the dominant element of modern life. Taking his cue from the Greek
dromos, or race, he coins the term "dromology" to characterize the method

by which he works through the critical role of brakes and accelerators as modernity moves "at speed from the confines of space to the exigencies of time."[17] Rosa, for whom "*the experience of modernization is an experience of acceleration,*"[18] is perhaps most comprehensive in his focus on acceleration as the quality that increasingly sets present apart from past. But all of these thinkers associate the perceived acceleration of the present with advances in technology and especially with the increased speed of successive communications media. Wordsworth also associates his contemporary moment with a speeding up linked to the spread of mass communications technology and the seeming explosion of newspapers, periodicals, and related publications. Romantic readers like Wordsworth, as shown by recent work grounded in contemporary media theory, very much understood themselves to be living through a media revolution as well as a political revolution.[19] For Wordsworth the excess demand for news created by its rapid communication produces a dearth of response; speed and slowness are locked into a recursive pattern akin to a feedback loop. What distinguishes Wordsworth's response to the perceived acceleration of modernity, then, is the complex manner in which he understands processes of acceleration and slowness to be conjoined.

Slowness

Wordsworth's understanding of acceleration and his association of the increasing speed of communications technologies with the diminished intellect of the audience for poetry circa 1800, I now want to suggest, has implications for how we read Wordsworth's poetry. If later eighteenth-century historical actors sensed the acceleration of time, and if some, like Wordsworth, were alarmed by it, we can begin to interpret what I would like to describe as a poetics of slowness as a carefully thought out response to this quickening. Wordsworth's poetry responds to this excess of speed by intentionally slowing things down. The poetry can thus be understood as minimally stimulating specifically in order reciprocally to heighten responsiveness. This suggests, in other words, a way of reading Wordsworth's poetry focused on its manifest content but also attuned to the effects it tries to create for its readers, where the deliberate production of a minimum of stimulation works to develop skills of attentiveness. Put slightly differently, we might say that Wordsworth's poetry takes up Rob Nixon's clarification of the representational challenges inherent in making "slow violence visible" while also challenging "the privileging of the visible."[20] Nixon adds that "In a world permeated by insidious, yet unseen or imperceptible violence, imaginative writing can help make the unapparent appear, making it accessible and tangible by humanizing drawn-out threats inaccessible to the immediate senses. Writing can challenge perceptual habits that downplay the damage slow violence inflicts and bring into imaginative focus apprehensions that elude sensory corroboration. The narrative imaginings of writer-activists may thus offer us a different kind of witnessing: of sights unseen."[21] The terms are Nixon's, but this might easily be read as the program for Wordsworth's contribution to the *Lyrical Ballads* project and for works like "The Ruined Cottage" and Wordsworth's poetry of the late 1790s more generally.

Read this way, Wordsworth's emphasis on the slow becomes a kind of hortatory slowness, one that responds to a perceived quickening, to the fast becoming faster, with an aesthetic and moral appreciation of the slow. This kind of attitude, for example, marks the development of the *Lyrical Ballads* project. I am thinking here about the speed and bustle of poems like "The Idiot Boy," whose effects are achieved not only through the description of speed but also through formal qualities like repetition and the use of galloping tetrameter, and "The Tables Turned," with its jarring and urgent opening appeal to haste aided and abetted by explanatory punctuation, "Up! Up!" "Nutting" perhaps most of all exemplifies the speed of sudden violence, when amidst the calm stillness of the nook of hazels marked by "quiet being" and "silent trees" the speaker rises up "And dragg'd to earth both branch and bough, with crash / And merciless ravage" (43–44).[22]

Such poems that turn on haste and rapid change contrast with the slowness and contemplation of "Tintern Abbey," the Lucy poems, and (later, in 1807) "The Leech Gatherer," but especially with "The Old Man Travelling" and "The Old Cumberland Beggar." In "Old Man Travelling," for example, the subject of the poem travels unregarded by the little hedgerow birds:

> He travels on, and in his face, his step,
> His gait, is one expression; every limb,
> His look and bending figure, all bespeak
> A man who does not move with pain, but moves
> With thought—He is insensibly subdued
> To settled quiet: he is one by whom
> All effort seems forgotten, one to whom
> Long patience has such mild composure given,
> That patience now doth seem a thing, of which
> He hath no need.   (3–12)

Though the language of the slow here is not explicit, the entire passage emphasizes particular qualities of stillness and calm. The old man moves, but he does so with singular purpose and with thought. A phrase like "settled quiet" serves to elicit qualities of stillness within movement and contributes to how the tenor of the passage builds to an emphasis on patience so marked and ingrained that it "now doth seem a thing, of which / He hath no need." A poem about traveling thus becomes a poem about traveling slowly with fixed purpose and settled quiet – the very picture of unspectacular time. The labored quality of the verse here, with its frequent use of pauses and midline caesuras and its patterns of repetition ("he is… he is," "one by whom… one to whom"), all underscore Wordsworth's attunement to the parallels between the steps of the traveler and the feet of the line, and, further, how the formal qualities of the verse and the pace of the traveler who moves "not with pain" but "with thought" both stand for a particular kind of slowness associated with the use of thought to overcome pain and invisible violence. Moreover, the slowness of the old man carries its own kind of intensification. Movement such as there is remains in the service of slowness and the wisdom of the old man is a quality indicated through pace. If one suffers into truth, it is a process that does not happen instantly, but over time as character comes to be ingrained in a particular slowness. Intensification is a quality generally associated with acceleration by theorists of modernity, especially Virilio and Rosa, but we see here that such intensification can also be part of an opposite and contrary formation, a result of slowing down as opposed to speeding up.

Perhaps the most remarkable emblem of slowness in the early Wordsworth is the Old Cumberland Beggar, who moves so slowly and with such little impact that,

> His staff trails with him, scarcely do his feet
> Disturb the summer dust, he is so still
> In look and motion that the cottage curs,
> Ere he have pass'd the door, will turn away
> Weary of barking at him.   (59–63)

This scene suggests a profound eventfulness – or uneventfulness – that happens so slowly, with such patient deliberation that the sound of the event, as marked by the barking dogs, ends before the event itself has concluded. In this way, it is a moment that we might compare to the famous opening of Pynchon's *Gravity's Rainbow*, one of the classic handbooks for the post-'68 media-theoretical establishment: "A screaming comes across the sky. It has happened before, but there is nothing to compare it to now. It is too late. The Evacuation still proceeds, but it's all theatre."[23] In Pynchon, the sound that marks the event comes after it is over and the event itself, the fall of a V2 rocket, happens so quickly that, by the time it is heard, "It is too late." The point for Pynchon is that knowledge of the event cannot keep pace with the event because the event itself, as registered on the senses, has always already happened. Though he does not discuss Pynchon, we might suggest that for a theorist like Paul Virilio the speed of the V2 as captured by Pynchon's description encapsulates the essence of modernity. It shows what Virilio calls "the extermination of space,"[24] which has lost its relevance due to developments in weapons technology to the point that "all that counts is the speed of the moving body and the undetectability of its path"; further, "without the violence of speed, that of weapons would not be so fearsome."[25] Speed here is understood as acceleration and intensification, which are conceived as part and parcel of the same formation. What I am suggesting, in contrast, is a more complex formation in which the increased speed associated with modernity is mutually generative of an increased slowness. This is why qualities associated with one are also so often present in the other. In contrast to the speed in Pynchon's opening, for Wordsworth the duration of the event is so drawn out, the pace of it so slow that the beggar almost becomes part of the landscape. Knowledge of the event – the barking dogs that we might consider a pastoral predecessor to Pynchon's screaming rockets – cannot keep pace with the event because it unfolds so slowly as almost perpetually not to have happened yet. The event is so slow that it ceases to be acknowledgeable.

Such slowness is not merely decorative or paradoxical. Rather, the figure of the beggar and that of the old man traveling achieve importance by the effect that they have on those who see these figures of long-suffering endurance picking their way through the landscape. The patience of the old man, for example, causes the young to behold him "with envy" (14). He serves as a model, as the epitome of a particular kind of slow patience. Ultimately, the effects of the Cumberland Beggar are also explicitly moral: he shows the inseparable links between "every mode of being," and

> ... the villagers in him
> Behold a record which together binds
> Past deeds and offices of charity
> Else unremembered. ...   (88–91)

The beggar stands as an emblem of the moral economy, one under attack by what Wordsworth describes in his note as the political economists' "war on mendacity." Philip Connell is therefore absolutely correct to link this poem to late eighteenth-century debates on poverty and alms in one of the best current readings of the poem.[26] But before Wordsworth describes the moral effect that the beggar has on the wider community, we see the particular effect that he has on three individual figures, each of whom break their pace and interrupt their work as a result of the encounter:

> The sauntering horseman-traveller does not throw
> With careless hand his alms upon the ground,
> But stops, that he may safely lodge the coin
> Within the old Man's hat...   (26–29)

Here, the interrupted rhythm of the line, the way the start of the third line forms a pause between two longer unpunctuated phrases causes the experience of the reader to mimic the stop of the horseman. The tollgate keeper similarly "quits her work" (35) while even the postboy "Turns with less noisy wheels to the road-side, / And passes gently by" (41–2). The "sauntering horseman-traveller," the tollroad, and especially the postboy are all markers of the increased mobility and speed that we associate with modernity, and yet the beggar causes each to brake. His slowness exists surrounded by acceleration but in deliberate relationship to it. This braking effect mimics also the experience of reading the poem as its deliberate lack of eventfulness forces qualities of attentiveness and scrutiny that demand slow reading.

Wordsworth's emphasis on the slow and his understanding of the complex and often fraught relationship between slowness and speed bears comparison with a range of other Romantic poems that also present slow time in dynamic relationship to more obvious processes of acceleration. William Cowper's 1785 poem *The Task*, for example, uses its position of retreat and removal – its sense of slow processes of repose – to make sense of the speed and hurry of urban life, especially as that haste is mediated by the newspaper. Additionally, if Wordsworth develops a poetry that, in Nixon's terms, "bring[s] into imaginative focus apprehensions that elude sensory corroboration" (15) then Keats, as we saw in Chapter 5, uses the classical as a general sign of the slow and offers an understanding of slowness in response to an explicit visual image and material object to which, however, he assigns a new temporal significance. We might think also of Charlotte Smith's *Beachy Head*, which combines Wordsworth and Keats by offering a version of pedestrianism that in its crisscrossing of the landscape works to excavate that which is buried or invisible and hence to turn up new understandings of time that arise from the interplay of the fast and the slow, the material and the immaterial, the concealed and the visible. The temporal emphasis of this kind of thinking includes the acceleration that Wordsworth and Keats associate with their contemporary media culture in its representation of the texture of everyday life, but Smith's poem also explicitly encompasses the expansion of time found in early geology. Collectively, these poems and others like them reveal how perceptions of speed are inherently related to perceptions of slowness, and how the comparative eventfulness and speed of the present emerge alongside an increasing awareness of intricate processes of slowness and invisible change related but not limited to the vastness of the timescale needed to grapple with the age of the earth. This, I have been suggesting, is a central concern in a Romantic poetics of slowness, one indicated by, but by no means limited to, my central examples from Wordsworth's poetry of the 1790s.

Wordsworth, Darwin, and the Slow

Robert Richards has argued for Darwin's thought as an extension of Romanticism. Though his contention is grounded in a German Romantic tradition, with Alexander von Humboldt as a key link, Richards acknowledges the additional influence of Wordsworth, who teaches Darwin the importance of poetry for scientific thought because it is through imagination that one tries out ideas for more analytical accounts. Further, in Richards's account, poetry – Milton's in particular – solves Darwin's metaphysical conundrum about struggle and death: in Milton's cosmos these very obstacles produce the higher creatures and the greatest perfection. Poetry thus helps Darwin recognize that nature "very gradually and over long periods of time refined and shaped her creatures."[27] Collectively, such claims underscore for Richards the aesthetic aspects of Darwin's thought and the close links between science and literature; more importantly for my account, Darwin's aesthetic sensibilities, according to Richards, help him reject the fits and starts, the sudden changes, of a mechanistic account of nature and to recognize instead the slow, gradual processes on which his theory depends.

My argument so far has shown the centrality of slowness for Wordsworth in particular, which can also be extended to much Romantic poetry more generally. I now want to suggest that Darwin inherits formal and representational problems related to slowness from

Wordsworth. My argument thus expands the sources of Richards's claims from a German to an English context in a manner less insistent on direct influence, though we can see overlap between Darwin and his Romantic precursors, especially Wordsworth. We know that Darwin in his early years was an avid reader of Wordsworth's poetry, and his writings are marked by resonances of Wordsworthian language. In the passage with which I began, the suggestion that all of the pebbles along the Uruguayan coast had been "slowly *rolled, rounded,* and far transported" echoes Wordsworth's Lucy "*Rolled round* in earth's diurnal course, / With rocks, and stones, and trees." Similarly, in Darwin's reference to "the face of nature *bright with gladness,*" the conjunction between the terms might also be thought of as Wordsworthian. In the "Ode," for example, Wordsworth addresses

> Ye that through your hearts today
>> Feel the *gladness* of the May!
> What though the radiance which was once so *bright*
> Be now for ever taken from my sight. . .   (173–76)

This is also a poem about suffering and disappearance, about the passing away of "a glory from the earth" (18) and the way in which a tree, a field, and a pansy all speak to the poet of immanent loss, of passing away, of an extinction that establishes the burden of the poem's eventual redemption. While telling, such echoes are admittedly limited and an argument for the relevance of a Wordsworthian poetics of slowness to the development of Darwin's thought will require more than a series of verbal echoes.

Beyond the particular resonances of Wordsworthian language, Alan Bewell has taught us to recognize how Wordsworth's poetry models a fascination with the marginal, with the dispossessed, and with a series of social and racial types on the verge of extinction.[28] These marginal figures contribute to what I have been describing as a poetics marked not only by figures nearly extinct but also by rocks and stones and by the interaction and frequent figural transposition between the marginal and the rocks. Indeed, the prominence of rocks in Wordsworth's poetry has prompted Paul Fry to ask whether "the nature poetry of Wordsworth is green or gray" given that "'rocks and stones' make up two thirds of the Wordsworthian cosmos."[29] Similarly, in *Romantic Things*, Mary Jacobus devotes a chapter to rocks, which she suggests provide Wordsworth with a key for reading nature's silences. Jacobus's attention to the resonances between rocks and the nearly extinct is clear in her argument that the Leech Gatherer "records the infinite slowness of glacial time."[30] These emphases on Wordsworth's fascination with rocks should come as no surprise, of course, after Noah Heringman's convincing argument that "the literary culture producing this poetry was fundamentally shaped by many of the same cultural practices that formed geology as a science during the period 1770–1820."[31] In this way, both Wordsworth's writing and the formation of geology might be understood as offering an archaeological framework for Darwin's appreciation of nature's slowness and the extinct former beings whose specimens Darwin collected on his voyage.

Wordsworth's "The Old Cumberland Beggar" is telling in this context. The beggar serves for those around him as both a container for sympathy and collective local memory and as a brake for the increasing speed and mobility of modern life, the class to which he belongs, as Wordsworth makes clear, "will probably soon be extinct." When Wordsworth used this term it would not have had the particular association with natural history and species extinction; rather, the term was mainly associated with the history of landed families. Darwin's concept of extinction, as Gillian Beer notes, "expanded the idea of family, away from the exclusiveness of 'pedigrees and armorial bearings' (*Origin*, 486), to embrace all 'the past and present inhabitants of the world' (488)."[32] In using the concept of extinction to describe a class of mendicant beggars, we might understand Wordsworth as anticipating Darwin's expansion of the concept. The link provides one instance of how Wordsworth's poetics of slowness contributes to the development of Darwin's thought.

We can further note how the beggar serves for the villagers as "a record" much the same way that for Darwin, as for Lyell, Cuvier, and others before him, fossils and rocks serve as a record of the prehuman history of the earth. Next, just as Darwin sees all organic beings, both extant and extinct, as belonging to the "same system,"[33] Wordsworth describes the beggar as part of a natural economy that is linked relationally and in which there is no waste:

> Tis Nature's law
> That none, the meanest of created things,
> Of forms created the most vile and brute,
> The dullest or most noxious, should exist
> Divorced from good, a spirit and a pulse of good,
> A life and soul to every mode of being
> Inseparably link'd.   (73–79)

The suggestion here is a less hierarchical version of the older concept of a great chain of being, one in which all matter and life, "every mode of being," are "inseparably linked." In this way, the slowness of the beggar, and Wordsworthian slowness more generally, is laden with moral value, with alternative ecosystems to the quickening of the wider world. Such slowness partakes in "a spirit and a pulse of good." Darwin, on the contrary, is eager to call our attention to the violence that lies beneath slow, drawn-out processes in the natural economy that he describes in his theory of evolution and extinction. If Wordsworth's slowness is often benevolent, Darwin's slowness is violent. I am suggesting, in other words, that Darwin adapts Wordsworth's poetics of slowness, but he abandons its chain-of-being suggestion in favor of a new model that sees such interdependence as part of a violent struggle for existence dissociated from moral values. Both are part of what I have earlier described as a structure of feeling predicated on a particular type of tension between the seemingly accelerated, fast time of modernity and the slow time of evolutionary change.

The fossils Darwin collected on the *Beagle* are literally indurate objects, bodies become rocks, that in their transformation tell us about duration, about time, and about the history of life on earth. If scholars like Heringman have placed their emphasis on induration, on the materiality of terrestrial history and geoformation in Romantic literature and science, my interest in the conjunction between Wordsworth, Darwin, and geology is more about duration, about time. In the passage set on the pebbled coastline of Uruguay with which this chapter opened, Darwin's rejection of sudden violence as a cause of extinction adapts Wordsworth's poetics of slowness. It is also an obvious reference to the French naturalist Georges Cuvier, who argued for a binary theory of life on earth. Applying his considerable skills in comparative anatomy to the fossil record, Cuvier suggested that, in a former age, a broad range of species like the famous *Megatherium* found in Paruguay (Darwin's "giant sloth"), populated the earth. At some point, however, a great catastrophe wiped out this entire range of life-forms. A second set of species, including humans, then developed after this catastrophe. One prominent opponent of Cuvier's theory was the botanist Jean-Baptiste Lamarck, who rejected the possibility of extinction in favor of a model of transformation and species adaptation. Lamarck essentially turns Cuvier on his head and suggests that the greater the contrast between fossils and living forms, the more it proves ubiquity of transmutation in a vast timescale rather than extinction. Despite its emphasis on unimaginably long swaths of time, Lamarck's theory forecloses the possibility of a true history of the earth because "at no point would the system be distinctive or characteristic of *that specific time*."[34]

The early nineteenth-century dispute between Cuvier and Lamarck centered on mummified ibis brought back as part of Napoleon's spoils from the conquest of Egypt. The identity between these 3,000-year-old birds and those still living was said by Cuvier to disprove the possibility of transmutation. Lamarck, however, insisted that a mere three millennia was way too brief a timescale in which to observe species transformation. Such changes happen too slowly to be observed by humans. As Lamarck notes, "for nature, time is nothing."[35] The dispute between the two hinges around how we understand the historical nature of life on earth, and, more importantly for my purposes here, on the problem of extinction as it relates to the scale of time in which we imagine the earth's development.

It will come as no surprise that Darwin developed his theory in relation to important precursors like Cuvier and Lamarck, and the point has been amply developed by scholars. We can locate this push toward larger time-scales not only in Lamarck and Cuvier, but also in Buffon, Saussure, de Luc, Hutton, Blumenbach, Demarest, and other savants discussed by Martin Rudwick in his magisterial *Bursting the Limits of Time*. Hence the perceived acceleration of modernity, commonly dated to the later eighteenth century, can be understood to develop in relationship to the longer timescales of natural or geological history, what Keats would call "slow time," but which is at present more commonly called "deep time."[36] For my purposes, however, the very changes that Rudwick describes in relation to the expansion of timescale by savants is part of a more widespread and less disciplinarily specific understanding of time that gains currency in the later eighteenth century and develops through the Romantic period. The accelerated time felt by Wordsworth and Coleridge and described by theorists of modernity and the slow time epitomized by Wordsworth's poetics of slowness and Darwin's ideas about extinction and evolution both emerge together. I am interested now in how Darwin addresses the representational problems framed by the interpellation between these two competing – but also, as I have suggested, complementary – ideas of time, and also in how the relationship between these two orders of time relate to the kind of measured, calibrated, and scalar time that formed the subject of Chapter 1 of this book.

Recall that the account of measured, scalar time began in Chapter 1 with Adam Smith's rejection of decline jeremiads. In rejecting these arguments, Smith's response aimed to identify quantifiable economic criteria through which decline might be measured, but it also emphasized the need to calibrate one's temporal perspective for the longer term – especially the unit of the century, the time frame that Smith thought most relevant for the exposure of economic trends. Similarly, as we also saw in Chapter 1, Gibbon's *Decline and Fall* explained Rome's decline as part of a long narrative of the advance of civilization and not as part of an inevitable cycle that Europe was doomed to repeat. Here, Gibbon's narrative of decline and fall transformed, from the broader scale of four millennia, into a story of the advance of civilization in which collapses like that of Rome proved less enduring than a broader pattern of progress. The shift in the understanding of time developed in that chapter was marked not only by an emphasis on new kinds of data measured over longer periods of time, but also by innovations in later eighteenth-century visual and print cultures like the charts of Joseph Priestley (Figure 1.1) and William Playfair (Figures 1.2–1.4) that attempt to convert spans of time that are virtually impossible to imagine into charts and graphs that can be grasped at a glance.

Perhaps not surprisingly, an emphasis on timescale and on the unimaginably slow movement of time that he inherited from his later eighteenth-century precursors marks Darwin's entire oeuvre. Despite scholarly emphasis on Darwin's idea of struggle, what Spencer would later term "survival of the fittest," Darwin uses variants of "slow" one and a half times more frequently than he uses "struggle." Slowness more even than struggle is what enables the theory of evolution. But, as Rob Nixon reminds us, slowness poses formal problems and requires figural resources. Just how slowly do the processes of extinction and adaptation take place and how can such processes be represented? The opening chapters of *On the Origin of Species* focus on the accumulation of minute variations over long periods of time that eventually produce marked divergences. When, for example, Darwin expresses his astonishment at those fanciers of pears and apples who refuse to believe that a Ribston Pippin or Codlin apple could have been produced from the seeds of the same tree, he notes that "they ignore all general arguments, and refuse to sum up in their minds slight differences accumulated during many successive generations" (*EW*, 119). The "many successive generations" here are soon qualified as the "centuries or thousands of years" (*EW*, 123) that Darwin suggests it has taken "to improve or modify most of our plants up their present standard of usefulness to man" (*EW*, 123). But, it quickly becomes clear, this is really not the timescale that Darwin has in mind in the *Origin*.

We can begin to grasp just how long the timescale Darwin's theory requires when we consider the diagram that Darwin offers us to show species differentiation over time (Figure 6.1). This image has fourteen horizontal lines. The interval between each line, Darwin tells us, represents

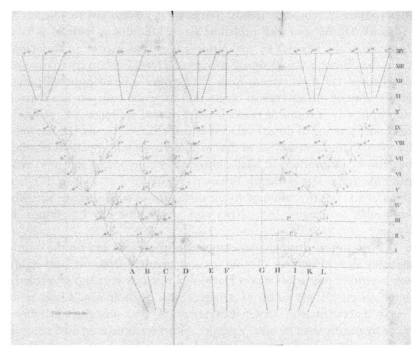

Figure 6.1: From Charles Darwin, *On the Origin of Species by Means of Natural Selection*. London: John Murray, 1859

a thousand generations, but he quickly adds that "it would have been better if each had represented ten thousand generations" (*EW*, 164). As Darwin begins to reach for the conclusions that can be drawn on the basis of this chart, he qualifies this figure yet again and says, "In the diagram, each horizontal line has hitherto been supposed to represent a thousand generations, but each may represent a million or hundred million generations" (*EW*, 169). A thousand, ten thousand, a million, a hundred million – numbers whose increase in ordinal power start to stretch the limits of our imagination, but which represent merely the start of the vast stretches of time that Darwin's theory requires.

Darwin himself was aware of this problem. His theory required "a lapse of time... so great as to be utterly inappreciable by the human intellect" (*EW*, 192). This, of course, is the problem of deep time: that it eludes representation and often requires a temporal span so large as to be almost without meaning. How, after all, can we comprehend the significant difference between ten million and a hundred million years, or, for that matter, even ten million and eleven million years? And yet this is also the representational problem that Darwin must confront if he wants to make the case for slow and gradual change within an almost incomprehensibly long time span that is nonetheless not infinite. In this context, slow time paves the way for the imaginative leap. Darwin understands the difference that deep time makes, and to render a vast timescale comprehensible he turns not to the kind of narrative thinking deployed by Wordsworth and Coleridge, but to a visual aid, a printed chart. Darwin's willingness to expand the significance of each horizontal line (those labeled with Roman numerals), then, indicates not a backsliding or confusion on his part, but rather underscores how the chart itself depends fundamentally upon a uniformity of scale. Scale is heterochronic. The same spatial representation can be used for very different experiences of time. What is interesting and innovative about Darwin's chart, then, is that it joins fast and slow into a variant of deep time that can now be made available to representation, that, like Playfair's charts but to an even greater extent, offers the possibility of accounting for vast swaths of time at a single glance, in the same amount of time that you can account for shorter periods of time.

In calling attention to the multiple temporalities enabled by Darwin's chart, I do not mean to suggest that Darwin has solved the representational problem of deep time; rather, I want to underscore how Wordsworth and Darwin face related formal problems in their attempts to call attention to unspectacular but not insignificant events, events that are characterized by an intensity of slowness that commonly escapes representation but that must nonetheless be shown in relationship to time. Such formal and representational problems, moreover, do not disappear, and, indeed, they continue into the present as attested by Rob Nixon's recent call for a redefinition of speed in relation to slow violence. The conditions for these ongoing problems, I have suggested, are set in the later eighteenth century when a sense of acceleration and eventfulness generated by print media – and revealed through a range of concerns about decline detailed in the previous chapters – develops in felt tension with new understandings of slowness and new awareness of the increasingly large estimates for the age of the earth that we now associate with deep time.

Notes

Introduction

1. For details of the painting and its eventual exhibition in 1832 as *Architectural Ruins—A Vision*, see Brian Lukacher, *Joseph Gandy: An Architectural Visionary in Georgian England* (New York: Thames & Hudson, 2006), esp. 161–66.

2. See especially Gibbon's "General Observations on the Fall of the Roman Empire in the West," the last chapter of the original third volume of *The History of the Decline and Fall of the Roman Empire*, ed. David Womersley, 3 vols. (London: Allen Lane, Penguin Press, 1994), 2: 508–516.

3. Isaac D'Israeli, *An Essay on the Manners and Genius of the Literary Character* (London: printed for T. Cadell, Junr. and W. Davies, 1795), vii.

4. Adam Smith, *An Inquiry into the Nature and Causes of the Wealth of Nations*, ed. Edwin Cannan (1904; reprint, Chicago: University of Chicago Press, 1976), 365 (hereafter cited in text as *WN*).

5. [William Hazlitt], "The Periodical Press," *Edinburgh Review* 38 (May, 1823): 349–78; quote from 357. On ephemerality, see "Ephemerality," chapter 8 of The Multigraph Collective, *Interacting with Print: Elements of Reading in the Era of Print Saturation* (Chicago: University of Chicago Press, forthcoming).

6. Ibid, 358.

7. William Wordsworth, "Preface" to *Lyrical Ballads* (1798, 1800), in *Wordsworth and Coleridge: Lyrical Ballads*, 2nd ed., eds. R. L. Brett-Smith and A. R. Jones (London: Routledge, 1991), 241–72, quote on 249 (hereafter cited in text as *LB*).

8. See William St. Clair, *The Reading Nation in the Romantic Period* (Cambridge: Cambridge University Press, 2004) and John Guillory, *Cultural Capital: The Problem of Literary Canon Formation* (Chicago: University of Chicago Press, 1993).

9. See, for example, Laurence Goldstein, *Ruins and Empire: The Evolution of a Theme in Augustan and Romantic Literature* (Pittsburgh, PA: University of Pittsburgh Press, 1977); Thomas McFarland, *Romanticism and the Forms of*

Ruin: Wordsworth, Coleridge, and Modalities of Fragmentation (Princeton, NJ: Princeton University Press, 1981); Anne Janowitz, *England's Ruins: Poetic Purpose and the National Landscape* (Cambridge, MA: Blackwell, 1990); Sophie Thomas, "Assembling History: Fragments and Ruins," *European Romantic Review* 14, no. 2 (2003): 177–86; and Nina Dubin, *Futures and Ruins: Eighteenth-Century Paris and the Art of Hubert Robert* (Los Angeles, CA: Getty, 2010).

10. *The Connoisseur by Mr. Town, Critic and Censor-General*, no. 3 (Thursday, February 14, 1754).

11. Maureen N. McLane, *Romanticism and the Human Sciences: Poetry, Population, and the Discourse of the Species* (Cambridge: Cambridge University Press, 2000). See also Philippe Lacoue-Labarthe and Jean-Luc Nancy, *The Literary Absolute: The Theory of Literature in German Romanticism*, translated by Michael Metteer with Chris Cullens (Stanford: Stanford University Press, 1988).

12. Adam Smith, *Lectures on Rhetoric and Belles Lettres*, ed. J. C. Bryce (Indianapolis, IN: Liberty Fund, 1985), 112; [William Hazlitt], "The Periodical Press," *Edinburgh Review* 38 (May, 1823): 358. This is also what the *Edinburgh Review* later described as the "universal hurry" of modern life, *Edinburgh Review* 17, no. 33 (1810): 170.

13. Stephen Arata, *Fictions of Loss in the Victorian Fin de Siecle* (Cambridge: Cambridge University Press, 1996), i.

14. Vincent Sherry, *Modernism and the Reinvention of Decadence* (Cambridge: Cambridge University Press, 2015), 200.

15. Sherry, *Modernism and the Reinvention of Decadence*, 60.

16. Sherry, *Modernism and the Reinvention of Decadence*, 60.

17. Jürgen Habermas, *The Philosophical Discourse of Modernity: Twelve Lectures* (Cambridge, MA: MIT Press, 1987), 6.

18. See David Spadafora, *The Idea of Progress in Eighteenth-Century Britain* (New Haven, CT: Yale University Press, 1990).

19. Reinhart Koselleck, *The Practice of Conceptual History: Timing History, Spacing Concepts*, trans. Todd Samuel Presner and others, (Stanford, CA: Stanford University Press, 2002), 164 (hereafter cited in text as *CH*).

20. Reinhart Koselleck, *Futures Past: On the Semantics of Historical Time*, trans. Keith Tribe (Cambridge, MA: MIT Press, 1985), 271 (hereafter cited in text as *FP*). See esp. "'Space of Experience' and 'Horizon of Expectation': Two Historical Categories," 267–88.

21. Koselleck, *Conceptual History*, 231.

22. Peter Fritzsche, *Stranded in the Present: Modern Time and the Melancholy of History* (Cambridge, MA: Harvard University Press, 2004), 5 (hereafter cited in text as *SP*).

23. Lynn Hunt, *Measuring Time, Making History* (Budapest: Central European University Press, 2008), 25.

24. Hunt, *Measuring Time, Making History*, 70.

25. Hunt, *Measuring Time, Making History*, 68.

26. Adam Smith, *Lectures on Rhetoric and Belles Lettres*, ed. J. C. Bryce (Indianapolis, IN: Liberty Fund, 1985), 112; *Edinburgh Review* 17, no. 33 (1810): 170.

27. D'Israeli, *Literary Character*, xviii–xix.

28. For important work on Romanticism and geology, see Noah Heringman, *Romantic Rocks, Aesthetic Geology* (Ithaca, NY: Cornell University Press, 2004), and Mary Jacobus, *Romantic Things: A Tree, A Rock, A Cloud* (Chicago: University of Chicago Press, 2012).

29. See Chandler, *England in 1819: The Politics of Literary Culture and the Case of Romantic Historicism* (Chicago: University of Chicago Press, 1998); Trumpener, *Bardic Nationalism: The Romantic Novel and the British Empire* (Princeton: Princeton University Press, 1997); Duncan, *Scott's Shadow: The Novel in Romantic Edinburgh* (Princeton: Princeton University Press, 2007; and Buckland, *Novel Science: Fiction and the Invention of Geology* (Chicago: University of Chicago Press, 2013).

30. Samuel Taylor Coleridge, *The Collected Works of Samuel Taylor Coleridge*, vol. 3, *Essays on His Times in "The Morning Post" and "The Courier,"* ed. David V. Erdman (Princeton, NJ: Princeton University Press, 1978), 3:316–17.

31. Coleridge, *Collected Works*, 3:312.

32. Reinhart Koselleck, *"Historia Magistra Vitae*: The Dissolution of the Topos into the Perspective of a Modernized Historical Process," in *Futures Past: On the Semantics of Historical Time* (Cambridge, MA: MIT Press, 1985), 21–38.

33. Charlotte Smith, *Charlotte Smith: Major Poetic Works*, ed. Claire Knowles and Ingrid Horrocks (Peterborough, ON: Broadview Press, 2017), 176, 178.

34. Anna Barbauld, *Anna Letitia Barbauld: Selected Poetry and Prose*, eds. William McCarthy and Elizabeth Kraft (Peterborough, ON: Broadview Press, 2001), 162; lines 33–34. Further references to this edition will be cited by line number in the text.

35. William Wordsworth, "Preface" to *Lyrical Ballads* (1798, 1800), in *Wordsworth and Coleridge: Lyrical Ballads*, 2nd ed., ed. R. L. Brett-Smith and A. R. Jones (London: Routledge, 1991), 241–72, citation from 249.

36. Kevis Goodman, *Georgic Modernity and British Romanticism: Poetry and the Mediation of History* (Cambridge: Cambridge University Press, 2004), 3–4.

37. Goodman, *Georgic Modernity*, 12.

38. Mary Favret, *War at a Distance: Romanticism and the Making of Modern Wartime* (Princeton, NJ: Princeton University Press, 2009), 9.

39. Favret, *War at a Distance*, 11.

40. Anne-Lise François, *Open Secrets: The Literature of Uncounted Experience* (Stanford, CA: Stanford University Press, 2007).

41. See, for example, Julian Go's *Patterns of Empire: The British and American Empires, 1688 to the Present* (New York: Cambridge University Press, 2011), with its development of the parallels between Britain and the US from 1688 to the present or, more popularly, Cullen Murphy's *Are We Rome?: The Fall of an Empire and the Fate of America* (Boston, MA: Houghton Mifflin, 2007), which looks at the contemporary US alongside the Roman Empire.

42. Examples here are legion, and increasingly common. Much recent attention has been paid to Éric Zemmour's *La suicide français* (Paris: Albin Michel, 2014), and we can think in the US case of similarly nostalgic works like Thomas Friedman and Michael Mandelbaum's *That Used to Be Us* (New York: Farrar, Straus and Giroux, 2011) or Patrick Buchanan's *Suicide of a Superpower: Will America Survive to 2025?* (New York: Thomas Dunne Books, 2011).

43. Paul Keen, *Revolutions in Romantic Literature: An Anthology of Print Culture, 1780–1832* (Peterborough, ON: Broadview Press, 2004), 184.

44. William St. Clair, *The Reading Nation in the Romantic Period* (Cambridge: Cambridge University Press, 2004), 172.

45. Anna Barbauld, *Eighteen Hundred and Eleven,* in *Anna Letitia Barbauld: Selected Poetry and Prose*, eds. William McCarthy and Elizabeth Kraft (Peterborough, ON: Broadview Press, 2001), 160–173.

Chapter I

1. Reinhart Koselleck, *Futures Past: On the Semantics of Historical Time*, trans. Keith Tribe (Cambridge, MA: MIT Press, 1985); see esp. "*Historia Magistra Vitae*: The Dissolution of the Topos into the Perspective of a Modernized Historical Process," 21–38, and "'Space of Experience' and 'Horizon of Expectation': Two Historical Categories," 267–88.

2. J. G. A. Pocock, *Virtue, Commerce, and History: Essays on Political Thought and History, Chiefly in the Eighteenth Century* (Cambridge: Cambridge University Press, 1985), 98, 99.

3. In Koselleck's account, this shift in the ways in which those living in the eighteenth century imagined the future is not limited to economic concepts like debt and credit, but can be extended also to science and related developments in technology and industry, and to the implications of the use of reason and rationality more generally.

4. Quoted by Donald Winch, *Riches and Poverty: An Intellectual History of Political Economy in Britain, 1750–1834* (Cambridge: Cambridge University Press, 1996), 50. The reply also gives Winch the title of a subsequent essay on Smith. See Winch, "A Great Deal of Ruin in a Nation," in *Understanding Decline: Perceptions and Realities of British Economic Performance*, eds. Peter Clarke and Clive Trebilcock (Cambridge: Cambridge University Press, 1997), 30–48.

5. Winch, "Great Deal of Ruin in a Nation," 39, 45.

6. Bernard Bailyn characterizes 1776 as a watershed year for its particular interpellation of "challenges of force and of statecraft" (445) with intellectual events like Gibbon's *Decline and Fall* and Smith's *Wealth of Nations*, but also Thomas Paine's *Common Sense*, Richard Price's *Observations on the Nature of Civil Liberty*, and Jeremy Bentham's *Fragment on Government*. For Bailyn, who relates all these events to economic and demographic shifts building through the Atlantic world in the eighteenth century, this is a "year of extraordinary, world-transforming challenges in every sphere of life—in ideology, in politics, in government, in religion, in economics, in law, in the uses of military force, and in the basic principles of international relations. In the annals of Western history there is probably no equivalent *annus mirabilis*, so far-reaching in its challenges and in the range of its ultimate consequences" (445). See Bailyn, "1776 A Year of Challenge—A World Transformed," *Journal of Law and Economics* 19, no. 3 (1976): 437–66.

7. This is one of the central arguments of Foucault's *The Order of Things: An Archaeology of the Human Sciences* (New York: Random House, 1970) and recurs repeatedly throughout as, for example, when Foucault claims that for "eighteenth-century thought, chronological sequences are merely a property and a more or less blurred expression of the order of beings; from the nineteenth century, they express, in a more or less direct fashion, and even in their interruptions, the profoundly historical mode of being of things and men" (276).

8. Here, as will become clear, I follow Mark Salber Phillips's recent work on historical distance. See *On Historical Distance* (New Haven, CT: Yale University Press, 2013). For an earlier version of this argument, see Mark Salber Phillips, "Rethinking Historical Distance: From Doctrine to Heuristic," *History and Theory* 50, no. 4 (2011): 11–23; for further reflection on historical distance, see the articles collected in the special issue, edited by Jaap den Hollander, Herman Paul, and Rik Peters, on "Historical Distance: Reflections on a Metaphor," *History and Theory* 50, no. 4 (2011).

9. Michael Sonenscher, *Before the Deluge: Public Debt, Inequality, and the Intellectual Origins of the French Revolution* (Princeton, NJ: Princeton University Press, 2007), 6.

10. Edward Gibbon, *The History of the Decline and Fall of the Roman Empire*, ed. David Womersley, 3 vols. (London: Allen Lane, Penguin Press, 1994), 1:103 (hereafter cited in text as *DF*).

11. See Arnoldo Momigliano, "Declines and Falls," *American Scholar* 49 (Winter 1979): 37–51.

12. In chapter 3 of *Decline and Fall*, for example, we learn that "A martial nobility and stubborn commons, possessed of arms, tenacious of property, and collected into constitutional assemblies, form the only balance capable of preserving a free constitution against the enterprises of an aspiring prince" (*DF*, 1:85). This reassuring explanation of the Glorious Revolution then expands to Europe later in the same chapter, when Gibbon notes in the final paragraph, "The division of Europe into a number of independent states, connected, however, with each other, by the general resemblance of religion, language, and manners, is productive of the most beneficial consequences to the liberty of mankind" (*DF*, 1:106).

13. J. G. A. Pocock, *Barbarism and Religion,* vol. 3, *The First Decline and Fall* (Cambridge: Cambridge University Press, 2003), 304.

14. Pocock, *Barbarism and Religion*, 314.

15. Reinhart Koselleck, "*Historia Magistra Vitae*: The Dissolution of the Topos into the Perspective of a Modernized Historical Process," in *Futures Past: On the Semantics of Historical Time*, trans. Keith Tribe (Cambridge, MA: MIT Press, 1985), 21–38.

16. "The greatest improvement in the productive powers of labour, and the greater part of the skill, dexterity, and judgment with which it is any where directed, or applied, seem to have been the effects of the division of labour" (*WN*, 7). As Duncan Forbes claims in his seminal essay on Smith, "The idea of the progress of society was the central theme and organizing principle of the social philosophy that he envisaged." Similarly, one of the main claims of Nicholas Phillipson's intellectual biography of Smith is that there is no Adam Smith problem: his work is completely of a piece and consistent with an attempt to develop a systematic science of man, one based on what Phillipson consistently refers to as a "theory of improvement." See Duncan Forbes, "'Scientific' Whiggism: Adam Smith and John Millar," *Cambridge Journal* 7 (1954): 649; and Nicholas T. Phillipson, *Adam Smith: An Enlightened Life* (New Haven, CT: Yale University Press, 2010).

17. Phillips, *On Historical Distance*, 6 and passim.

18. On relations between Smith's *Theory of Moral Sentiments* (1759) and *The Wealth of Nations* see John Dwyer, who argues that the "concept of the impartial spectator was a metaphor for moral judgment in *Theory of Moral Sentiments* and... entirely consistent with the combined economic and ethical role that Smith attributed to the gentry in *Wealth of Nations*."

Dwyer, "Ethics and Economics: Bridging Adam Smith's *Theory of Moral Sentiments* and *Wealth of Nations*," *Journal of British Studies*, 44 (Oct. 2005): 662–87, quote from 679. See also, Jonathan Sachs, "Scales of Time and the Anticipation of the Future: Gibbon, Smith, Playfair," *Modern Intellectual History* 11.3 (2014): 697–718; esp. 704–09.

19. This point brings to mind Zhao Enlai's response when asked in the early 1970s about the impact of the French Revolution: "Too early to say." Though this is now thought to have been a mistranslation of a question about the 1968 uprisings in Paris, the point stands.

20. Records of Smith's *Lectures on Jurisprudence*, as subsequent notes will show, make it clear that Smith had been thinking of this issue at least since the 1760s.

21. There, Smith insists that "No nation can be ruined by the ballance of trade being against them." Adam Smith, *Lectures on Jurisprudence*, ed. Ronald L. Meek, David D. Raphael, and Peter G. Stein (1978; repr., Indianapolis, IN: Liberty Fund, 1982), 392. References to this edition are hereafter cited in text as *LJ*. He refers explicitly to Joshua Gee's *The Trade and Navigation of Great Britain Considered* (1729) and Jonathan Swift's *A Short View of the State of Ireland* (1727–1728):

> If we look into Gee's book we find that trade to all the nations of Europe had a ballance against us excepting Spain, Portugall, and Ireland, besides the American plantations, for the West Indian islands had a vast ballance against us. This he represents as threatening us with immediate ruin; and as Swift imagined that in six or seven years there would not be a shill. or a guinea left in Ireland, notwithstanding of which Ireland is improving very fast, so he seems to have imagined that England would be utterly ruined in a short time if some stop was not put to this destructive and ruinous forreign trade. (*LJ*, 392–93)

Such arguments, Smith continues, are part of a general pattern:

> This indeed has been the cry, that the forreign trade would be the ruin of England, ever since the time of Ch. 2d, and notwithstanding of this the nation has continually improved in riches, in strength, and opulence.... The case is the same in other countries: France, Holland, Italy have all complained that the ballance of trade would ruin them, and yet they are continually improving. (*LJ*, 393)

Balance of trade is, for Smith, never a cause of ruin; instead, "The same thing ruins nations as individualls, viz their consumption being greater than their produce" (*LJ*, 393). This is clearly an early version of the passage analyzed subsequently from *Wealth of Nations*, book 2. Smith again notes the prolific prediction of imminent ruin and then seeks to diffuse panic about decline. Whereas the published passage identified only general malaise and responded with an insistence on concrete, measurable data collected over a broad period of time, this passage acknowledges efforts to use measure and quantity to identify decline. It then rejects one measure, balance of trade, in favor of another, the balance between domestic production and consumption.

In the later transcript of these lectures, from 1766, Smith makes the point with less concision, but with more emphasis on the annual as a period of relevant measurement:

> When a man consumes more than he gains by his industry, he must impoverish himself unless he has some other way of subsistence. In the same manner, if a nation consume more than it produces, poverty is inevitable. If it's annual produce be 90 millions and it's annual consumption an 100, then it spends, eats and drinks, tears, wears, 10 millions more than it produces, and its stock of opulence must gradually <?come> to nothing. (*LJ*, 513)

In both versions of the lectures, Smith expands this point to engage Mandeville's argument concerning the public benefits of private vices (luxury) on the basis of which the common argument emerges that national wealth consists of money and that whatever is consumed at home cannot diminish such wealth. By Smith's reckoning, however, what is spent on domestic consumption can impoverish the nation because it does not contribute to the promotion of industry; by contrast, to consume the interest of an investment does no harm as the "capital still remains and is employed in promoting industry" (*LJ*, 513). According to Smith, by virtue of this argument, "Brittain should by all means be made a free port" and "there should be no interruptions of any kind made to forreign trade" (*LJ*, 514). This is a point taken up in both extant sets of lectures as published in *LJ*. Because the 1762–63 record is more detailed about balance of trade issues, I focus my discussion on it. The similar passage from notes dated 1765 can be found in *LJ*, 513.

22. On the connection, see Winch, *Riches and Poverty*, 80–85.
23. Smith's understanding of how a collective series of disasters is part of a longer process of progress and improvement might be likened to debates in what we now call geology and earth sciences that explain catastrophic events as both destructive and productive and in which, in Mary Ashburn Miller's formulation, "Natural tropes provided a way of integrating apparent *disorder* into a narrative of eventual order." Mary Ashburn Miller, *A Natural History of Revolution: Violence and Nature in the French Revolutionary Imagination, 1789–1794* (Ithaca, NY: Cornell University Press, 2011), 10.

24. With, however, certain limitations. See Giovanni Arrighi, *The Long Twentieth Century: Money, Power, and the Origins of Our Times*, 2nd ed. (London: Verso, 2010).

25. This is because, in Condorcet's terms, "It is . . . impossible to pronounce for or against the future realization of an event which cannot take place but at an era when the human race will have attained improvements, of which we can at present scarcely form a conception." Quoted by T. R. Malthus in *An Essay on the Principle of Population*, ed. Geoffrey Gilbert (Oxford: Oxford University Press, 1993), 65.

26. T. R. Malthus, *An Essay on the Principle of Population*, ed. Geoffrey Gilbert (Oxford: Oxford University Press, 1993), 61. (Further references to this edition, whose source text is the initial 1798 version of Malthus's argument, will be cited in the text as *EPP*.)

27. Charlotte Sussman, *Peopling the World: Representing Human Mobility from Milton to Malthus*, unpublished book manuscript. Quoted with permission.

28. On this point, see Howard J. Bell, "*The Deserted Village* and Goldsmith's Social Doctrines," *PMLA* 59, no. 3 (1944): 747–72, and Winch, *Riches and Poverty*, 80–85.

29. Winch, *Riches and Poverty*, 83.

30. All of these binary divisions are reinforced by the formal qualities of Goldsmith's use of the smooth couplet verse that dominated eighteenth-century prosody. In describing the change between past and present, for example, Goldsmith notes, "Sweet smiling village, loveliest of the lawn, / Thy sports are fled, and all thy charms withdrawn." The lines sharply divide now from then, a separation that they enact formally in the division between the sweet village in the first line and the withdrawal of its charms as the rhyme is completed. This kind of division plays throughout the poem, sometimes within rhyming couplets and other times in between couplets or, as in the opening thirty-four lines, between a long series of couplets. See Oliver Goldsmith, *Collected Works of Oliver Goldsmith*, ed. Arthur Friedman, 5 vols. (Oxford: Oxford University Press, 1966), 4:289, lines 35–36; further references to this edition will be cited by line number in the text.

31. Goldsmith, *Collected Works*, 4:286.

32. The *Monthly Review*, for example, rehashed arguments for the employment created by luxury before concluding "That luxury is at present depopulating our country, not only by preventing marriage, but driving our villagers over the Western Ocean, we may perhaps be disposed to deny with the best and wisest of Dr. Goldsmith's friends, but we do not therefore read his poem with the less pleasure." The *Critical Review* concurred that "a fine poem may be written upon a false hypothesis," and defended urban life as a scene not of

vice, as Goldsmith insisted, but rather as a source of genius and virtue. "He who reads the *Deserted Village*," the reviewer noted, "and is not acquainted with the face of our country, may imagine, that there are many deserted villages to be found in it, and many more tracts of uncultivated land than formerly. England wears now a more smiling aspect than she ever did; and few ruined villages are to be met with except on poetical ground." This suggests that Goldsmith's deserted village is an anomaly and not representative of the state of the nation as a whole, and the reviewer anticipates Smith's insistence that Goldsmith encourages conflation of the local with the national. See G. S. Rousseau, ed., *Goldsmith: The Critical Heritage* (London: Routledge and Kegan Paul, 1974), 84, 78, 77.

33. Peter Fritzsche, *Stranded in the Present: Modern Time and the Melancholy of History* (Cambridge, MA: Harvard University Press, 2004), 53 (hereafter cited in text as *SP*).

34. On this point, see Martin J. S. Rudwick, *Bursting the Limits of Time: The Reconstruction of Geohistory in the Age of Revolution* (Chicago: University of Chicago Press, 2005), 127–29.

35. My understanding of these developments relies on Martin Rudwick's *Bursting the Limits of Time*, which begins in 1787, shortly after the publication of the *Wealth of Nations* and the initial volumes of *Decline and Fall*, with what Rudwick calls a golden spike, a baseline from which to trace the emergence of a new geohistorical outlook.

36. Rudwick, *Bursting the Limits of Time*, 131.

37. As Maureen McLane and Laura Slatkin argue in connection with Homeric orality, "Intellectual history likes its currents to flow forward and downward. Yet there are thresholds of emergence that might still benefit from something along the lines of a Foucauldian archaeology of discourse rather than a sources-and-influence model." In my account, the recalibration of timescale is one such threshold. See Maureen N. McLane and Laura M. Slatkin, "British Romantic Homer: Oral Tradition, 'Primitive Poetry' and the Emergence of Comparative Poetics in Britain, 1760–1830," *ELH* 78, no. 3 (2011): 687–714; quote on 703.

38. E. P. Thompson, "Time, Work-Discipline, and Industrial Capitalism," *Past & Present* 38, no. 1 (1967): 56–97.

39. Joseph Priestley, *A Description of a New Chart of History*, 6th ed. (London: printed for J. Johnson, 1786), 8 (emphasis in original).

40. Priestley, *Description*, 11.

41. One drawback to this chart, Priestley explained, was that, while it could show which empires occupied which territories, it had no way accurately to show the size of an empire's territory in comparative scale with other empires. To include large spaces like Tartary, Siberia, and America, places that he describes as "barren of events," would make the chart "immoderately large."

Priestley, *Description*, 16. This is a problem that would subsequently be solved by William Playfair, who enhanced Priestley's historical chart and extended its linear and geometric principles to the financial measurement of relative prosperity and decline.

42. William Playfair, *Inquiry into the Permanent Causes of the Decline and Fall of Powerful and Wealthy Nations* (London: Printed for Greenland and Norris, 1805), xv.

43. Anthony Grafton and Daniel Rosenberg, *Cartographies of Time: A History of the Timeline* (New York: Princeton Architectural Press, 2010), 136.

44. *Oxford Dictionary of National Biography*, accessed September 12, 2017, www .oxforddnb.com/view/printable/22370.

45. For a recent reprint of this 1805 edition, which shows how Playfair repeatedly took issue with many of Smith's claims see Adam Smith, *An Inquiry into the Nature and Causes of the Wealth of Nations*, edited by William Playfair, new introduction by William Rees-Mogg, 3 vols. (London: W. Pickering, 1995). In the story of decline that this book sets out to frame, Playfair functions as a Zelig-like character; his traces recur seemingly everywhere. He was a popularizer and critic of Adam Smith, an orphan with links to key figures of the Scottish Enlightenment, a pioneer of graphic design whose work was referred to favorably by Alexander von Humboldt, was rumored to have been present at the storming of the Bastille, the partner of the American epic poet Joel Barlow in the notorious Scioto land swindle, the editor (briefly) of *Galignani's Messenger* (from which the exiled Byron took his British news), and the author of a formidable folio volume on decline. Rogue, scoundrel, convict, opportunist, genius, whatever terms one chooses to describe him, Playfair was clearly an intriguing character who led a colorful life. Playfair was the younger brother of John Playfair, the champion of James Hutton's *Theory of the Earth* (1788) who succeeded Dugald Stewart as professor of mathematics at the University of Edinburgh. William's career, however, was much less conventional than that of his older brother. While John Playfair stayed in Scotland, William Playfair apprenticed first for three years with Andrew Meikle (the inventor of the drum threshing machine in 1789) and then with Matthew Boulton and James Watt (the improver of the steam engine) in Birmingham. Eventually, he abandoned engineering for enterprise, and set off for France, where the 1789 translation into French of his *Commercial and Political Atlas* (1786) had attracted the attention of Louis XVI. In France, he stayed through the Revolution and left to escape prosecution for his part in the Scioto land swindle just before the Terror. Back in London, his various enterprises included a bank, a newspaper, gun-carriage making, and a series of dubious efforts to supplement his income by blackmail, extortion, and one outright swindle that led to his conviction at the court of the King's Bench in

1805—the same year that he published his most ambitious work, the *Inquiry into the Permanent Causes of the Decline and Fall of Powerful and Wealthy Nations*, and also the first critical edition of Smith's *Wealth of Nations*, which included corrections and extensions of Smith's ideas. Today, Playfair is best known for his contributions to statistical graphics, especially the time-series line graph, the bar chart, and the pie chart. See the online version of the *Oxford Dictionary of National Biography*, accessed September 12, 2017, www .oxforddnb.com/view/printable/22370.

46. For a comprehensive account of the differences between the three editions of the *Atlas*, see Ian Spence and Howard Wainer's introduction to William Playfair's *The Commercial and Political Atlas and Statistical Breviary*, eds. Ian Spence and Howard Wainer (Cambridge: Cambridge University Press, 2005), 16–23.

47. The title in full is *The Commercial and Political Atlas, Representing by Means of Stained Copper-Plate Charts, the Progress of the Commerce, Revenues, Expenditure, and Debts of England, During the Whole of the Eighteenth Century*.

48. Ian Spence, "William Playfair and the Psychology of Graphs," in *Proceedings of the American Statistical Association, Section on Statistical Graphics* (Alexandria, VA: American Statistical Association, 2006), 2426–36, quote on 2427.

49. For more on Playfair and the psychology of graphs, see Spence, "William Playfair and the Psychology of Graphs."

50. On "information overload," see Ann Blair, *Too Much to Know: Managing Scholarly Information Before the Modern Age* (New Haven, CT: Yale University Press, 2011), Chad Wellmon, *Organizing Enlightenment: Information Overload and the Invention of the Modern Research University* (Baltimore: Johns Hopkins University Press, 2015), and also the articles collected by Daniel Rosenberg on "Early Modern Information Overload," *Journal of the History of Ideas* 64.1 (January 2003): 1–72. We should note, furthermore, it was the lack of data that produced Playfair's first bar chart, of Scotland's imports and exports from 1780 to 1781, which did not include a time element because there was not enough data to support a time-series graph. Playfair observed that "This chart... does not comprehend any portion of time, and is much inferior in utility to those that do" (*CPA*, 1786; 101), and he removed it from subsequent editions of the *Atlas*.

51. See Hartmut Rosa, *Social Acceleration: A New Theory of Modernity* (New York: Columbia University Press, 2013).

52. Stuart Sherman, *Telling Time: Clocks, Diaries, and English Diurnal Form, 1660–1785* (Chicago: University of Chicago Press, 1996).

53. E. P. Thompson, "Time, Work-Discipline, and Industrial Capitalism," *Past & Present* 38, no. 1 (1967): 56–97.

54. Lynn Hunt, *Measuring Time, Making History* (Budapest: Central European University Press, 2008), 119.

55. Mark W. Turner, "Periodical Time in the Nineteenth Century," *Media History* 8, no. 2 (2002): 183–96, quote on 188.

56. Walter Benjamin, *Illuminations*, eds. Hannah Arendt and Harry Zohn (New York: Harcourt, Brace & World, 1968); Benedict Anderson, *Imagined Communities: Reflections on the Origin and Spread of Nationalism*, rev. ed. (London: Verso, 1991).

57. Sherman, *Telling Time*, 35–36.

58. Sherman, *Telling Time*, 35. In adapting Sherman's claims about the date for Playfair's version of the annual, I paraphrase Sherman's terms here.

59. On this point, see Jonathan Sachs, "1786/1801: William Playfair, Statistical Graphics, and the Meaning of an Event," *BRANCH: Britain, Representation and Nineteenth-Century History*, ed. Dino Franco Felluga, an extension of *Romanticism and Victorianism on the Net*, accessed April 3, 2015, www .branchcollective.org/?ps_articles=jonathan-sachs-17861801-william-playfair-statistical-graphics-and-the-meaning-of-an-event. Indeed, in later editions, Playfair – who, as the brief sketch of his life above suggests, was in a number of his ventures something of a con man, or, in the words of one solicitor, "a daring worthless fellow" (Ian Spence and Howard Wainer, "William Playfair: A Daring Worthless Fellow," *Chance* 10, no. 1 [1997]: 31–34; quote on 34) – insisted that his work was widely recognized and cited Dr. Gilbert Stuart from the *Political Herald* to the effect that "The new method in which accounts are stated in this work has attracted very general notice" (*CPA*, 1801, vii–viii, footnote). But as late as 1937, a history of graphic representation noted the "common opinion shared by layman and statistician alike, that the graphic method in statistics is of recent origin" (H. Gray Funkhouser, "Historical Development of the Graphical Representation of Statistical Data," *Osiris* 3 [1937]: 269–404; quote on 270). The author explains that despite Playfair's attempt to articulate the value of his charts and to popularize their use, through the first half of the nineteenth century, English statistical publications ignored charts in favor of tables or figures: "The *Journal of the London Statistical Society* was established in 1837. Graphs began to appear in it in 1841. In the first fifty volumes, graphic representations occur fourteen times. Nine of these deal with vital statistics. The first graphs of economic data in this journal appeared in 1847 and are crudely drawn" (294). Not surprisingly, Playfair remained uncited by an English statistician or economist until William Stanley Jevons insisted to the London Statistical Society in 1879 that

"Englishmen have lost sight of the fact that William Playfair who has never been heard of in this generation produced statistical atlases and statistical curves that ought to be treated by some writer in the same way that Dr Guy has treated the method of Dr Todd" (quoted in Funkhouser, "Historical Development," 293). For a discussion of Jevons as a statistician, and his development of statistical graphics, see Stephen M. Stigler, *Statistics on the Table: The History of Statistical Concepts and Methods* (Cambridge, MA: Harvard University Press, 1999), 66–79.

60. Adam Smith, *Lectures on Rhetoric and Belles Lettres*, ed. J. C. Bryce (Indianapolis, IN: Liberty Fund, 1985), 112.

61. On this point, see Phillips, *Society and Sentiment*, 187–233.

62. Cited by Phillips, *Society and Sentiment*, 234.

63. Adam Ferguson, *An Essay on the History of Civil Society*, ed. Fania Oz-Salzberger (Cambridge: Cambridge University Press, 1995), 200 (hereafter cited in text as *CS*). Matters of public concern for Ferguson include: the "public safety, and the relative interests of states; political establishments, the pretensions of party, commerce, and arts," and "The advantages gained in some of these particulars, determine the degree of national prosperity" (*CS*, 200).

64. "Institutions that fortify the mind, inspire courage, and promote national felicity, can never tend to national ruin" (*CS*, 213). The point is further elaborated in the sixth part of Ferguson's essay, in which luxury and refined tastes are characterized as the source of national corruption.

65. Theodore M. Porter, *The Rise of Statistical Thinking, 1820–1900* (Princeton, NJ: Princeton University Press, 1986); Mary Poovey, *A History of the Modern Fact: Problems of Knowledge in the Sciences of Wealth and Society* (Chicago: University of Chicago Press, 1998).

66. The Dutchman Christiaan Huygens used John Graunt's data on English mortality rates to construct a rudimentary time-series graph of the data in a letter to his brother in 1669. See Biderman, "Playfair Enigma," for the claim that "neither the Cartesian system, nor any geometry that did not exist before Euclid was at all needed for any of Playfair's forms" (11). This is part of Biderman's larger argument that formal mathematical geometry was likely an impediment to the development of statistical graphing, which relied on raw as opposed to abstract data.

67. In book 1, for example, after noting that Rome fell when it began to rely on a mercenary standing army, he explains, "In nations that obtain wealth by commerce, manufactures, or any other means than by conquests, the corruption of the state is not naturally so great. The wealth originates in the people, and not in the state; and, besides that they are more difficult to purchase, there is less means of doing so, and less inducement". *William*

Playfair, An Inquiry into the Permanent Causes of the Decline and Fall of Powerful and Wealthy Nations (London: printed for Greenland and Norris, 1805), 41 (hereafter cited as *IPC*)(*IPC*, 41).

68. Playfair acknowledges the problem only to brush past it: "This plan would be unexceptionably correct, if the materials for it could be procured; but if they were, it would not lead to any very different conclusion from what it does in the present state. The times, when the elevation began, and its duration are exact" (*IPC*, 78). At moments like this, Playfair exposes the paradox of what Mary Poovey calls "the modern fact" with its seeming reverence for empirical observation and inductive reasoning that works to cover the deductive premises of a theory formed before the gathering of evidence. See Poovey, note 65 above.

69. Playfair might further be understood as a projector in a different, and more post-Restoration sense: his ambition to publicize and promote his graphic charts as the basis for government policy that could prevent decline align him with "projectors," those who devise schemes designed mutually for both public improvement and their own advancement. In his *Characters*, Samuel Butler describes a projector as preferring "the public Good before his own Advantage, until he has joined them both in some Monopoly, and then he thinks he has done his Part, and may be allowed to look after his own Affairs in the second Place." Playfair's colorful history and the broad claims made for his graphic techniques largely fit this description. On projectors, see Butler, *Characters and Passages from Note-Books*, ed. A. R. Waller (Cambridge: Cambridge University Press, 1908), 116. On projecting more generally, see Maximillian E. Novak, ed., *The Age of Projects* (Toronto: University of Toronto Press, 2008). For especially insightful work on projecting and its relationship to enthusiasm, see Joanne Myers, "Defoe and the Project of 'Neighbours Fare,'" *Restoration: Studies in English Literary Culture, 1660–1700* 35, no. 2 (2011): 1–19, and Myers, *Projecting Agents: Epistemological Critique and the Rhetoric of Belief in Eighteenth-Century British Projects* (PhD dissertation, University of Chicago, 2005).

70. On the significance of such transpositions of time and space, see Johannes Fabian, *Time and the Other: How Anthropology Makes Its Object* (New York: Columbia University Press, 1983); on uneven development, see, among others, James Chandler, *England in 1819: The Politics of Literary Culture and the Case of Romantic Historicism* (Chicago: University of Chicago Press, 1998), 127–35.

71. On this point, see Kevis Goodman's intervention into Foucault's account of classification, in which the classificatory systems of natural history in the Classical age (prior to Cuvier) were "a non-temporal rectangle" in

which "creatures present themselves one beside the other" for visual analysis without respect to time, in what Goodman calls "an ineluctably spatial system." In her reading of Charlotte Smith, Goodman underscores how that space itself can serve as a record of temporal change. See Kevis Goodman, "Conjectures on Beachy Head: Charlotte Smith's Geological Poetics and the Ground of the Present," *ELH* 81, no. 3 (2014): 983–1006; quote on 992.

Chapter 2

1. George Crabbe, *The Complete Poetical Works*, edited by Norma Dalrymple-Champneys and Arthur Pollard, 3 vols. (Oxford: Clarendon Press, 1988), 1: 181; [William Hazlitt], "The Periodical Press," *Edinburgh Review* 38 (May 1823), 358.
2. Clifford Siskin and William Warner, eds., *This Is Enlightenment* (Chicago: University of Chicago Press, 2010), 15–21.
3. Siskin and Warner, *This is Enlightenment*, 16.
4. John Brown, *An Estimate of the Manners and Principles of the Times*, 2nd ed. (London: printed for L. Davis and C. Reymers, 1757), 15.
5. Adam Smith, *An Inquiry into the Nature and Causes of the Wealth of Nations*, ed. Edwin Cannan (1904; reprint, Chicago: University of Chicago Press, 1976), 365 (hereafter cited in text as *WN*).
6. Paul Keen, *Literature, Commerce, and the Spectacle of Modernity, 1750–1800* (Cambridge: Cambridge University Press, 2012), 18–19, italics in original.
7. Oliver Goldsmith, *Collected Works of Oliver Goldsmith*, ed. Arthur Friedman, 5 vols. (Oxford: Oxford University Press, 1966), 1:257 (hereafter cited in text as *GCW*).
8. See, for example, Alvin B. Kernan, *Samuel Johnson & the Impact of Print* (Princeton, NJ: Princeton University Press, 1989).
9. See, for example, William St. Clair, *The Reading Nation in the Romantic Period* (Cambridge: Cambridge University Press, 2004); James Raven, *The Business of Books: Booksellers and the English Book Trade, 1450–1850* (New Haven, CT: Yale University Press, 2007); Andrew Piper, *Dreaming in Books: The Making of the Bibliographic Imagination in the Romantic Age* (Chicago: University of Chicago Press, 2009).
10. Marcus Walsh, "The Superfoetation of Literature: Attitudes to the Printed Book in the Eighteenth Century," *Journal for Eighteenth-Century Studies* 15, no. 2 (1992): 151–61.
11. James Boswell, *Life of Johnson*, ed. R. W. Chapman (1904; Oxford: Oxford University Press, 2008), 979.

12. Stuart Sherman, *Telling Time: Clocks, Diaries, and English Diurnal Form, 1660–1785* (Chicago: University of Chicago Press, 1996).

13. C. John Sommerville, *The News Revolution in England: Cultural Dynamics of Daily Information* (New York: Oxford University Press, 1996).

14. Deidre Lynch, *Loving Literature: A Cultural History* (Chicago: University of Chicago Press, 2015), 178.

15. Ann Blair, *Too Much to Know: Managing Scholarly Information before the Modern Age* (New Haven: Yale University Press, 2010), 3.

16. Vicesimus Knox, *Essays, Moral and Literary*, 2 vols. (London: Edward and Charles Dilly, 1778), 1:35 (hereafter cited in text as *EML*). Note here that the remark also echoes Smith's response to the decline jeremiad. See *WN*, 365.

17. Vicesimus Knox, *Winter Evenings, Or, Lucubrations on Life and Letters*, 3 vols. (London: Charles Dilly, 1788), 3:120 (hereafter cited in text as *WE*).

18. Sianne Ngai, *Ugly Feelings* (Cambridge: Harvard University Press, 2005), 7.

19. James Ralph, *The Case of Authors by Profession or Trade, Stated. With Regard to Booksellers, the Stage, and the Public. No Matter by Whom…* (London: R. Griffiths, 1758), 65.

20. Catharine Macaulay, *A Modest Plea for the Property of Copy Right* ([Bath]: printed by R. Cruttwell in Bath for Edward and Charles Dilly, London, 1774), 33.

21. Goldsmith, *CW*, 2:124–25.

22. William Wordsworth, "Preface" to *Lyrical Ballads* (1798, 1800), in *Wordsworth and Coleridge: Lyrical Ballads*, 2nd ed., eds. R. L. Brett-Smith and A. R. Jones (London: Routledge, 1991), 241–72, quote on 249 (hereafter cited in text as *LB*).

23. Note here that the 1802 version omits "his taste exalted," but the point remains.

24. Maureen N. McLane, *Romanticism and the Human Sciences: Poetry, Population, and the Discourse of the Species* (Cambridge: Cambridge University Press, 2000), 13–30.

25. Philippe Lacoue-Labarthe and Jean-Luc Nancy, *The Literary Absolute: The Theory of Literature in German Romanticism*, translated by Michael Metteer and Chris Cullens. Stanford: Stanford University Press, 1988).

26. Percy Bysshe Shelley, *Shelley's Poetry and Prose: Authoritative Texts, Criticism*, eds. Donald H. Reiman and Neil Fraistat, 2nd ed. (New York: Norton, 2002), 531 (hereafter cited in text as *SPP*).

27. Thomas Love Peacock, "The Four Ages of Poetry," in *The Works of Thomas Love Peacock*, eds. H. F. B. Brett-Smith and C. E. Jones, 10 vols. (1924; reprinted, New York: AMS Press, 1967), 8:3–25; quote on 20.

28. Peacock, "Four Ages," 12.

29. Thomas De Quincey, "The Works of Alexander Pope," in *The Works of Thomas De Quincey*, ed. Grevel Lindop, 21 volumes (London: Pickering and Chatto, 2000–2003), 16: 334–364, citation from 338 (hereafter cited in the text as *WDQ*).

30. John Stuart Mill, *Collected Works of John Stuart Mill*, 33 vols. (Toronto: University of Toronto Press, 1963–91), 27:410 (hereafter cited in text as *MCW*).

31. Smith, *Wealth of Nations*, 351–71.

32. Keen, *Literature, Commerce, and the Spectacle*, 1–39, esp. page 5.

33. Keen, *Revolutions in Romantic Literature*, 164.

34. St. Clair, *Reading Nation*.

35. John Guillory, *Cultural Capital: The Problem of Literary Canon Formation* (Chicago: University of Chicago Press, 1993); Jonathan Brody Kramnick, *Making the English Canon: Print-Capitalism and the Cultural Past, 1700–1770* (Cambridge: Cambridge University Press, 1998).

36. William Hazlitt, *The Complete Works of William Hazlitt*, ed. P. P. Howe, 21 vols. (London: J. M. Dent and Sons, Ltd, 1930–34), 17:327.

37. Hazlitt, *Complete Works*, 17:324.

Chapter 3

1. William Hazlitt, *The Selected Writings of William Hazlitt*, ed. Duncan Wu, 9 vols. (London: Pickering and Chatto, 1998), 9:208.

2. See William St. Clair, *The Reading Nation in the Romantic Period* (Cambridge: Cambridge University Press, 2004) and John Guillory, *Cultural Capital: The Problem of Literary Canon Formation* (Chicago: University of Chicago Press, 1993).

3. This is a central concept in Reinhart Koselleck's oeuvre. See, for example, essays in *Future's Past: On the Semantics of Historical Time*, trans. Keith Tribe (Cambridge, MA: MIT Press, 1985), especially "*Historia Magistra Vitae*: The Dissolution of the Topos into the Perspective of a Modernized Historical Process" and "'Space of Experience' and 'Horizon of Expectation': Two Historical Categories" and Koselleck, *The Practice of Conceptual History: Timing History, Spacing Concepts*, trans. Todd Samuel Presner and others (Stanford, CA: Stanford University Press, 2002), especially "The Unknown Future and the Art of Prognosis." See also Pocock's claim that the growth of public credit "obliged capitalist society to develop as an ideology something society had never possessed before, the image of a secular and historical future." He characterizes this future as "the spectacle of a society advancing at high speed into a world it can only imagine as existing in the forms which it may desire." J. G. A. Pocock,

Virtue, Commerce, and History: Essays on Political Thought and History, Chiefly in the Eighteenth Century (Cambridge: Cambridge University Press, 1985), 98, 99. See also the introduction and opening of Chapter 1 in this book.

4. François Hartog, *Regimes of Historicity: Presentism and Experiences of Time* (New York: Columbia University Press, 2015), 17.

5. For an especially useful discussion of thinking about the present as the future's past, see Kevis Goodman, *Georgic Modernity and British Romanticism: Poetry and the Mediation of History* (Cambridge: Cambridge University Press, 2004), 1–16.

6. In this sense, Romantic fantasies of decline share a recuperative element of Romantic historicism that, while grounded in the recognition that normative standards are bound by time and place and hence change their meanings, commonly seeks consolation from loss and death in the perceived immortality and autonomy of the field of culture. On the fascination with the afterlife and the compensatory belief in the immortality of an autonomous cultural field, see Ted Underwood, "Romantic Historicism and the Afterlife," *PMLA* 117 (2002): 237–51.

7. All references to Barbauld's poem come from Anna Barbauld, *Anna Letitia Barbauld: Selected Poetry and Prose*, eds. William McCarthy and Elizabeth Kraft (Peterborough, ON: Broadview Press, 2001). Line numbers from this edition will be provided in parenthesis.

8. Mary Favret, *War at a Distance: Romanticism and the Making of Modern Wartime* (Princeton: Princeton University Press, 2009), 18. Further page references provided parenthetically in the text.

9. The secondary literature on this concept is considerable. The phrase itself can be found in Nigel Leask, *Curiosity and the Aesthetics of Travel Writing, 1770–1840: 'From an Antique Land'* (Oxford: Oxford University Press, 2004), 46. See also Clara Tuite, "Maria Edgeworth's Déjà-Voodoo: Interior Decoration, Retroactivity, and Colonial Allegory in *The Absentee*," *Eighteenth Century Fiction* 20, no. 3 (2008): 385–413; and Christoph Bode, "Ad Fontes! Remarks on the Temporalization of Space in Hemans (1829), Bruce (1790), and Barbauld (1812)," *Romanticism* 10, no. 1 (2004): 63–78.

10. For this point, see Koselleck, "The Eighteenth Century as the Beginning of Modernity," in *Conceptual History*, 154–69; esp. 162–65.

11. Percy Bysshe Shelley, *Shelley's Poetry and Prose: Authoritative Texts, Criticism*, eds. Donald H. Reiman and Neil Fraistat, 2nd ed. (New York: Norton, 2002), 109–10.

12. Mary Wollstonecraft, *A Vindication of the Rights of Men; With A Vindication of the Rights of Woman*, ed. Sylvana Tomaselli (Cambridge: Cambridge University Press, 1995), 37.

13. Suvir Kaul, *Poems of Nation, Anthems of Empire: English Verse in the Long Eighteenth Century* (Charlottesville, VA: University of Virginia Press, 2000), 127.

14. See Shelley, *Shelley's Poetry and Prose*, 341. The poem was composed in 1819, and published in 1839.

15. Shelley writes: "when St. Paul's and Westminster Abbey shall stand, shapeless and nameless ruins in the midst of an unpeopled marsh; when the piers of Waterloo bridge shall become. . . isles of reeds and osiers and cast the jagged shadows of their broken arches on the solitary stream, —and when some transatlantic commentator will be weighing in the scales of some new and now unimagined system of criticism the respective merits of the Bells and the Fudges and their historians" (341).

16. James Chandler, *England in 1819: The Politics of Literary Culture and the Case of Romantic Historicism* (Chicago: University of Chicago Press, 1998), 96, 105.

17. Chandler, *England in 1819*, 107.

18. Chandler, *England in 1819*, 118. For a full description of uneven development and its relationship to the evenness of time as represented by annual dates, see Chandler, *England in 1819*, 127–35.

19. For a fuller description of the events of 1811–12, see William Keach, "A Regency Prophecy and the End of Anna Barbauld's Career," *Studies in Romanticism* 33, no. 4 (1994): 569–77; esp. 573.

20. Indeed, Emma Clery's recent account of the poem insists that the poem responds not to Barbauld's general concerns with war and commerce, as I have been discussing it here, but to a very particular economic crisis linked to specific Parliamentary legislation. See E. J. Clery, *Eighteen Hundred and Eleven: Poetry, Protest and Economic Crisis* (Cambridge: Cambridge University Press, 2017). Clery's book came out too late for its arguments to be integrated into this chapter.

21. Anne Grant, *Eighteen Hundred and Thirteen: A Poem, in Two Parts* (Edinburgh: J. Ballantyne, 1814).

22. John Wilson Croker, review of *Eighteen Hundred and Eleven*, by Anna Barbauld, *Quarterly Review* 7 (June 1812): 309. Clery's argument with its sustained emphasis on the particularity of Barbauld's critique in relation to the economic crisis of 1811, cited above in note 20, ultimately insists that the joke here is on Croker, contrary to most scholarly accounts.

23. See Chandler, *England in 1819*, 114; Lucy Newlyn, *Reading, Writing, Romanticism: The Anxiety of Reception* (Oxford: Oxford University Press, 2000), 164–69. My thinking about Barbauld has benefited from the extraordinary work on Barbauld in recent years, especially: Keach, "Prophecy"; Anne K. Mellor, *Mothers of the Nation: Women's Political Writing in England, 1780–1830* (Bloomington, IN: Indiana University

Press, 2000); Anne Janowitz, *Women Romantic Poets: Anna Barbauld and Mary Robinson* (Tavistock: Northcote House, 2004); Josephine McDonagh, "Barbauld's Domestic Economy," in *Romanticism and Gender*, ed. Anne Janowitz (Cambridge: D. S. Brewer, 1998), 62–77; and William McCarthy, *Anna Letitia Barbauld: Voice of the Enlightenment* (Baltimore: Johns Hopkins University, 2008).

24. Keach, "A Regency Prophecy," 573.

25. Favret, *War at a Distance*, 123–24.

26. For a more general discussion of "historical process as a present participle... rather than as a past perfect" (3), see Goodman, *Georgic Modernity*.

27. Though we might wonder here when we can say that Barbauld predicts ruin and gets it wrong – in a sense, it is always far too early.

28. Koselleck, *Conceptual History*, 131–47.

29. See Koselleck, *Future's Past*, 21–38 and 267–88.

30. Review of *Eighteen Hundred and Eleven*, by Anna Barbauld, *Monthly Review*, n.s., 671 (1812): 428.

Chapter 4

1. William Wordsworth, "The Ruined Cottage," in *Wordsworth's Poetry and Prose: Authoritative Texts, Criticism*, ed. Nicholas Halmi (New York: Norton, 2014), 448–494, citation from page 458. Line numbers for citations from this edition (which is based on MS D for its source text) will be provided parenthetically in the text.

2. Christopher Woodward, *In Ruins* (London: Chatto and Windus, 2001), 139.

3. Denis Diderot, in *Diderot on Art*, vol. 2, *The Salon of 1767*, ed. and trans. John Goodman (New Haven, CT: Yale University Press, 1995), 197.

4. Thomas McFarland, *Romanticism and the Forms of Ruin: Wordsworth, Coleridge, and Modalities of Fragmentation* (Princeton, NJ: Princeton University Press, 1981).

5. Anne Janowitz, *England's Ruins: Poetic Purpose and the National Landscape* (Cambridge, MA: Blackwell, 1990); see also Laurence Goldstein, *Ruins and Empire: The Evolution of a Theme in Augustan and Romantic Literature* (Pittsburgh, PA: University of Pittsburgh Press, 1977).

6. Janowitz, *England's Ruins*, 7.

7. Sophie Thomas, "Assembling History: Fragments and Ruins," *European Romantic Review* 14, no. 2 (2003): 177–86, quote on 181.

8. Thomas, "Assembling History," 179–80.

9. Nina L. Dubin, "Robert des Ruines: Speculating in the Market for Ruins," *Cabinet* 20 (Winter 2005/06): 1–11, quote on 2. See also Dubin, *Futures*

and *Ruins: Eighteenth-Century Paris and the Art of Hubert Robert* (Los Angeles, CA: Getty, 2010).

10. Dubin, "Robert des Ruines," 4, referring to J. G. A. Pocock, *Virtue, Commerce, and History: Essays on Political Thought and History, Chiefly in the Eighteenth Century* (Cambridge: Cambridge University Press, 1985), 91–92.

11. Andrew Piper, "Vertiginous Life: Goethe, Bones, and Italy," in *Marking Time: Romanticism and Evolution*, ed. Joel Faflak (Toronto: University of Toronto Press, forthcoming). See Matthias Schöning, "Zeit der Ruinen: Tropologische Stichproben zu Modernität und Einheit der Romantik," *Internationales Archiv für Sozialgeschichte der deutschen Literatur* 34, no. 1 (2009): 75–93.

12. Diderot, *Salon of 1767*, 201.

13. Diderot, *Salon of 1767*, 196.

14. See Jonathan Sachs, "Scales of Time and the Anticipation of the Future: Gibbon, Smith, Playfair," part of a forum on historical distance in *Modern Intellectual History* 11, no. 3 (2014): 697–718. See also Chapter 1.

15. Janowitz, *England's Ruins*, 118.

16. Jerome McGann, *The Romantic Ideology: A Critical Investigation* (Chicago: University of Chicago Press, 1985); Marjorie Levinson, *The Romantic Fragment Poem: A Critique of Form* (Chapel Hill: University of North Carolina Press, 1986); Alan Liu, *Wordsworth: The Sense of History* (Stanford, CA: Stanford University Press, 1989); Janowitz, *England's Ruins*; Karen Swann, "Suffering and Sensation in *The Ruined Cottage*," *PMLA* 106, no. 1 (1991): 83–95; Celeste Langan, *Romantic Vagrancy: Wordsworth and the Simulation of Freedom* (Cambridge: Cambridge University Press, 1995); David Simpson, *Wordsworth, Commodification and Social Concern: The Poetics of Modernity* (Cambridge: Cambridge University Press, 2009).

17. Kevis Goodman, *Georgic Modernity and British Romanticism: Poetry and the Mediation of History* (Cambridge: Cambridge University Press, 2004), 12.

18. Simpson, *Wordsworth, Commodification and Social Concern*, 53.

19. E. P. Thompson, "Time, Work-Discipline, and Industrial Capitalism," *Past & Present* 38, no. 1 (1967): 56–97; Mark W. Turner, "Periodical Time in the Nineteenth Century," *Media History* 8, no. 2 (2002): 183–96.

20. James Chandler, *Wordsworth's Second Nature: A Study of the Poetry and Politics* (Chicago: University of Chicago Press, 1984), 142.

21. Chandler, *Wordsworth's Second Nature*, 143.

22. Chandler, *Wordsworth's Second Nature*, 143.

23. Liu, *Wordsworth*, 317.

24. Swann, "Suffering and Sensation," 93.

25. William Wordsworth, "Preface" to *Lyrical Ballads* (1798, 1800), in *Wordsworth and Coleridge: Lyrical Ballads*, 2nd ed., eds. R. L. Brett-Smith and A. R. Jones (London: Routledge, 1991), 241–72, quote on 249. For a fuller discussion of this point, see Chapter 6.
26. Claude Lévi-Strauss, "History and Dialectic," in *The Savage Mind* (Chicago: University of Chicago Press, 1966), 258.
27. McGann, *Romantic Ideology*, 91.
28. Liu, *Wordsworth*, 325.
29. Swann, "Suffering and Sensation," 90.
30. For citations from "Lines Composed a Few Miles above Tintern Abbey, On Revisiting the Banks of the Wye during a Tour. July 13, 1798," I use William Wordsworth, *Lyrical Ballads*, in *Wordsworth and Coleridge: Lyrical Ballads*, 2nd ed., eds. R. L. Brett-Smith and A. R. Jones (London: Routledge, 1991), 113–17. Line numbers are provided parenthetically in the text.
31. Lévi-Strauss, "History and Dialectic," 259.
32. Lévi-Strauss, "History and Dialectic," 259; Chandler, *England in 1819, The Politics of Literary Culture and the Case of Romantic Historicism* (Chicago: University of Chicago Press, 1998), 70.
33. Lévi-Strauss, "History and Dialectic," 260.
34. See James Chandler, *England in 1819*.
35. Georg Simmel, "Two Essays: The Handle, and The Ruin," *Hudson Review* 11, no. 3 (1958): 371–85.
36. Reinhart Koselleck, *Futures Past: On the Semantics of Historical Time*, trans. Keith Tribe (Cambridge, MA: MIT Press, 1985), 279.
37. Koselleck, *Futures Past*, 282.
38. Dubin, "Robert des Ruines," 2.

Chapter 5

1. Samuel Taylor Coleridge, *The Collected Works of Samuel Taylor Coleridge, Volume 3: Essays on His Times in The Morning Post and The Courier*, ed. David Erdman, 3 vols. (Princeton: Princeton University Press, 1978), 3:316–17. Further references to this edition will be provided parenthetically in the text with the initials *CW*.
2. Michael Sonenscher, *Before the Deluge* (Princeton: Princeton University Press, 2007), 6.
3. Reinhart Koselleck, "*Historia Magistra Vitae*: The Dissolution of the Topos into the Perspective of a Modernized Historical Process," in *Futures Past: On the Semantics of Historical Time* (Cambridge, MA: MIT Press, 1985), 23.
4. Ibid.
5. William Eden, *Some Remarks on the Apparent Circumstances of the War in the Fourth Week of October 1795* (London, 1795), 38.

6. The chapter, in other words, does not follow the influence or uses of particular classical authors, nor does it seek to answer questions about what specific invocations of particular classical texts do in the various contexts in which they are reused. The seminal work for this first, hermeneutic approach is Charles Martindale, *Redeeming the Text: Latin Poetry and the Hermeneutics of Reception* (Cambridge: Cambridge University Press, 1993). For a more recent account of its claims, see Martindale, "Reception – A New Humanism? Receptivity, Pedagogy, the Transhistorical," *Classical Receptions Journal* 5.2 (2013): 169–83. The second approach is commonly linked to Simon Goldhill. See, for example, *Who Needs Greek?: Contests in the Cultural History of Hellenism* (Cambridge: Cambridge University Press, 2002).

7. Simon Goldhill, *Victorian Culture and Classical Antiquity: Art, Opera, Fiction and the Proclamation of Modernity* (Princeton: Princeton University Press, 2011), 161.

8. For fascinating recent work on the calendar, see Sanja Perovic, *The Calendar in Revolutionary France: Perceptions of Time in Literature, Culture, Politics* (Cambridge: Cambridge University Press, 2012).

9. Lynn Hunt, *Measuring Time, Marking History* (Budapest and New York: Central European University Press, 2008), 68.

10. Peter Fritzsche, *Stranded in the Present: Modern Time and the Melancholy of History* (Cambridge, MA: Harvard University Press, 2004), 53–54.

11. These are Koselleck's terms.

12. Karl Marx, *The Eighteenth Brumaire of Louis Bonaparte* (New York: International Publishers, 1963), 16–17.

13. Ibid, 17.

14. On the French appropriation of Rome, see Harold T. Parker, *The Cult of Antiquity and the French Revolutionaries* (Chicago: University of Chicago Press, 1937); Robert L. Herbert, *David, Voltaire, Brutus and the French Revolution: An Essay in Art and Politics* (New York: The Viking Press, 1972); Mona Ozouf, *Festivals and the French Revolution* (Cambridge: Harvard University Press, 1988), 271–78; Norman Vance, *The Victorians and Ancient Rome* (Oxford: Blackwell, 1997), 24–26.

15. Marx, *Eighteenth Brumaire*, 15.

16. William Wordsworth and Samuel Taylor Coleridge, *Lyrical Ballads*, eds. R. L. Brett and A. R. Jones, 2nd edition (London: Routledge, 1991), 239.

17. Rolf Engelsing, *Der Bürger als Leser: Lesergeschichte in Deutschland 1500–1800* (Stuttgart: Meltzler, 1974). Engelsing's argument, briefly, is that there was a revolutionary shift circa 1750 from intensive reading, where readers read repeatedly the few books that they owned, to extensive reading, where readers began to read as many books as they could.

18. Andrew Piper, *Dreaming in Books: The Bibliographic Imagination in the Romantic Age* (Chicago: University of Chicago Press, 2009), 4, 5. For

additional arguments about Romanticism's "media revolution," see Celeste Langan and Maureen McLane, "The Medium of Romantic Poetry," in *The Cambridge Companion to British Romantic Poetry*, ed. James Chandler and Maureen McLane (Cambridge: Cambridge University Press, 2008); and Maureen McLane, *Balladeering, Minstrelsy, and the Making of British Romantic Poetry* (Cambridge: Cambridge University Press, 2008), esp. pp. 112–16.

19. From "Bonaparte. III: The Hope for Peace," *CW*, 3:214.

20. From "On Peace. II: Overtures," *CW*, 3:67.

21. Samuel Taylor Coleridge, *The Collected Works of Samuel Taylor Coleridge, Volume 6: Lay Sermons*, ed. R. J. White (Princeton: Princeton University Press, 1972), 9.

22. In addition to Koselleck, as discussed above, and Giovanni Arrighi, discussed below, I have in mind here also Hartmut Rosa, Jürgen Habermas, and Paul Virilio. See Hartmut Rosa, "The Speed of Global Flows and the Pace of Democratic Politics," *New Political Science* 27.4 (2005): 445–459, esp. 443; Hartmut Rosa, *Social Acceleration: A New Theory of Modernity* (New York: Columbia University Press, 2013), and "Social Acceleration: Ethical and Political Consequences of a De-Synchronized High-Speed Society", with comments by William Scheuerman, Barbara Adam and Carmen Leccardi, *Constellations: An International Journal of Critical and Democratic Theory* 10:1 (2003), pp. 3–52; Jürgen Habermas, *The Philosophical Discourse of Modernity* (Cambridge, MA: MIT Press, 1987), especially "Modernity's Consciousness of Time and Its Need for Self-Reassurance," 1–22; and Paul Virilio, *The Virilio Reader*, ed. James Der Derian (London: Wiley Blackwell, 1998).

23. Walter Benjamin, "Theses on the Philosophy of History," in *Illuminations*, ed. Hannah Arendt (New York: Schocken Books, 1969), 261.

24. Giovanni Arrighi, *The Long Twentieth Century: Money, Power, and the Origins of Our Time*, 2nd ed. (London: Verso, 2010), 221–22. Further page references to this edition are given parenthetically in the text.

25. Ian Baucom, *Specters of the Atlantic: Finance Capital, Slavery, and the Philosophy of History* (Durham: Duke University Press, 2005), 29.

26. Ibid, 24.

Chapter 6

1. Charles Darwin, *Evolutionary Writings*, ed. James A. Secord (Oxford: Oxford University Press, 2008), 10 (hereafter cited in text as *EW*). Emphasis mine.

2. The passage quoted here was added in 1845 for the second edition. Darwin must have liked this point because it also appears, nearly

verbatim, in *On the Origin of Species.* See *On the Origin of Species: A Facsimile Reprint of the First Edition* (Cambridge: Harvard University Press, 1964), 320. With thanks to Ian Duncan for pointing out this overlap.

3. Martin J. S. Rudwick, *Bursting the Limits of Time: The Reconstruction of Geohistory in the Age of Revolution* (Chicago: University of Chicago Press, 2005), 124–29.

4. Coinage of this term is often credited to John McPhee, *Basin and Range* (New York: Farrar, Strauss and Giroux, 1981). The term, whose use has been widespread in geology, became a contested topic in literary studies with the appearance of Wai Chee Dimock's *Through Other Continents: American Literature Across Deep Time* (Princeton, NJ: Princeton University Press, 2006) and Mark McGurl's critique of Dimock in "The Posthuman Comedy," *Critical Inquiry* 38, no. 3 (2012): 533–53. Dimock uses "deep time" to mark a Braudelian *longue durée*; my usage is closer to that of McGurl, though I am not convinced that either elicits fully the role of literary writing in developing the metaphorical force of the concept.

5. For a powerful argument that draws upon deep time to join human history and natural history, see Noah Heringman, "Deep Time at the Dawn of the Anthropocene," *Representations* 129.1 (Winter 2015): 55–85.

6. The point is widely repeated and acknowledged. I have in mind, among others, theorists of modernity including Reinhart Koselleck, Hartmut Rosa, Jürgen Habermas, Paul Virilio, and Giovanni Arrighi. See discussion below for further details and sources.

7. Here I follow Maureen N. McLane and Laura M. Slatkin, who argue that "Intellectual history likes its currents to flow forward and downward. Yet there are thresholds of emergence that might still benefit from something along the lines of a Foucauldian archaeology of discourse rather than a sources-and-influence model." See "British Romantic Homer: Oral Tradition, 'Primitive Poetry' and the Emergence of Comparative Poetics in Britain, 1760–1830," *ELH* 78, no. 3 (2011): 687–714, quote on 703.

8. Raymond Williams, *Politics and Letters: Interview with the New Left Review* (London: Verso, 1981), 167.

9. Ursula K. Heise, *Chronoschisms: Time, Narrative, and Postmodernism* (Cambridge: Cambridge University Press, 1997), 5–6.

10. Rob Nixon, *Slow Violence and the Environmentalism of the Poor* (Cambridge, MA: Harvard University Press, 2011), 8.

11. Nixon, *Slow Violence*, 13.

12. William Wordsworth and Samuel Taylor Coleridge, *Wordsworth and Coleridge: Lyrical Ballads*, 2nd ed., eds. R. L. Brett-Smith and A. R. Jones (London: Routledge, 1991), 249.

13. See Claude Lévi-Strauss, "History and Dialectic," in *The Savage Mind* (Chicago: University of Chicago Press, 1966), 259.

14. See Chapter 2.

15. For more on the use of "torpor" circa 1800, see Robert Mitchell, *Experimental Life: Vitalism in Romantic Science and Literature* (Baltimore, MD: Johns Hopkins University Press, 2013), 56–60.

16. I am thinking here of Reinhart Koselleck "'Space of Experience' and 'Horizon of Expectation': Two Historical Categories," in *Futures Past: On the Semantics of Historical Time*, trans. Keith Tribe (Cambridge, MA: MIT Press, 1985), 267–88, esp. 279–84; Hartmut Rosa, "The Speed of Global Flows and the Pace of Democratic Politics," *New Political Science* 27, no. 4 (2005): 445–59; Hartmut Rosa, "Social Acceleration: Ethical and Political Consequences of a Desynchronized High-Speed Society," with comments by Carmen Leccardi, William Scheuerman, and Barbara Adam, *Constellations: An International Journal of Critical and Democratic Theory* 10, no. 1 (2003): 3–52; and Giovanni Arrighi, whose *The Long Twentieth Century: Money, Power, and the Origins of Our Times*, 2nd ed. (London: Verso, 2010) describes processes of acceleration and compression and suggests explicitly that, "as we move from the earlier to the later stages of capitalist development, it has taken less and less time for systemic regimes of accumulation to rise, develop fully, and be superseded" (221). Most recently, Jonathan Crary, in *24/7: Late Capitalism and the Ends of Sleep* (London: Verso, 2013), characterizes modernity through the acceleration of novelty into a regime of the 24/7: "The contemporary phenomenon of acceleration is not simply a linear succession of innovations in which there is a substitution of a new item for something out of date. Each replacement is always accompanied by an exponential increase beyond the previous number of choices and options. It is a continuous process of distention and expansion, occurring simultaneously on different levels and in different locations, a process in which there is a multiplication of the areas of time and experience that are annexed to new machinic tasks and demands" (43).

17. Paul Virilio, *The Virilio Reader*, ed. James Der Derian (Malden, MA: Blackwell, 1998), vi.

18. See Hartmut Rosa, *Social Acceleration: A New Theory of Modernity*, trans. Jonathan Trejo-Mathys (New York: Columbia University Press, 2013), 21, emphasis original.

19. I have in mind here Celeste Langan and Maureen N. McLane's "The Medium of Romantic Poetry," in *The Cambridge Companion to British Romantic Poetry*, ed. James Chandler and Maureen N. McLane (Cambridge: Cambridge University Press, 2008), 239–62; Maureen N. McLane's *Balladeering, Minstrelsy, and the Making of British Romantic Poetry* (Cambridge: Cambridge University Press, 2008), esp. 112–16; Andrew Piper's *Dreaming in Books: The Making of the Bibliographic Imagination in the Romantic Age* (Chicago: University of Chicago Press, 2009); as well as the work of the research group "Interacting with Print: Cultural Practices of Intermediality, 1700–1900." See http://interacting withprint.org.

20. Nixon, *Slow Violence*, 15.

21. Nixon, *Slow Violence*, 15.

22. All references to Wordsworth's poetry will be cited parenthetically by line number from: William Wordsworth and Samuel Taylor Coleridge, *Wordsworth and Coleridge: Lyrical Ballads*, 2nd ed., eds. R. L. Brett-Smith and A. R. Jones (London: Routledge, 1991).

23. Thomas Pynchon, *Gravity's Rainbow* (London: Cape, 1973), 3.

24. *Virilio Reader*, 51.

25. *Virilio Reader*, 47, 48.

26. Philip Connell, *Romanticism, Economics and the Question of 'Culture'* (Oxford: Oxford University Press, 2001), 16–25.

27. Robert Richards, *The Romantic Conception of Life: Science and Philosophy in the Age of Goethe* (Chicago: University of Chicago Press, 2002), 539.

28. Alan Bewell, *Wordsworth and the Enlightenment: Nature, Man, and Society in the Experimental Poetry* (New Haven, CT: Yale University Press, 1989).

29. Paul H. Fry, *Wordsworth and the Poetry of What We Are* (New Haven, CT: Yale University Press, 2008), 72.

30. Mary Jacobus, *Romantic Things: A Tree, A Rock, A Cloud* (Chicago: University of Chicago Press, 2012).

31. Noah Heringman, *Romantic Rocks, Aesthetic Geology* (Ithaca, NY: Cornell University Press, 2004), xii.

32. Gillian Beer, "Darwin and the Uses of Extinction," *Victorian Studies* 51, no. 2 (Winter 2009): 321–31, quote on 322. The page numbers referred to in Beer's quotation are from the original 1859 edition of Darwin's *On the Origin of Species* (London: John Murray, 1859). See *The Complete Work of Charles Darwin Online*. ed. John van Wyhe. May 21, 2015, http://darwin-online.org .uk.

33. "The grand fact that all extinct organic beings belong to the same system with recent beings, falling either into the same or into inter-mediate

groups, follows from the living and the extinct being the offspring of common parents." See the original 1859 edition of Darwin's *On the Origin of Species* (London: John Murray, 1859), 476. *The Complete Work of Charles Darwin Online.* ed. John van Wyhe. May 21, 2015, http://darwin-online.org.uk.

34. Rudwick, *Bursting the Limits of Time*, 390.
35. Quoted by Rudwick, *Bursting the Limits of Time*, 391.
36. See note above.

Bibliography

Adam, Barbara. "Comment on 'Social Acceleration' by Hartmut Rosa." *Constellations: An International Journal of Critical and Democratic Theory* 10, no. 1 (2003): 49–52.

Anderson, Benedict. *Imagined Communities: Reflections on the Origin and Spread of Nationalism.* Rev. ed. London: Verso, 1991.

Anon. *The Connoisseur by Mr. Town, Critic and Censor-General*, no. 3 (Thursday, February 14, 1754).

Arata, Stephen. *Fictions of Loss in the Victorian Fin de Siecle.* Cambridge: Cambridge University Press, 1996.

Arrighi, Giovanni. *The Long Twentieth Century: Money, Power, and the Origins of Our Times.* 2nd ed. London: Verso, 2010.

Bailyn, Bernard. "1776 A Year of Challenge—A World Transformed." *Journal of Law and Economics* 19, no. 3 (1976): 437–66.

Barbauld, Anna. *Anna Letitia Barbauld: Selected Poetry and Prose.* Edited by William McCarthy and Elizabeth Kraft. Peterborough, ON: Broadview Press, 2001.

Barbauld, Anna. *Eighteen Hundred and Eleven, a Poem.* In Anna Barbauld, *Anna Letitia Barbauld: Selected Poetry and Prose*, ed. William McCarthy and Elizabeth Kraft, 160–73. Peterborough, ON: Broadview Press, 2001.

Baucom, Ian. *Specters of the Atlantic: Finance Capital, Slavery, and the Philosophy of History.* Durham, NC: Duke University Press, 2005.

Beer, Gillian. "Darwin and the Uses of Extinction." *Victorian Studies* 51, no. 2 (Winter 2009): 321–31.

Bell, Howard J. "*The Deserted Village* and Goldsmith's Social Doctrines." *PMLA* 59, no. 3 (1944): 747–72.

Benjamin, Walter. *Illuminations.* Edited by Hannah Arendt and Harry Zohn. New York: Harcourt, Brace & World, 1968.

Berry, Christopher J. *The Idea of Luxury: A Conceptual and Historical Investigation.* Ideas in Context. Cambridge: Cambridge University Press, 1994.

Bewell, Alan. *Wordsworth and the Enlightenment: Nature, Man, and Society in the Experimental Poetry.* New Haven, CT: Yale University Press, 1989.

Biderman, Albert. "The Playfair Enigma: The Development of the Schematic Representation of Statistics." *Information Design Journal* 6, no. 1 (1990): 3–25.

Blair, Ann. *Too Much to Know: Managing Scholarly Information Before the Modern Age*. New Haven, CT: Yale University Press, 2010.

Bode, Christoph. "Ad Fontes! Remarks on the Temporalization of Space in Hemans (1829), Bruce (1790), and Barbauld (1812)." *Romanticism* 10, no. 1 (2004): 63–78.

Boswell, James. *Life of Johnson*, ed. R. W. Chapman. Oxford World's Classics. 1904. Oxford: Oxford University Press, 2008.

Brewer, John. "Between Distance and Sympathy: Dr John Moore's Philosophical Travel Writing." *Modern Intellectual History* 11, no. 3 (2014): 655–75.

Brewer, John. "Microhistory and the Histories of Everyday Life." *Cultural and Social History* 7, no. 1 (2010): 87–109.

Brown, John. *An Estimate of the Manners and Principles of the Times*. 2nd ed. London: printed for L. Davis and C. Reymers, 1757.

Buchanan, Patrick. *Suicide of a Superpower: Will America Survive to 2025?* New York: Thomas Dunne Books, 2011.

Buckland, Adelene. *Novel Science: Fiction and the Invention of Geology*. Chicago: University of Chicago Press, 2013.

Butler, Samuel. *Characters and Passages from Note-Books*. Edited by A. R. Waller. Cambridge English Classics. Cambridge: Cambridge University Press, 1908.

Chandler, James. *England in 1819: The Politics of Literary Culture and the Case of Romantic Historicism*. Chicago: University of Chicago Press, 1998.

Chandler, James. *Wordsworth's Second Nature: A Study of the Poetry and Politics* Chicago: University of Chicago Press, 1984.

Clery, E. J. *Eighteen Hundred and Eleven: Poetry, Protest and Economic Crisis*. Cambridge: Cambridge University Press, 2017.

Coleridge, Samuel Taylor. *The Collected Works of Samuel Taylor Coleridge*. Vol. 3, *Essays on His Times in "The Morning Post" and "The Courier."* Edited by David V. Erdman. Princeton, NJ: Princeton University Press, 1978.

Connell, Philip. *Romanticism, Economics and the Question of "Culture."* Oxford: Oxford University Press, 2001.

Crabbe, George. *The Complete Poetical Works*. Edited by Norma Dalrymple-Champneys and Arthur Pollard. 3 vols. Oxford: Clarendon Press, 1988.

Crary, Jonathan. *24/7: Late Capitalism and the Ends of Sleep*. London: Verso, 2013.

Croker, John Wilson. "Review of Anna Barbauld, 'Eighteen Hundred and Eleven.'" *Quarterly Review* 7 (June 1812): 309–13.

Darwin, Charles. *Evolutionary Writings*. Edited by James A. Secord. Oxford World's Classics. Oxford: Oxford University Press, 2008.

De Bruyn, Frans. "From Georgic Poetry to Statistics and Graphs: Eighteenth-Century Representations and the 'State' of British Society." *Yale Journal of Criticism* 17, no. 1 (2004): 107–39.

De Quincey, Thomas. "The Works of Alexander Pope," in *The Works of Thomas De Quincey*, ed. Grevel Lindop, 21 volumes (London: Pickering and Chatto, 1999–2003), 16: 334–364

den Hollander, Jaap, Paul Herman, and Rik Peters, eds. "Historical Distance: Reflections on a Metaphor." Special issue, *History and Theory* 50, no. 4 (2011).

Diderot, Denis. *Diderot on Art, Vol. 2, The Salon of 1767*. Edited and Translated by John Goodman. New Haven, CT: Yale University Press, 1995.

Dimock, Wai Chee. *Through Other Continents: American Literature across Deep Time*. Princeton, NJ: Princeton University Press, 2006.

D'Israeli, Isaac. *An Essay on the Manners and Genius of the Literary Character*. London: printed for T. Cadell, Junr. and W. Davies, 1795.

Dubin, Nina L. *Futures and Ruins: Eighteenth-Century Paris and the Art of Hubert Robert*. Los Angeles, CA: Getty, 2010.

Dubin, Nina L. "Robert des Ruines: Speculating in the Market for Ruins." *Cabinet* 20 (Winter 2005/06): 1–11.

Duncan, Ian. *Scott's Shadow: The Novel in Romantic Edinburgh*. Princeton: Princeton University Press, 2007.

Dwyer, John. "Ethics and Economics: Bridging Adam Smith's *Theory of Moral Sentiments* and *Wealth of Nations*." *Journal of British Studies* 44, no. 4 (2005): 662–87.

Eden, William. *Some Remarks on the Apparent Circumstances of the War in the Fourth Week of October 1795*. London, 1795.

Engelsing, Rolf. *Der Bürger als Leser: Lesergeschichte in Deutschland 1500–1800*. Stuttgart: Meltzler, 1974.

Fabian, Johannes. *Time and the Other: How Anthropology Makes Its Object*. New York: Columbia University Press, 1983.

Favret, Mary. *War at a Distance: Romanticism and the Making of Modern Wartime*. Princeton, NJ: Princeton University Press, 2009.

Ferguson, Adam. *An Essay on the History of Civil Society*. Edited by Fania Oz-Salzberger. Cambridge Texts in the History of Political Thought. Cambridge: Cambridge University Press, 1995.

Forbes, Duncan. "'Scientific' Whiggism: Adam Smith and John Millar." *Cambridge Journal* 7 (1954): 643–70.

Foucault, Michel. *The Order of Things: An Archaeology of the Human Sciences*. New York: Random House, 1970.

François, Anne-Lise. *Open Secrets: The Literature of Uncounted Experience*. Meridian: Crossing Aesthetics. Stanford, CA: Stanford University Press, 2007.

Friedman, Thomas, and Michael Mandelbaum. *That Used to Be Us: How America Fell Behind in the World It Invented and How We Can Come Back*. New York: Farrar, Straus and Giroux, 2011.

Fritzsche, Peter. *Stranded in the Present: Modern Time and the Melancholy of History*. Cambridge, MA: Harvard University Press, 2004.

Fry, Paul H. *Wordsworth and the Poetry of What We Are*. Yale Studies in English. New Haven, CT: Yale University Press, 2008.

Funkhouser, H. Gray. "Historical Development of the Graphical Representation of Statistical Data." *Osiris* 3 (1937): 269–404.

Gibbon, Edward. *The History of the Decline and Fall of the Roman Empire*. Edited by David Womersley. 3 vols. London: Allen Lane, Penguin Press, 1994.

Go, Julian. *Patterns of Empire: The British and American Empires, 1688 to the Present*. New York: Cambridge University Press, 2011.

Goldhill, Simon. *Victorian Culture and Classical Antiquity: Art, Opera, Fiction and the Proclamation of Modernity*. Princeton: Princeton University Press, 2011.

Goldhill, Simon. *Who Needs Greek?: Contests in the Cultural History of Hellenism*. Cambridge: Cambridge University Press, 2002.

Goldsmith, Oliver. *Collected Works of Oliver Goldsmith*. Edited by Arthur Friedman. 5 vols. Oxford: Oxford University Press, 1966.

Goldstein, Laurence. *Ruins and Empire: The Evolution of a Theme in Augustan and Romantic Literature*. Pittsburgh, PA: University of Pittsburgh Press, 1977.

Goodman, Kevis. "Conjectures on Beachy Head: Charlotte Smith's Geological Poetics and the Ground of the Present." *ELH* 81, no. 3 (2014): 983–1006.

Goodman, Kevis. *Georgic Modernity and British Romanticism: Poetry and the Mediation of History*. Cambridge Studies in Romanticism. Cambridge: Cambridge University Press, 2004.

Grafton, Anthony and Daniel Rosenberg. *Cartographies of Time: A History of the Timeline*. New York: Princeton Architectural Press, 2010.

Grant, Anne. *Eighteen Hundred and Thirteen: A Poem, in Two Parts*. Edinburgh: J. Ballantyne, 1814.

Grossman, Henryk. "W. Playfair, the Earliest Theorist of Capitalist Development." *Economic History Review* 18 (1948): 65–83.

Guillory, John. *Cultural Capital: The Problem of Literary Canon Formation*. Chicago: University of Chicago Press, 1993.

Habermas, Jürgen. *The Philosophical Discourse of Modernity: Twelve Lectures*. Studies in Contemporary German Social Thought. Cambridge, MA: MIT Press, 1987.

Hartog, François. *Regimes of Historicity: Presentism and Experiences of Time*. New York: Columbia University Press, 2015.

Hazlitt, William. *The Complete Works of William Hazlitt*. Edited by P. P. Howe. 21 vols. London: J. M. Dent and Sons, Ltd, 1930–34.

Hazlitt, William. *The Selected Writings of William Hazlitt*. Edited by Duncan Wu. 9 vols. London: Pickering and Chatto, 1998.

Hazlitt, William. "The Periodical Press." In Paul Keen, *Revolutions in Romantic Literature: An Anthology of Print Culture, 1780–1832*, 11–12. Broadview Anthologies of English Literature. Peterborough, ON: Broadview Press, 2004.

Heise, Ursula K. *Chronoschisms: Time, Narrative, and Postmodernism*. Literature, Culture, Theory. Cambridge: Cambridge University Press, 1997.

Herbert, Robert L. *David, Voltaire, Brutus and the French Revolution: An Essay in Art and Politics*. New York: The Viking Press, 1972.

Heringman, Noah. *Romantic Rocks, Aesthetic Geology*. Ithaca, NY: Cornell University Press, 2004.

Heringman, Noah. "Deep Time at the Dawn of the Anthropocene," *Representations* 129.1 (Winter 2015): 55–85.

Hunt, Lynn. *Measuring Time, Making History*. Natalie Zemon Davis Annual Lecture Series. Budapest: Central European University Press, 2008.

Jacobus, Mary. *Romantic Things: A Tree, A Rock, A Cloud*. Chicago: University of Chicago Press, 2012.

Janowitz, Anne. *England's Ruins: Poetic Purpose and the National Landscape.* Cambridge, MA: Blackwell, 1990.

Janowitz, Anne. *Women Romantic Poets: Anna Barbauld and Mary Robinson.* Tavistock: Northcote House, 2004.

Jordheim, Helge. "Against Periodization: Koselleck's Theory of Multiple Temporalities." *History and Theory* 51, no. 2 (2012): 151–71.

Kaul, Suvir. *Poems of Nation, Anthems of Empire: English Verse in the Long Eighteenth Century.* Charlottesville, VA: University of Virginia Press, 2000.

Keach, William. "A Regency Prophecy and the End of Anna Barbauld's Career." *Studies in Romanticism* 33, no. 4 (1994): 569–77.

Keen, Paul. *Literature, Commerce, and the Spectacle of Modernity, 1750–1800.* Cambridge Studies in Romanticism. Cambridge: Cambridge University Press, 2012.

Kernan, Alvin B. *Samuel Johnson & the Impact of Print.* Princeton, NJ: Princeton University Press, 1989.

Knox, Vicesimus. *Essays, Moral and Literary.* 2 vols. London: Edward and Charles Dilly, 1778.

Knox, Vicesimus. *Winter Evenings, Or, Lucubrations on Life and Letters.* 3 vols. London: Charles Dilly, 1788.

Koselleck, Reinhart. *Futures Past: On the Semantics of Historical Time.* Translated by Keith Tribe. Studies in Contemporary German Social Thought. Cambridge, MA: MIT Press, 1985.

Koselleck, Reinhart. "*Historia Magistra Vitae*: The Dissolution of the Topos into the Perspective of a Modernized Historical Process." In Koselleck, *Futures Past,* 21–38.

Koselleck, Reinhart. *The Practice of Conceptual History: Timing History, Spacing Concepts.* Translated by Todd Samuel Presner and others. Cultural Memory in the Present. Stanford, CA: Stanford University Press, 2002.

Koselleck, Reinhart. "'Space of Experience' and 'Horizon of Expectation': Two Historical Categories." In Koselleck, *Futures Past,* 267–88.

Kramnick, Jonathan Brody. *Making the English Canon: Print-Capitalism and the Cultural Past, 1700–1770.* Cambridge: Cambridge University Press, 1998.

Lacoue-Labarthe Philippe and Jean-Luc Nancy. *The Literary Absolute: The Theory of Literature in German Romanticism.* Translated by Michael Metteer with Chris Cullens. Stanford: Stanford University Press, 1988.

Langan, Celeste. *Romantic Vagrancy: Wordsworth and the Simulation of Freedom.* Cambridge Studies in Romanticism. Cambridge: Cambridge University Press, 1995.

Langan, Celeste and Maureen N. McLane. "The Medium of Romantic Poetry." In *The Cambridge Companion to British Romantic Poetry*, edited by James Chandler and Maureen N. McLane, 239–62. Cambridge: Cambridge University Press, 2008.

Leask, Nigel. *Curiosity and the Aesthetics of Travel Writing, 1770–1840: 'From an Antique Land.'* Oxford: Oxford University Press, 2004.

Leccardi, Carmen. "Resisting 'Acceleration Society.'" *Constellations: An International Journal of Critical and Democratic Theory* 10, no. 1 (2003): 34–41.

Levinson, Marjorie. *The Romantic Fragment Poem: A Critique of Form*. Chapel Hill: University of North Carolina Press, 1986.

Lévi-Strauss, Claude. "History and Dialectic." In *The Savage Mind*. Nature of Human Society. Chicago: University of Chicago Press, 1966.

Liu, Alan. *Wordsworth: The Sense of History*. Stanford, CA: Stanford University Press, 1989.

Lukacher, Brian. *Joseph Gandy: An Architectural Visionary in Georgian England*. New York: Thames & Hudson, 2006.

Lynch, Deidre. *Loving Literature: A Cultural History*. Chicago: University of Chicago Press, 2015.

Maas, Harro and Mary S. Morgan. "Timing History: The Introduction of Graphical Analysis in 19th-Century British Economics." *Revue d'histoire des sciences humaines* 7 (2002/2): 97–127.

Macaulay, Catharine. *A Modest Plea for the Property of Copy Right*. [Bath]: printed by R. Cruttwell in Bath for Edward and Charles Dilly, London, 1774.

Malthus, T. R. *An Essay on the Principle of Population*. Edited by Geoffrey Gilbert. World's Classics. Oxford: Oxford University Press, 1993.

Marshall, P. J., ed., *The Oxford History of the British Empire, vol. 2, The Eighteenth Century*. New York: Oxford University Press, 2001.

Martindale, Charles. "Reception – A New Humanism? Receptivity, Pedagogy, the Transhistorical," *Classical Receptions Journal* 5.2 (2013): 169–83.

Martindale, Charles. *Redeeming the Text: Latin Poetry and the Hermeneutics of Reception*. Cambridge: Cambridge University Press, 1993.

Marx, Karl. *The Eighteenth Brumaire of Louis Bonaparte*. New York: International Publishers, 1963.

McCarthy, William. *Anna Letitia Barbauld: Voice of the Enlightenment*. Baltimore: Johns Hopkins University, 2008.

McDonagh, Josephine. "Barbauld's Domestic Economy." In *Romanticism and Gender*. Edited by Anne Janowitz. Cambridge: D. S. Brewer, 1998, 62–77.

McFarland, Thomas. *Romanticism and the Forms of Ruin: Wordsworth, Coleridge, and Modalities of Fragmentation*. Princeton, NJ: Princeton University Press, 1981.

McGann, Jerome. *The Romantic Ideology: A Critical Investigation*. Chicago: University of Chicago Press, 1985.

McGurl, Mark. "The Posthuman Comedy." *Critical Inquiry* 38, no. 3 (2012): 533–53.

McLane, Maureen N. *Balladeering, Minstrelsy, and the Making of British Romantic Poetry*. Cambridge Studies in Romanticism. Cambridge: Cambridge University Press, 2008.

McLane, Maureen N. *Romanticism and the Human Sciences: Poetry, Population, and the Discourse of the Species*. Cambridge Studies in Romanticism Cambridge: Cambridge University Press, 2000.

McLane, Maureen N. and Laura M. Slatkin, "British Romantic Homer: Oral Tradition, 'Primitive Poetry' and the Emergence of Comparative Poetics in Britain, 1760–1830." *ELH* 78, no. 3 (2011): 687–714.

McPhee, John. *Basin and Range*. New York: Farrar, Strauss and Giroux, 1981.

Mellor, Anne K. *Mothers of the Nation: Women's Political Writing in England, 1780–1830*. Bloomington, IN: Indiana University Press, 2000.

Mill, John Stuart. *Collected Works of John Stuart Mill*. 33 vols. Toronto: University of Toronto Press, 1963–1991.

Miller, Mary Ashburn. *A Natural History of Revolution: Violence and Nature in the French Revolutionary Imagination, 1789–1794*. Ithaca, NY: Cornell University Press, 2011.

Mitchell, Robert. *Experimental Life: Vitalism in Romantic Science and Literature* Baltimore, MD: Johns Hopkins University Press, 2013.

Momigliano, Arnoldo. "Declines and Falls." *American Scholar* 49 (Winter 1979): 37–51.

Monthly Review n.s., 67 (1812): 428–32. Review of *Eighteen Hundred and Eleven*, by Anna Barbauld.

Moretti, Franco. *Graphs, Maps, Trees: Abstract Models for a Literary History*. London: Verso, 2005.

Multigraph Collective, The. *Interacting with Print: Elements of Reading in the Era of Print Saturation*. Chicago: University of Chicago Press, forthcoming.

Murphy, Cullen. *Are We Rome?: The Fall of an Empire and the Fate of America*. Boston, MA: Houghton Mifflin, 2007.

Myers, Joanne. "Defoe and the Project of 'Neighbours Fare.'" *Restoration: Studies in English Literary Culture, 1660–1700* 35, no. 2 (2011): 1–19.

Myers, Joanne. *Projecting Agents: Epistemological Critique and the Rhetoric of Belief in Eighteenth-Century British Projects*. PhD dissertation, University of Chicago, 2005.

Newlyn, Lucy. *Reading, Writing, Romanticism: The Anxiety of Reception*. Oxford: Oxford University Press, 2000.

Ngai, Sianne. *Ugly Feelings*. Cambridge: Harvard University Press, 2005.

Nixon, Rob. *Slow Violence and the Environmentalism of the Poor*. Cambridge, MA: Harvard University Press, 2011.

Novak, Maximillian E., ed. *The Age of Projects*. UCLA Clark Memorial Library Series. Toronto: University of Toronto Press, 2008.

Ozouf, Mona. *Festivals and the French Revolution*. Cambridge: Harvard University Press, 1988.

Parker, Harold T. *The Cult of Antiquity and the French Revolutionaries*. Chicago: University of Chicago Press, 1937.

Peacock, Thomas Love. "The Four Ages of Poetry." In *The Works of Thomas Love Peacock*, edited by H. F. B. Brett-Smith and C. E. Jones, 8:3–25. 10 vols. 1924; reprint, New York: AMS Press, 1967.

Perovic, Sanja. *The Calendar in Revolutionary France: Perceptions of Time in Literature, Culture, Politics*. Cambridge: Cambridge University Press, 2012.

Phillips, Mark Salber. "History Painting Redistanced: From Benjamin West to David Wilkie." *Modern Intellectual History* 11, no. 3 (2014): 611–29.

Phillips, Mark Salber. *On Historical Distance*. Lewis Walpole Series in Eighteenth-Century Culture and History. New Haven, CT: Yale University Press, 2013.

Phillips, Mark Salber. "Rethinking Historical Distance: From Doctrine to Heuristic." *History and Theory* 50, no. 4 (2011): 11–23.

Phillips, Mark Salber. *Society and Sentiment: Genres of Historical Writing in Britain, 1740–1820*. Princeton, NJ: Princeton University Press, 2000.

Phillipson, Nicholas T. *Adam Smith: An Enlightened Life*. New Haven, CT: Yale University Press, 2010.

Piper, Andrew. *Dreaming in Books: The Making of the Bibliographic Imagination in the Romantic Age*. Chicago: University of Chicago Press, 2009.

Piper, Andrew. "Vertiginous Life: Goethe, Bones, and Italy." In *Marking Time: Romanticism and Evolution*, edited by Joel Faflak. Toronto: University of Toronto Press, forthcoming.

Playfair, William. *An Inquiry into the Permanent Causes of the Decline and Fall of Powerful and Wealthy Nations*. London: printed for Greenland and Norris, 1805.

Playfair, William. *The Commercial and Political Atlas, Representing by Means of Stained Copper-Plate Charts, the Progress of the Commerce, Revenues, Expenditure, and Debts of England, During the Whole of the Eighteenth Century*. 3rd ed. London: printed for Greenland and Norris, 1801.

Playfair, William. *The Commercial and Political Atlas and Statistical Breviary*. 3rd ed. London: J. Wallis, 1801.

Pocock, J. G. A. *Barbarism and Religion*, vol. 3, *The First Decline and Fall*. Cambridge: Cambridge University Press, 2003.

Pocock, J. G. A. *The Machiavellian Moment: Florentine Political Thought and the Atlantic Republican Tradition*. Princeton, NJ: Princeton University Press, 1975.

Pocock, J. G. A. *Virtue, Commerce, and History: Essays on Political Thought and History, Chiefly in the Eighteenth Century*. Ideas in Context. Cambridge: Cambridge University Press, 1985.

Poovey, Mary. *A History of the Modern Fact: Problems of Knowledge in the Sciences of Wealth and Society*. Chicago: University of Chicago Press, 1998.

Porter, Theodore M. *The Rise of Statistical Thinking, 1820–1900*. Princeton, NJ: Princeton University Press, 1986.

Priestley, Joseph. *A Description of a New Chart of History*. 6th ed. London: printed for J. Johnson, 1786.

Pynchon, Thomas. *Gravity's Rainbow*. London: Cape, 1973.

Ralph, James. *The Case of Authors by Profession or Trade, Stated. With Regard to Booksellers, the Stage, and the Public. No Matter by Whom...* London: R. Griffiths, 1758.

Raven, James. *The Business of Books: Booksellers and the English Book Trade, 1450–1850*. New Haven, CT: Yale University Press, 2007.

Richards, Robert. *The Romantic Conception of Life: Science and Philosophy in the Age of Goethe*. Chicago: University of Chicago Press, 2002.

Rosa, Hartmut. *Social Acceleration: A New Theory of Modernity*. Translated by Jonathan Trejo-Mathys. New York: Columbia University Press, 2013.

Rosa, Hartmut. "Social Acceleration: Ethical and Political Consequences of a Desynchronized High-Speed Society." *Constellations: An International Journal of Critical and Democratic Theory* 10, no. 1 (2003): 3–33.

Rosa, Hartmut. "The Speed of Global Flows and the Pace of Democratic Politics." *New Political Science* 27, no. 4 (2005): 445–59.

Rosenberg, Daniel, ed. "Early Modern Information Overload." *Journal of the History of Ideas* 64.1 (2003): 1–72.

Rousseau, G. S., ed. *Goldsmith: The Critical Heritage*. Critical Heritage Series. London: Routledge and Kegan Paul, 1974.

Rousseau, Jean-Jacques. *The Discourses and Other Early Political Writings*. Edited by Victor Gourevitch. Cambridge Texts in the History of Political Thought. Cambridge: Cambridge University Press, 1997.

Royston, Erica. "Studies in the History of Probability and Statistics: III. A Note on the History of the Graphical Presentation of Data." *Biometrika* 43, nos. 3–4 (1956): 241–47.

Rudwick, Martin J. S. *Bursting the Limits of Time: The Reconstruction of Geohistory in the Age of Revolution*. Chicago: University of Chicago Press, 2005.

Sachs, Jonathan. "1786/1801: William Playfair, Statistical Graphics, and the Meaning of an Event." *BRANCH: Britain, Representation and Nineteenth-Century History*, edited by Dino Franco Felluga, an extension of *Romanticism and Victorianism on the Net*. Accessed April 3, 2015. www.branchcollective.org/?ps_articles=jonathan-sachs-17861801-william-playfair-statistical-graphics-and-the-meaning-of-an-event.

Sachs, Jonathan. *Romantic Antiquity: Rome in the British Imagination, 1789–1832*. Classical Presences. New York: Oxford University Press, 2010.

Sachs, Jonathan. "Scales of Time and the Anticipation of the Future: Gibbon, Smith, Playfair." *Modern Intellectual History* 11, no. 3 (2014): 697–718.

Sachs, Jonathan. "The Time of Decline." *European Romantic Review* 22, no. 3 (June 2011): 305–12.

Scheuerman, William. "Speed, States, and Social Theory: A Response to Hartmut Rosa." *Constellations: An International Journal of Critical and Democratic Theory* 10, no. 1 (2003): 42–48.

Schöning, Matthais. "Zeit der Ruinen: Tropologische Stichproben zu Modernität und Einheit der Romantik." *Internationales Archiv für Sozialgeschichte der deutschen Literatur* 34, no. 1 (2009): 75–93.

Sekora, John. *Luxury: The Concept in Western Thought, Eden to Smollett*. Baltimore: Johns Hopkins University Press, 1977.

Shelley, Percy Bysshe. *Shelley's Poetry and Prose: Authoritative Texts, Criticism*. Edited by Donald H. Reiman and Neil Fraistat. 2nd ed. A Norton Critical Edition. New York: Norton, 2002.

Sherman, Stuart. *Telling Time: Clocks, Diaries, and English Diurnal Form, 1660–1785*. Chicago: University of Chicago Press, 1996.

Sherry, Vincent. *Modernism and the Reinvention of Decadence*. Cambridge: Cambridge University Press, 2015.

Simmel, Georg. "Two Essays: The Handle, and The Ruin." *Hudson Review* 11, no. 3 (1958): 371–85.

Simpson, David. *Wordsworth, Commodification and Social Concern: The Poetics of Modernity*. Cambridge Studies in Romanticism. Cambridge: Cambridge University Press, 2009.

Siskin, Clifford and William Warner, eds. *This is Enlightenment* (Chicago: University of Chicago Press, 2010).

Smith, Adam. *An Inquiry into the Nature and Causes of the Wealth of Nations*. Edited by Edwin Cannan. 1904. Reprint, Chicago: University of Chicago Press, 1976.

Smith, Adam. *An Inquiry into the Nature and Causes of the Wealth of Nations*. Edited by William Playfair. New introduction by William Rees-Mogg. 3 vols. 1805; reprint, London: W. Pickering, 1995.

Smith, Adam. *Lectures on Jurisprudence*. Edited by Ronald L. Meek, David D. Raphael, and Peter G. Stein. The Glasgow edition of the works and correspondence of Adam Smith. 1978. Reprint, Indianapolis, IN: Liberty Fund, 1982.

Smith, Adam. *Lectures on Rhetoric and Belles Lettres*. Edited by J. C. Bryce. Indianapolis, IN: Liberty Fund, 1985.

Smith, Adam. *The Theory of Moral Sentiments*. Edited by David D. Raphael and Alec L. Macfie. The Glasgow edition of the works and correspondence of Adam Smith. Indianapolis, IN: Liberty Classics, 1982.

Smith, Charlotte. *Charlotte Smith: Major Poetic Works*. Edited by Claire Knowles and Ingrid Horrocks. Peterborough, ON: Broadview Press, 2017.

Sommerville, C. John. *The News Revolution in England: Cultural Dynamics of Daily Information*. New York: Oxford University Press, 1996.

Sonenscher, Michael. *Before the Deluge: Public Debt, Inequality, and the Intellectual Origins of the French Revolution*. Princeton, NJ: Princeton University Press, 2007.

Spadafora, David. *The Idea of Progress in Eighteenth-Century Britain*. Yale Historical Publications. New Haven, CT: Yale University Press, 1990.

Spence, Ian. "William Playfair and the Psychology of Graphs." In *Proceedings of the American Statistical Association, Section on Statistical Graphics*, 2426–36. Alexandria, VA: American Statistical Association, 2006.

Spence, Ian and Howard Wainer. Introduction to *The Commercial and Political Atlas and Statistical Breviary*, by William Playfair, 16–23. Edited by Ian Spence and Howard Wainer. Cambridge: Cambridge University Press, 2005.

Spence, Ian and Howard Wainer. "William Playfair: A Daring Worthless Fellow." *Chance* 10, no. 1 (1997): 31–34.

St. Clair, William. *The Reading Nation in the Romantic Period*. Cambridge: Cambridge University Press, 2004.

Stewart, Dugald. *Account of the Life and Writings of Adam Smith*, edited by I. S. Ross. In Adam Smith, *Essays on Philosophical Subjects*, edited by W. P. D. Wightman and J. C. Bryce, 312–14. The Glasgow edition of the works and correspondence of Adam Smith. Oxford: Clarendon Press, 1980.

Stewart, Dugald. *Elements of the Philosophy of the Human Mind*. London: printed for A. Strahan and T. Cadell, 1792.

Stigler, Stephen M. *Statistics on the Table: The History of Statistical Concepts and Methods*. Cambridge, MA: Harvard University Press, 1999.

Sussman, Charlotte. *Peopling the World: Representing Human Mobility from Milton to Malthus*, unpublished book manuscript.

Swann, Karen. "Suffering and Sensation in *The Ruined Cottage*." *PMLA* 106, no. 1 (1991): 83–95.

Thomas, Sophie. "Assembling History: Fragments and Ruins." *European Romantic Review* 14, no. 2 (2003): 177–86.

Thompson, E. P. "Time, Work-Discipline, and Industrial Capitalism." *Past & Present* 38, no. 1 (1967): 56–97.

Trumpener, Katie. *Bardic Nationalism: The Romantic Novel and the British Empire*. Princeton: Princeton University Press, 1997.

Tucker, Herbert F. "In the Event of a Second Reform." In *BRANCH: Britain, Representation and Nineteenth-Century History*, edited by Dino Franco Felluga, an extension of *Romanticism and Victorianism on the Net*. Accessed April 2, 2015. www.branchcollective.org/?ps_articles=herbert-f-tucker-on-event.

Tufte, Edward R. *The Visual Display of Quantitative Information*. Cheshire, CT: Graphics Press, 1983.

Tuite, Clara. "Maria Edgeworth's Déjà-Voodoo: Interior Decoration, Retroactivity, and Colonial Allegory in *The Absentee*." *Eighteenth Century Fiction* 20, no. 3 (2008): 385–413.

Turner, Mark W. "Periodical Time in the Nineteenth Century." *Media History* 8, no. 2 (2002): 183–96.

Uglow, Jenny. *The Lunar Men: Five Friends Whose Curiosity Changed the World*. New York: Farrar, Strauss and Giroux, 2002.

Underwood, Ted. "Romantic Historicism and the Afterlife." *PMLA* 117 (2002): 237–51.

Vance, Norman. *The Victorians and Ancient Rome*. Oxford: Blackwell, 1997.

Virilio, Paul. *The Virilio Reader*. Edited by James Der Derian. Malden, MA: Blackwell, 1998.

Walsh, Marcus. "The Superfoetation of Literature: Attitudes to the Printed Book in the Eighteenth Century." *Journal for Eighteenth-Century Studies* 15, no. 2 (1992): 151–61.

Wellmon, Chad. *Organizing Enlightenment: Information Overload and the Invention of the Modern Research University*. Baltimore: Johns Hopkins University Press, 2015.

Winch, Donald. "A Great Deal of Ruin in a Nation." In *Understanding Decline: Perceptions and Realities of British Economic Performance*, edited by Peter Clarke and Clive Trebilcock, 30–48. Cambridge: Cambridge University Press, 1997.

Winch, Donald. *Riches and Poverty: An Intellectual History of Political Economy in Britain, 1750–1834*. Ideas in Context. Cambridge: Cambridge University Press, 1996.

Wollstonecraft, Mary. *A Vindication of the Rights of Men; With a Vindication of the Rights of Woman*. Edited by Sylvana Tomaselli. Cambridge Texts in the History of Political Thought. Cambridge: Cambridge University Press, 1995.

Woodward, Christopher. *In Ruins*. London: Chatto and Windus, 2001.

Wordsworth, William. "Preface" to "Lyrical Ballads" (1798, 1800). In *Wordsworth and Coleridge: Lyrical Ballads*, 2nd ed., edited by R. L. Brett-Smith and A. R. Jones, 241–72. London: Routledge, 1991.

Wordsworth, William and Samuel Taylor Coleridge. *Wordsworth and Coleridge: Lyrical Ballads*. 2nd ed. Edited by R. L. Brett-Smith and A. R. Jones. London: Routledge, 1991.

Wordsworth, William. *Wordsworth's Poetry and Prose: Authoritative Texts, Criticism*. Edited by Nicholas Halmi. New York: Norton, 2014.

Zemmour, Éric. *La suicide français*. Paris: Albin Michel, 2014.

Index

CAMBRIDGE STUDIES IN ROMANTICISM

General Editor
James Chandler, *University of Chicago*

For EU product safety concerns, contact us at Calle de José Abascal, 56–1°,
28003 Madrid, Spain or eugpsr@cambridge.org.

www.ingramcontent.com/pod-product-compliance
Ingram Content Group UK Ltd.
Pitfield, Milton Keynes, MK11 3LW, UK
UKHW020330140625
459647UK00018B/2095